GORBACHEV'S GAMBLE

To Alena, and to my grandson Maxim,
with the hope that one day he will read this book and will
be struck by the contrast between the world in which he
will be living and the absurdity and fears of the one that
had been inherited by his grandparents.

# GORBACHEV'S GAMBLE

## Soviet Foreign Policy and the End of the Cold War

Andrei Grachev

polity

First published in 2008 by Polity Press

Polity Press
65 Bridge Street
Cambridge CB2 1UR, UK

Polity Press
350 Main Street
Malden, MA 02148, USA

ISBN-13: 978-07456-4345-8

A catalogue record for this book is available from the British Library.

Typeset in 11 on 13pt Palatino
by Servis Filmsetting Ltd, Stockport, Cheshire
Printed and bound in the United States of America by Maple Vail

The publisher has used its best endeavours to ensure that the URLs for
external websites referred to in this book are correct and active at the time
of going to press. However, the publisher has no responsibility for the
websites and can make no guarantee that a site will remain live or that the
content is or will remain appropriate.

Every effort has been made to trace all copyright holders, but if any have
been inadvertently overlooked the publishers will be pleased to include
any necessary credits in any subsequent reprint or edition.

For further information on Polity, visit our website: www.polity.co.uk

# CONTENTS

# THE GORBACHEV YEARS: A CHRONOLOGY

**1982**

- **November.** Brezhnev dies, replaced by Andropov as Soviet leader

**1983**

- **March.** Reagan denounces the USSR as 'the evil empire'; announces the Strategic Defense Intitative
- **August.** KAL flight 007 shot down over the Sea of Okhotsk
- **November.** NATO 'Able Archer' 'nuclear scare' (nuclear war gaming) exercise

**1984**

- **February.** Andropov dies, replaced by Chernenko
- **December.** Gorbachev goes to the UK at the head of a Soviet Parliamentarian delegation. First meeting with Margaret Thatcher

**1985**

- **March.** Chernenko dies. Gorbachev is elected Party's General Secretary
- **October.** Gorbachev's official visit to France at the invitation of François Mitterrand
- **November.** US–Soviet summit meeting in Geneva. First meeting of Gorbachev with Reagan

**1986**

- **January.** Soviet government's Declaration proposing to rid the world of nuclear weapons by the year 2000
- **February–March.** 27th Congress of Communist Party of the Soviet Union (CPSU). Announcement of reforms in internal life and radical changes in Soviet foreign policy
- **April.** Explosion of nuclear reactor at the Chernobyl power plant
- **October.** Gorbachev–Reagan meeting in Reykjavik
- **December.** Andrei Sakharov returns to Moscow from his forced exile in Gorky.

**1987**

- **May.** West German amateur pilot Mathias Rust lands on Red Square near the Kremlin. Gorbachev fires the Minister of Defence Marshal Sokolov and top commanders of the Soviet air-defence
- **December.** Gorbachev's official visit to the USA. Signing of the INF Treaty in Washington

**1988**

- **April.** Signing of Geneva Agreements on Afghanistan
- **June–July.** 19th Party Conference in Moscow. Gorbachev proposes major reform of state institutions, including competitive elections for a new legislature
- **September.** Andrei Gromyko 'resigns' from the post of Chairman of Praesidium of Supreme Soviet, replaced by Gorbachev
- **7 December.** Gorbachev addresses the UN General Assembly with a speech in which he announces the de-ideologization of Soviet foreign policy, proposes the renunciation of the use of force in international relations and confirms respect for the right of each people to freely chose their political system

**1989**

- **February.** The Soviet government announces the completion of the withdrawal of Soviet troops from Afghanistan
- **May.** Bush in his first presidential speech on the Soviet Union pledges to move 'beyond containment'

- Gorbachev's visit to the People's Republic of China – first Sino-Soviet summit in 30 years
- **June.** Election in Poland becomes a political triumph for Solidarity
- **August–September.** Massive exodus of East Germans after the opening of the Hungarian border
- **October.** Gorbachev comes to the GDR for the celebration of its 40th anniversary
- **9 November.** The Berlin Wall comes down
- **December.** Gorbachev meets Bush at the 'seasick' summit in Malta
- Václav Havel is elected the new President of Czechoslovakia
- Nicolae Ceauşescu and his wife are executed by a firing squad after a hasty trial

## 1990
- **February.** American, Soviet, British and French foreign ministers during a meeting in Ottawa agree on a '2 + 4' formula of negotiations to solve the problem of German reunification
- **March.** In elections East German voters back the pro-unification party allied with Helmut Kohl
- **May–June.** Bush–Gorbachev summit in Washington and at Camp David
- **July.** Kohl comes to Moscow and is invited by Gorbachev to his native region in the North Caucasus, where the two leaders finalize the agreement on the reunification of Germany and the future Germany's affiliation to NATO.
- **August.** Iraqi troops invade Kuwait. Baker and Shevardnadze issue a joint condemnation of the invasion
- **September.** Bush–Gorbachev meeting in Helsinki to discuss the Persian Gulf
- **October.** East and West Germany unite
- **Gorbachev is awarded the Nobel Peace Prize**
- **November.** Paris Conference on Security and Cooperation in Europe adopts the Charter of a New Europe. NATO and Warsaw Pact leaders sign a Treaty on Conventional Forces in Europe
- The UN Security Council passes Resolution 678 authorizing the use of force to impose on Saddam Hussein the

implementation of the UN resolutions on the evacuation of Kuwait

- **December.** Shevardnadze resigns as Foreign Minister

**1991**

- **January.** In Vilnius Soviet troops storm the local TV station, killing 14 Lithuanians
- Bessmertnykh appointed Foreign Minister
- The Persian Gulf War begins with an air strike on Baghdad
- **February.** The leaders of the Warsaw Pact announce their decision to dissolve the military structure of the alliance on 1 April. (The Political Consultative Council is dissolved on 1 July.)
- **March.** Soviet citizens (in nine republics) vote massively in a referendum in favour of retaining a federal Union
- **June.** Yeltsin elected President of the Russian Republic
- **July.** G7 leaders invite President Gorbachev to their summit in London
- **July–August.** During a US–Soviet summit in Moscow, Gorbachev and Bush sign the START I Treaty.
- **18–21 August.** Attempted coup against Gorbachev by hard-liners
- Upon his return to Moscow from Crimea, where he was sequestrated by the putschists for three days, Gorbachev resigns from his post of the General Secretary of the Communist Party. The activity of the CPSU is suspended at the instigation of Yeltsin
- **October.** Gorbachev and Bush meet in Madrid on the occasion of the Conference on the Middle East
- **November.** Gorbachev reappoints Shevardnadze to the post of Minister of Foreign Affairs
- **8 December.** The leaders of Russia, Ukraine and Belarus meeting in a forest near Minsk declare the dissolution of the Soviet Union and the formation of the Commonwealth of Independent States (CIS)
- **25 December.** Gorbachev resigns from the post of the President of the USSR. The Soviet Union ceases to exist

# PREFACE AND ACKNOWLEDGEMENTS

I owe this book to a combination of various, occasionally accidental circumstances as well as the important contribution and assistance of certain specific persons and institutions. It was certainly chance – indeed, the chance of a lifetime – that gave me the privilege of assisting and participating, to the degree of my capabilities, in an exceptional political adventure: Soviet *perestroika*. Initiated by Mikhail Gorbachev and a group of his followers, it radically transformed the former Soviet Union and played a crucial role in the course of world history at the end of the twentieth century.

As a member of the circle of Gorbachev's advisers, I could closely observe the unfolding scenario of an exciting, unpredictable drama, the political 'revolution from above' that had as its goal the return of an immense country to the course of its natural history, reconciling it with the rest of the world. Conscious that I was witnessing History in the making, I started to take notes during my conversations with Mikhail Gorbachev and at numerous sessions and meetings with his closest colleagues, aides and political allies (some of whom later became his most severe critics or even political adversaries).

These notes and observations served me well during the preparation of my several previous books, where I tried to explore the origins and internal roots of *perestroika*, a phenomenon which otherwise may have seemed to arrive as a sudden thunderbolt within an apparently all-powerful, one-dimensional totalitarian universe. This book, a continuation of these reflections, has been written with the intention of establishing the link between the attempt to democratize the political system and the transformation of foreign policy, a transformation that resulted in the end of the Cold War.

If my first stimulus for writing this book was to record and try to explain a turning point of modern politics, to examine a historic episode that had a profound effect on the world political scene, there was another motive as well. In my view, despite the enormous literature over what is now almost two decades since the end of the Cold War, despite the various explanations and versions of events found in numerous analytical publications, research studies and memoirs (of the principal as well as secondary actors), the origins of this unprecedented historic upheaval are still inadequately explored or understood.

Given a political shock of such dimension, it is not surprising that there have been various, sometimes conflicting interpretations of the end of the Cold War. Yet the particular feature of the events that shook the world in the late 1980s and early 1990s is their contemporary relevance, their continuing effect on the current international situation and even on today's politics. For this reason it is important to have a better understanding of what really happened during those years and why. In the relations of the Soviet Union with its Western partners, what were the motivations and the intentions of the new Soviet leadership after the election of Gorbachev? How was the delicate process of relinquishing the era of confrontation actually handled? Answers to these questions could be of interest not only for historians but also for the decision-makers of today and perhaps of tomorrow as well.

Thus, my intention has been to try to complete the existing picture with the provision of missing details, new information and additional touches that I hope will help to increase our understanding of the meaning of these complex events and draw useful lessons from this unique episode of recent history. Yet it would not have taken the form of a book if I had not been encouraged by others to undertake necessary additional research and to proceed with the realization of this project.

I wish first of all to thank Alex Pravda, the former Director of the Russian and Eurasian Studies Centre at St Antony's College, Oxford, who participated in the original formulation of the concept and joined me in the process of interviewing and recording for posterity the testimony of numerous Soviet decision-makers who were personally involved in the implementation of the policies of those years.

I am profoundly grateful to the many outstanding figures of *perestroika*, starting with President Gorbachev and his principal colleagues, advisers and aides, but also the many diplomatic, military and academic experts and analysts who agreed to answer our questions and to provide us with precious and exclusive insider information about the functioning and mechanisms of Soviet foreign policy.

I would like also to thank their foreign colleagues, who agreed to share their own recollections with us, in this way allowing us to compare and contrast Western and Soviet versions of what happened behind the scenes. Among them I want to mention particularly the contributions of Presidents Jaruzelski and Iliescu from Poland and Romania, the former Hungarian Prime Minister, Gyula Horn, the former French Foreign Ministers, Roland Dumas and Hubert Vedrine, the foreign policy adviser to Chancellor Kohl, Horst Teltschik, and also the US and UK Ambassadors to Moscow, Jack Matlock and Rodric Braithwaite.

At the time of the final revision and editing of this book I received most valuable expert advice from two anonymous readers who were invited to comment on the manuscript by my publisher, and I want to sincerely thank both of them for the encouragement they have given.

I am enormously indebted to Ellen Dahrendorf for the inestimable contribution she has made to give to my writing a more readable form and also for her enthusiastic support which inspired me to go ahead with the research and book project.

The academic assistance and hospitality offered to me by St Antony's College, Oxford, which generously accepted me as a senior fellow during the period of my research, was exceptional and extremely helpful.

In conclusion I would like to express my warmest thanks for the support offered to this research by the Leverhulme Trust, without which this book would probably never have appeared.

# INTRODUCTION

Since wars begin in the minds of men, it is in the minds of men
that the defences of peace must be constructed.

Constitution of UNESCO

The radical shift of Soviet foreign policy and the subsequent
chain of events that eventually led to what later came to be
called 'the end of the Cold War' are justly associated with the
name of Mikhail Gorbachev. No one – whether his former
political partners in the West or his opponents or most severe
critics in his own country – contests the significance of the
change he managed to bring about in the world political arena.
Most observers seem ready to recognize the value of his strategic vision as well as the tactical skill that allowed him to extir-
pate ideological antagonism from East–West relations, putting
an end to military confrontation and eliminating, it is hoped
forever, the danger of a third world war.

There is, however, disagreement about certain aspects of the
events in question which continue to provoke debate within
Russia and abroad, largely concerned with a limited set of
questions, namely: was Gorbachev free to chose other variants
for his foreign policy? Could he not have obtained a better
'price' from the West in return for introducing such an unprecedented transformation of the foreign policy of the second
world superpower? Could the 'reward' eventually offered to

Gorbachev by the West in the form of more vigorous political support and, in particular, economic assistance have helped him to secure his internal power position which would have enabled him to take his reform project further? Finally, and perhaps the most crucial question: what were the basic internal and external factors that pushed the Soviet leadership and Gorbachev personally to engage in such a breathtaking, politically risky adventure – the promotion of a qualitatively new foreign policy that with great solemnity was designated as the 'new political thinking'?

Gorbachev's practical activity in the field of foreign policy produced controversial results. It brought about the end of the Cold War as well as unprecedented change on the international scene, contributing to the advance of democratic forces, the liberation of oppressed nations and an acceleration of the natural course of world history. At the same time, the implosion of a country that had constituted one of the props of the postwar international order contributed to the rise of political instability and a return of old tensions with a proliferation of breeding grounds for new conflicts.

Gorbachev's own statements on the subject do not always provide absolute answers, including comments made several years after these historic events unfolded. The same can be said of the numerous memoirs by other key political players of the period that have been published in the course of the last fifteen years. Naturally each contribution adds its own particular angle to the recapitulation of the course of events, sometimes confirming but quite often contradicting the versions provided by other decision-makers. Taken together these accounts represent a gold-mine of information about these exciting years of historic change. Yet they do not provide an answer to the main question: 'Why did it happen?' To this day, therefore, the sudden ending of the Cold War, surely the dominant feature of the second half of the twentieth century, continues to be one of the most unexpected and perplexing phenomena of our time.

Most Western scholars, with hindsight, have sought to rationalize tumultuous developments that quite often were spontaneous in character; their books tend to present the Soviet leadership's policies of these years against a monochrome, rather flat background, rarely referring to the difficult compromises that had to be reached on each occasion behind the scenes.[1] What also appears to be a common feature of various analyses is a tendency to ignore the fact that the frequent zigzags of Soviet foreign policy during the Gorbachev years represented, above all, one of the most important components of the tremendous political struggle that accompanied the realization of his global project of *internal reform*.[2]

Several years after his resignation, in an interview with the author, Gorbachev confirmed that from the very beginning he regarded the radical improvement of relations between the Soviet Union and the West as a basic precondition for the success of *perestroika*, 'since without putting an end to the fatal spiral of the arms race we could have drawn the whole world into an abyss and would have had to abandon all our plans for internal reform'.[3] This statement by Gorbachev was corroborated by his closest political ally and the chief ideologist of *perestroika*, Aleksandr Yakovlev. For Yakovlev also, the introduction of radical change in the Soviet Union's relations with the West and establishment of cooperative relations between the USSR and the outside world represented an integral part of a much broader project: the democratic transformation of the Soviet political system.[4]

This explanation certainly differs from interpretations of the reasons for the new Soviet foreign policy given by most Western political leaders and analysts, more or less summarized in the formula of Michael R. Beschloss and Strobe Talbott in their book *At the Highest Levels*. They argue that 'the improvements in the Kremlin's behavior were a direct result of forty years of consistent pressure from the West and particularly, for the previous eight years, from the Reagan administration'.[5] A more laconic expression of the same view appears in James Baker's memoirs: 'Containment had worked,' announced the US State Secretary, speaking at Princeton on 12 December 1991 in the presence of George Kennan, the author of the 'long telegram' sent from Moscow in 1946 in the first months of the Cold War, where the formula appeared for the first time.[6]

This amounts to a rather simplistic reading of an extremely complicated and controversial historical episode. Explanation of the unexpected ending of decades of ideological and military confrontation between East and West is reduced to one dimension – the determination of Western hard-liners. Having rejected the pacification course advocated by naïve promoters of *détente* as well as the hopes of 'realists' to re-educate communist leaders according to the standards of Western civilization, they chose to wear out the Soviet totalitarian system by imposing on it the unbearable arms race and in this way compel it to capitulation.[7]

There is an alternative Western interpretation according to which the triumph of the West was not in fact achieved by frontal pressure on the USSR, which only served to encourage the totalitarian regime to maintain the atmosphere of a besieged fortress inside the country as well as throughout the zone of Soviet influence; rather it was the peaceful 'managed cohabitation' which in its different forms – from Willy Brandt's *Ostpolitik* to the provisions of the Helsinki Final Act – managed to stage a trap for the Soviet leaders, obliging them to compete with the West not just in the field of weapons production, where their system proved to be quite efficient, but also in a totally different area. The Soviet Union proved unable to compete when it came to assuring individual freedom and civil rights, or, above all, the creation of decent conditions for everyday life. It was largely this policy that eventually led to the internal decomposition of the Soviet monolith, giving birth to the viruses of pro-Western reformist currents. The shell was bound to crack.

Even a combination of these apparently divergent explanations presents just a part of the picture. It should not be forgotten that the Soviet leaders were just as enthusiastic as their Western adversaries in their efforts to speed up the arms race while hoping to make use of the fruits of political *détente*. However, the main point is this: those who award the prize for bringing about the downfall of the communist project in the USSR exclusively to Western actors tend to present the Soviet colossus merely as an object to be manipulated by alternative versions of 'hard' and 'soft' Western (primarily American) power. The most crucial factor is ignored if there is no proper analysis of the dynamics of the evolution and internal transformation of Soviet society, a transformation that has followed a logic of its own, quite apart from externally imposed influence and pressure.

It is understandable that Gorbachev and members of his 'team' (Aleksandr Yakovlev, Eduard Shevardnadze, Anatoli Chernyaev, Vadim Medvedev . . .) have challenged the thesis that the West can claim sole credit for an unconditional victory in the Cold War, in view of their personal involvement in the decision-making processes during the years of *perestroika*. Given the fall of the Berlin Wall, the unification of Germany and the withdrawal from Afghanistan as well as the unprecedented achievements in the field of disarmament, they have convincing arguments to plead their case.[8] However there are other quite different Soviet voices – some who from the outset were sceptical of Gorbachev's project and strategy, others who only later became critics or political adversaries (Yegor Ligachev, Vladimir Kryuchkov, Georgi Kornienko, Anatoli Dobrynin, Valentin Falin . . .), whose testimony confirms, as the reader will see, the endogenous roots of the process that led to a qualitative change in Soviet foreign policy when a new national leader appeared on the scene.[9]

Nor can we ignore the opinions of Russian politicians, experts and commentators, increasingly audible in Putin's Russia, who, speaking with hindsight and for evident internal political reasons, prefer to present the end of the Cold War as the result of the naïve or, even worse, the consciously 'capitulationist' policy of Gorbachev and his supporters, who 'betrayed' their country's national interests by surrendering to the perennial Western enemy. Paradoxically, their interpretation of the end of the Cold War as a historic defeat for the Soviet Union or Putin's description of the disintegration of the country as 'the biggest geo-strategic catastrophe of the last century' coincides with the most arrogant Western position that proclaims the absolute triumph of the West over its Soviet strategic rival. Such a view leaves no room for doubt: what happened to the Soviet Union and to the communist regime in general was the result of 'high treason' by the initiators of *perestroika*.

In defence of their political and foreign policy choices, Gorbachev, Shevardnadze, Yakovlev and their other allies argue that what once had been an *'arms* wrestling' contest between the two superpowers had escalated into a quest for strategic domination via a monstrous arms race that had become a major threat for the whole of humankind. This is why all responsible politicians had to regard the ending of the Cold War as their first priority. It is this assumption that led to the conception of the 'new political thinking', soon to be followed by unprecedented practical initiatives by the Soviet leadership under Gorbachev. The extraordinary political moves, the proposals for unexpected compromise, the unilateral gestures and concessions all would have been inconceivable in the framework of the traditional logic of superpower confrontation.

Acting in accordance with the principles and spirit of the new political philosophy, but also, as stated on a number of occasions by Gorbachev, merely following the criteria of the common sense and universal norms of human morality, the authors of the new Soviet foreign policy would not admit that they acted under constraint or were borrowing Western values. The theorists and practitioners of the 'new thinking' considered it to be a home-grown product, conditioned mostly by internal problems, and if they referred to Western sources of influence and inspiration, they would mention first of all the ideas to be found in the Russell–Einstein Manifesto, the reports of the Palme Commission or the Club of Rome or other similar appeals calling for an end to the absurd logic of nuclear confrontation and demanding that the attention of world politics be turned to the global problems and challenges facing the human species. For example, such terms and notions in the vocabulary of the 'new thinking' as 'reasonable security' and 'non-offensive defence' were promoted mainly by the Western peace movements and peace research networks in the USA and Western Europe (for example, the Pugwash group or Physicians for Nuclear Disarmament) and not taken from the West's strategic doctrines.

Moreover, if they admit that there was indeed effective pressure coming from the West which had an influence on the subsequent development of Soviet policy, it was not a question of the military threat or the politics of 'containment' but rather the example of successful economic development along with the attractiveness of ideas of political freedom which were, in fact, becoming important factors in the *internal evolution of Soviet society*.

Paradoxically enough, at least during the first years of *perestroika*, the new Soviet leaders failed to see the danger of possible economic ruin if the Soviet Union were to follow the United States in a new round of the arms race. Leaders of *perestroika*, particularly at its initial stage, were barely conscious of the scale of disaster unfolding within the national economy and had only a rather vague idea about its capacity to survive if there were to be an abolition of centralized planning and an end to the administrative command system. One explanation for this, as Gorbachev admitted later, was the fact that even the members of the new Politburo, himself included, had yet to discover the monstrous size of the Soviet military-industrial complex.

> Already at the time when I became a member of the Secretariat and later of the Politburo of the Central Committee I was conscious of the fact that neither I nor other members of the Soviet political leadership were getting full information about the real figures for our defence spending. Even at the next stage in my capacity as General Secretary and *de facto* head of the Soviet state, I had enormous difficulty squeezing out of our military lobby genuine information about the amount of money being poured into this bottomless barrel. First of all, this was because the people in charge had got accustomed to not having to report to anybody about how the money was being used and they certainly did not want to sacrifice their privileged status. Secondly, quite often they themselves did not possess total information.[10]

*    *    *

Analysing the motives and expectations of the initiators of the 'new thinking' and then comparing them to its balance sheet, one is tempted to conclude that the whole construction rested on a rather shaky foundation. The pioneer reformers of the totalitarian system expected a smooth evolution from rigid Soviet communism to some vague political model combining the social paternalism of the centralized state with a modern social democratic version of capitalism; obviously they were unable to envision all the consequences for the functioning of the highly centralized economy when they attempted simultaneously to impose profound political reform along with the introduction of the logic of the market. Still less could they have foreseen the implosion of the multinational state accompanied by the free-fall of the USSR's international authority and, with that, the credibility of its foreign policy.

In addition to the above, the Soviet missionaries of 'new thinking' also idealistically (some would say, naïvely) believed that once they had proclaimed themselves to be new *partners of the West* in the quest for peace and stability, their former adversaries would eagerly accept Soviet pledges at face value and would adapt their own policies in a practical way. They hoped that once relieved from the fear of the Soviet threat, the West not only would resist the temptation to profit strategically from the transition crisis of post-communist society, it also would meet them halfway in a common effort to remodel international relations along the lines of their messianic project. However, the fact that the results of their actions proved to be quite different from their initial aspirations does not mean that such an outcome was inevitable.

In order to provide a more stereoscopic image of this unprecedented political adventure, it seemed useful to collect and compare the testimony of a large number of varied political players and top functionaries of the former Soviet Union, the men who were involved in the elaboration and application of major foreign policy decisions. They have often been asked to comment on the same events. The people who were interviewed come from various levels of the Soviet power hierarchy and represent the most important political and state institutions and think-tanks of the Soviet epoch: the Party apparatus, the Ministry of Foreign Affairs, the Ministry of Defence, the KGB, academics and military industry specialists. Each one of them played an appreciable role on the level of decision-making at different stages, offering expertise or counselling the political leaders. Together with the personal testimony of Mikhail Gorbachev and remarks by a number of former Politburo members who share with him the political and personal responsibility for the remarkable shift of the Soviet foreign policy at the end of the 1980s, these statements provide a multi-voice chorus that allows us better to understand the origin and trajectory of events leading to the overall reshuffle of the world power balance by the beginning of the 1990s.

# I

# PREPARING THE CHANGE

We reformers dreamed of ending . . . the division between East
and West, of halting the insanity of the arms race and ending the
'Cold War'.

Aleksandr Yakovlev, *'Gor'kaia chasha'*[1]

## Dual-Track Diplomacy

In order to understand what made possible the emergence of
'new thinking' as a conceptual base for Soviet foreign policy in
the Gorbachev years, it is necessary to explore the political and
intellectual 'soil' from which it arose. It is also essential to recall
the basic characteristics of the 'old political thinking' that determined USSR behaviour on the world scene during the long
years of the Cold War period. How had it influenced the international position of the USSR at the time of Gorbachev's election to the position of General Secretary in March 1985? An
analysis of this kind should identify the ideas that began to
ferment within circles of the Soviet political elite several years
before 1985. It would otherwise be impossible to explain the
colossal change that occurred in Soviet political behaviour with
the arrival of Mikhail Gorbachev, other than by the caprice of a
Providence that chose him as its arm.

One of the most crucial factors paving the way for future changes in Soviet foreign policy at the end of Brezhnev's reign was a growing feeling within Soviet society that the *civilization project* initiated at the time of the 1917 October Revolution had reached a stage of general exhaustion, if not fiasco. Associated with initial Bolshevik political ambition, its main message consisted initially in proposing an alternative model of societal organization founded on an ideological base imposed and supervised by the state: its protagonists were absolutely convinced that this model was destined to prevail throughout the world.

However, the initial messianic ambitions of the founding fathers of the Soviet state soon had to be revised. Not long after his death, Lenin's hopes of unleashing the world communist revolution were rapidly reduced by his more sober and disillusioned successors to Stalin's project of building 'socialism in one country'.

In accordance with this evolution of ideology, the command centre of Soviet foreign policy gradually moved from the structures of the Communist International (created in March 1919) to a much more traditional state institution – the People's Commissariat (later Ministry) for Foreign Affairs. But a congenital contradiction remained at the heart of the Soviet state. Throughout its entire history, Soviet foreign policy never abandoned the 'double track', constantly oscillating between support for 'revolutionary forces' (thus challenging the existing world order) and a quest for stability that required traditional great power behaviour and the application of *realpolitik*.

The innate duplicity of this policy was carefully managed by the Soviet Party-state leadership's highest political '*instance*' (a term usually used in Soviet bureaucratic jargon to identify the Party apparatus), and found its reflection in the parallel handling of the different aspects of foreign policy by its two 'arms' – mutually complementary and at the same time rival structures – the Ministry of Foreign Affairs (MID) and the International Department of the Central Committee (ID), the unofficial heir of the Secretariat of the Communist International.

While the MID was charged with looking after 'stability' and assuring the Soviet state's presence and position in the world 'concert of powers', the ID was supposed to encourage and introduce the 'change' needed to provide evidence of the advance of the world 'revolutionary process' and of the continuous shift of the world balance of power to the advantage of the USSR. These two dimensions of Soviet foreign policy, the 'realist' and the 'ideological', not only often were in competition with each other but also regularly changed places in the hierarchy of the Soviet leadership's political priorities depending upon internal policy concerns.

The curious amalgam of ideological ambition and permanent fear within a Soviet leadership obsessed by the danger of being 'crushed' (a term used by Stalin) by the powerful capitalist enemy quite often provoked an ostentatiously aggressive image of the country's foreign policy, even at times when the real intentions of its leaders (and certainly their capacities) were rather modest. As prisoners of communist dogma, the leaders of the USSR regarded the capitalist world and its member states as historic enemies with which one was obliged to coexist and sometimes even to cooperate only because of the (temporary) unfavourable balance of forces. Even the solemnly proclaimed Khrushchev policy of peaceful coexistence[2] was perceived to be forced by circumstances and was intended to fill in an interval in the expectation that ultimately the capitalist rival would disappear, condemned by history in accordance with Marxist doctrine. Thus, even after initial hopes of world revolution evaporated, the 'coexistence' façade of USSR foreign policy directed at the Western world remained largely an expression of political tactics, while competition, confrontation and worldwide 'continuous class struggle' represented the real political strategy that would lead to the happy ending of History.

However, from the end of the 1960s, even the most convincing ideological arguments or persuasive citations from Marx and Lenin could no longer obscure the reality of the economic situation of the Soviet Union for the leadership of the country. Unable to nourish any hope of being able to do away with the capitalist world by military means, especially since the 1962 Cuban missile crisis, they nevertheless continued to use ideological jargon stressing the 'antagonistic conflict' between the two systems, mostly as a means of legitimizing the totalitarian regime within Soviet society and in order to justify the state of the permanent economic disaster produced by administrative mismanagement of the economy.

In fact, having started out in the first post-revolutionary years as fundamentalist missionaries of Marxist doctrine, by the 1970s and 1980s Soviet leaders had become its prisoners. The 'dual-track' foreign policy of the USSR quite naturally became the programmed victim of a broadening gap between the requirements of a sterile ideological project and the reality of a changing world. More and more often obliged to deal with the aggravating internal problems of the communist regime, Soviet leaders were forced to sacrifice official strategy based on ideology, replacing it with survival tactics. And although formally the declared strategic horizon of the Soviet state's long-term policy continued to be the predetermined victory over capitalism, this hypothetical goal virtually disappeared from the field of practical policy, passing to the sphere of propaganda, while the foreign policy sector was exclusively engaged in the daily exercise of obligatory coexistence.

After Khrushchev, who was perhaps the last sincere believer in the possible victory of the world communist cause, the ideological dimension of Soviet foreign policy was gradually reduced to rhetoric and propaganda while the conservative structure of the MID, headed by Andrei Gromyko, definitely gained the upper hand over the International Department (led by Boris Ponomarev) in the handling of foreign affairs. The MID's new status was confirmed in 1973 by Gromyko's elevation to the position of full member of Politburo, which demonstrated his superiority over Ponomarev, who continued to remain a candidate member.

Of course, rhetoric devoted to the continuous advance of the 'world revolutionary process' still could be heard in the public statements of Soviet leaders and continued to occupy an honourable place in the political reports of the General Secretary to Party congresses. Yet it was mostly meant for internal consumption and used as one of the elements of the stabilization mechanism of the system. It was increasingly evident that the actual foreign policy of the Soviet Union, although maintaining some relation to its ideological origin, had sacrificed its revolutionary ambition for the sake of great power pragmatism.

\* \* \*

It could be argued that the institutionalized confrontation with the West became one of the basic factors assuring the survival of regime, at least until the time it reached the stage of virtual collapse at the beginning of the 1980s with a succession of deaths among its ailing top leaders.[3] By this time the logic of superpower competition had so tightly chained together the military-industrial complexes of the Soviet Union and the United States that their functioning and development became *de facto* interconnected. Because it was rather obscurely defined, the mutually accepted formula of strategic balance offered large margins of interpretation for both sides, allowing each to present the other's moves as a real or potential breach of the strategic equilibrium. And despite the fact that political calculations or corporate and financial interests on each side must have played an important role in the misinterpretation of the opponent's acts and intentions, in many cases it was based on genuine mutual misgivings.

In fact it was only after the end of the Cold War, when decision-makers of both sides (with their experts and advisers) could confront and compare the mutual suspicions of those times, that the unprecedented, jointly constructed 'hoax of the century' was gradually unveiled. A striking incident of this kind took place when top political and military advisers of the US and the former Soviet Union met during an Oral History Conference, 'Understanding the End of the Cold War', that took place at Brown University, in the USA, between 7 and 10 May 1998. At this conference, President Reagan's former National Security Adviser, Robert McFarlane, argued that the character of the defence spending of the Soviet Union in this period could hardly be justified by feelings of insecurity since 'much of the money was going not into defensive systems but into force projection'. For the former US Ambassador to the USSR, Jack Matlock, Soviet foreign and security policy 'did not seem to be one of retrenchment but rather expansionist with the situations in Angola, Ethiopia, South Yemen, Mozambique and especially Afghanistan providing apparent proof of it'.

At the same time their Soviet colleague, Anatoli Chernyaev, maintained that since the Cuban missile crisis, any support for 'revolutionary change' remained largely a 'hollow shell', verbal ideological wrapping destined (and designed) mostly for internal consumption to support the image of the Soviet Union as an mighty superpower. 'No one would seriously think of going to war with the West over Angola or Ethiopia.'[4]

For the Soviet experts of the war-time generation (Anatoli Chernyaev, Georgi Shakhnazarov, Georgi Arbatov – the former two served as principal political aides to the President while the latter played the role of an *ad hoc* adviser to Gorbachev), one of the explanations for a seemingly irrational 'obsession' with security concerns that characterized Soviet behaviour in the postwar years could be found in the '1941 syndrome'. This of course was the year of Hitler's surprise attack on the Soviet Union which provoked the disorderly retreat of the Red Army, caused heavy losses among the military and the civilian population and almost resulted in the seizure of Moscow by the rapidly advancing German army. After the experience of 1941, an obsession with the danger of sudden invasion or a 'disarming strike' coming from the West continued to condition the political behaviour of an entire generation of Soviet leaders such as Brezhnev, Ustinov and Andropov; they were programmed to give absolute priority to the question of national defence and to accept the logic of an exhausting arms race not only with the United States but also, more or less, with the rest of the world. 'While talking about "equal security", it was the ambition of the Soviet leaders to match not only US capabilities but also those of America's European allies in NATO and China as well,' states General Viktor Starodubov.[5]

This kind of paranoiac policy started to produce devastating effects on the Soviet economy, which could ill afford the expense of an unlimited arms race, especially after the fall of world oil prices. It was also at this time that the entire Soviet political and economic model began to show signs of systemic crisis. As confirmed by one of the chief analysts of the former KGB, Nikolai Leonov, 'the people from the military-industrial complex or its representatives didn't take economics into account at all. They thought that our resources were unlimited. As if they had not been informed as to the country's real situation.'[6]

After almost sixty years in power, the communist regime proved incapable of keeping its initial promises and was apparently losing its historic bet against its capitalist rival. Rejecting the very idea of any reform or modernization, the ailing Soviet Party leadership and state bureaucracy comfortably settled into the climate of 'stagnation', seeking to perpetuate the status quo.

The only sphere in which the decaying regime could hope to produce any sign of 'historic dynamism' was in the foreign policy arena, and particularly with regard to the expansion of the Soviet presence and influence in the 'third world'. Soviet leaders preferred to rely on 'external' success to demonstrate the 'historic superiority' of the communist project for a number of reasons. First of all, it was a way of diverting the attention of the Soviet population from the rather obvious failures inside the country. Secondly, they believed that indirect confrontation with their main Western rival, the United States, in the 'no man's land' of 'third world' countries was relatively safe and presented no risks of a dangerous military conflict between the two superpowers. Furthermore, the military-industrial complex remained the only sector of the Soviet economy that was rapidly increasing its production, was competitive on the world market and apparently supplied the political leadership with 'cheap', convincing arguments capable of winning the favour of a number of 'third world' leaders, dragging them into the Soviet sphere of influence.

Finally, Soviet Party and military bosses convinced themselves that the Western world, and above all the US, especially after the humiliating defeat in Vietnam, was being pushed into strategic retreat, leaving them a chance to gain the offensive. During the 25th Party Congress in February 1976, Leonid Brezhnev could boast that the historical 'correlation of forces' was shifting in favour of socialism'.[7]

The events that followed in the late 1970s seemed to confirm this conclusion, including the April 1978 coup staged by the radical leftist officers in Afghanistan, the June 1978 'anti-imperialist' coup in South Yemen, the toppling of the Shah and Khomeini's accession to power in Iran in February 1979, and in July the victory of the Nicaraguan Sandinistas over Somoza. All these developments in the 'third world' could be considered to be American defeats, along with the impressive scale of the anti-nuclear movement in Western Europe that forced President Carter to abort his neutron bomb programme.

It was in these years that the Soviet military, backed by the monstrous industrial complex, gained a position of almost unrestrained domination of the political and economic life of the country, able to prevail over the Party apparatus. This process was strengthened and accelerated by two parallel events – the beginning of the rapid physical decay of the General Secretary of the Central Committee, Leonid Brezhnev, and the appointment of Dimitri Ustinov to the post of Minister of Defence in 1976. Since he had been Weapons Minister under Stalin and subsequently, putting Ustinov at the head of the Ministry of Defence combined the functions of purchaser and supplier; this had the effect of exempting the giant military-industrial complex, of which he became the sole ruler, from any political control. As confirmed by the International Department's military expert, General Viktor Starodubov:

> Ustinov brought the psychology of the producer of armaments into the strategic planning of the Defence Ministry. Since it was customary in his previous role to devise excessive, 'reserve', budget demands, he continued to do the same except that now he was addressing these demands not to the government or to the Party leadership but to himself. As a result there was an arms over-saturation with an unnecessary duplication of similar armaments systems, which was regarded critically even by military professionals.[8]

Profiting from his direct access to the ailing Brezhnev, Ustinov was guaranteed to get the formal approval of the Politburo for his demands, virtually without discussion. According to Anatoli Chernyaev, from the beginning of the 1980s

> the military were pressuring our politicians so strongly that when Ustinov stood up in the Politburo to demand new billions of roubles for something, nobody dared to say anything against it. Such practice resulted in the almost routine acceptance by the Politburo of practically every demand of the military without any regard for potential political consequences or the possibility of retaliatory measures that could be taken by the other side.[9]

Attempting to account for this obviously bizarre situation, Andrei Gromyko (who in his role as the Minister of Foreign Affairs normally would have been responsible for preventing it) provided the following explanation to his son:

> Ustinov's presentation of new demands to the Politburo was usually preceded by a *tête-à-tête* consultation with Brezhnev, who almost always gave his consent to anything. After that no one would dare to object. To obtain Brezhnev's approval, Ustinov, who knew him well, would not hesitate to profit from the fact that for the General Secretary a quantitative approach to the evaluation of military might normally would prevail over a qualitative one.[10]

Yet this is a rather facile version that should not be taken as the whole truth. Brezhnev's 'simplistic' approach toward the complicated question of maintaining geo-strategic parity with the West would not have prevailed had it not been shared and exploited by other members of the Soviet political leadership. In addition to Ustinov, this would have included Andropov and also Gromyko himself.

## The Military-Diplomatic Complex

The rapid development of the Soviet military-industrial complex was accompanied by the formation of another coalition, a 'military-diplomatic complex' forged between the Ministry of Defence and the MID. Certainly it was not just personal friendship that lay at the base of the close political alliance between Dimitri Ustinov and Andrei Gromyko; there was also a community of corporate interests and a shared belief that only a military build-up would assure real great power status for the Soviet Union as well as the best political bargaining position in its relations with the US. In the next decade these considerations would transform 'Mr Nyet' (Gromyko's nickname given to him by his Western colleagues due to the legendary rigidity of his negotiating behaviour) into the *de facto* 'Minister of Foreign Affairs of the Soviet Military'.

Each party to this alliance benefited from it. The Soviet military build-up provided the MID with necessary arguments in order forcefully to assert the USSR's importance on the world scene. Consequently Gromyko himself was upgraded to the position of the nasty but unavoidable partner of his Western colleagues, above all the Americans. The Minister of Defence could in his turn rely on the MID to supply political justification for his military programmes. (In later years when Ustinov and afterwards Gromyko departed from the political scene, their alliance was reproduced by political complicity between their former first deputies – Marshal Sergei Akhromeev and Georgi Kornienko.)

The Gromyko–Ustinov alliance was soon reinforced by the association of the KGB Chairman, Yuri Andropov. Like Ustinov, Gromyko and Andropov were promoted to the position of full Politburo members in 1973. All three had similar views, sharing a 'hawkish' approach toward handling Soviet policy on the world scene.[11] The constitution of this new 'troika' confirmed the changed balance of forces within the Politburo that began to evolve after 1975 when Brezhnev suffered the first stroke that considerably diminished his physical and intellectual capacities.[12]

It was at this time that the Soviet leaders' new assertive behaviour on the international scene was exemplified in a most spectacular fashion by two defiant moves: first, the decision to replace medium range SS-4 and SS-5 missiles deployed in the European part of the USSR by the much more powerful and precise SS-20 'euro-missiles', thus considerably increasing the Soviet nuclear offensive potential; next, the invasion of Afghanistan. Both initiatives were imposed on Brezhnev along with the rest of Politburo by the *troika*. Trying to justify these decisions in the later, 'Gorbachev years', Gromyko, who had been largely responsible for both actions, said the following in a kind of repentance speech during a session of the Politburo (on 20 June 1988):

In Khrushchev's time we produced 600 nuclear bombs. Khrushchev himself from time to time asked the question: 'When should we stop?' Later under Brezhnev we should have taken a more reasonable position. But we remained attached to the same principle: since they [the US] are running ahead, we should do the same, as if it was a sports competition. . . . It was an evidently primitive approach but our supreme military commanders were convinced that if a war was started, we could win it. That was evidently an erroneous position, completely erroneous. And the political leadership was fully responsible for it.[13]

To this day, former experts of the Soviet General Staff involved in military planning as well as functionaries in the Party apparatus responsible for the defence sector continue to argue that Soviet senior army commanders as well as political leaders 'were all convinced that the USSR was merely catching up with the USA in the strategic arms race since the Americans were always ahead of us by 20–30 per cent'.[14] At the same time they claim that ever since the Cuban missile crisis in 1962, Soviet military doctrine excluded the launching of the first nuclear strike and that such an option was never considered at the highest level within the Soviet political leadership.[15]

While the Soviet side pointed to US supremacy over the Soviet Union in the total number of warheads, the Americans insisted that the USSR had an advantage in 'throw-weight' capacity and in the number of land-based strategic missiles. Each side suspected and accused the other of intending to build up a first-strike potential, while both sought any excuse to continue the upwards spiral of the arms race. The two super-powers engaged in this exercise were obviously motivated more by a common interest in preserving the status quo (including the positions of their respective military lobbies and industrial complexes) than by real defence concerns. A major distinction between the two positions lay only in the fact that the US could at least justify this strategy with the hope of bringing the Soviet economy to ruin. As for the Soviet Union, according to Anatoli Chernyaev, 'the inner logic of self-destruction hardly required an arms race in order for the Soviet system to reach its inevitable terminal stage'.[16]

Thus for some top-level members of the Reagan administration, in the words of Robert McFarlane (a former Deputy National Security Adviser in 1982–3 and National Security Adviser from 1983 to 1986) aside from their strategic value, new armaments programmes represented 'an economic argument', since 'the leverage that it would give us and the amount it would require you to spend would favor our side'.[17] Seen from this perspective, President Reagan's SDI (Strategic Defense Initiative) programme (often referred to as 'Star Wars'), apart from its formally declared goal to put pressure on the Soviet leadership, compelling it to agree to more far-reaching arms reductions, was also supposed to have the effect of a 'last straw breaking the back of the Russian camel' by pushing the Soviet economy 'beyond the level it could afford',[18] while its strategic role was highly hypothetical.

It fact, neither approach produced the desired result or impressed the Soviet leadership enough to make it curtail its strategic ambitions or reduce its military spending. And this despite the fact that, contrary to the United States, which was allocating roughly 6 per cent of GNP to defence, the Soviet Union, with an economy of only half the size (according to optimistic evaluations), was officially spending around 16 per cent of its GNP on military purposes.[19]

Reasons for such 'politically irresponsible behavior', in the words of Georgi Arbatov, former Director of the Institute of the USA and Canada Studies, were multiple. The most important probably were *ideological*: the Soviet leadership of Brezhnev's time remained the hostage of anti-Western complexes, convinced by its own propaganda about the 'aggressive nature of imperialism' and its capacity to resort to military force in order to destroy the socialist community. Hence the obligation for the Soviet state and its citizens to pay whatever price necessary for its defence.[20] Yet the ideological wrapping was less an explanation than a cover; there were other *political and corporate* motives for pursuing this line, since the Soviet regime used the bugaboo of an 'external threat' as an essential psychological tool in support of the totalitarian system.

In the seemingly favourable international context of the 1970s, the governing *troika* within the Soviet leadership saw no reason to refrain from a more 'muscular' foreign policy. On the diplomatic front, following the instructions of Gromyko, the Soviet MID was doing its best to clear the way for the new appetites of the Soviet military. According to one of the USSR negotiators at the US–Soviet disarmament negotiations, Oleg Grinevsky, the treaties that Soviet diplomacy was busy trying to extract from the US would 'give us an opportunity to change the structure of the Soviet military profoundly. . . . We had the clear feeling that the US was losing the arms race and were determined to profit from it.'[21]

Naturally the *troika* of hard-liners in the Politburo advocated this policy as an 'obligatory' defensive move by the USSR, which was forced on Soviet policy-makers by the 'aggressive designs' of world imperialism and was necessary in order to protect allies and secure the status of the Soviet Union as the second world superpower. And just as additional military spending was justified by the need to 'catch up' with the US in the arms race, Soviet leaders viewed their own behaviour in the 'third world' as merely a replica of traditional American conduct.

Commenting on the spectacular shift in American policy toward the Soviet Union under Ronald Reagan at the beginning of the 1980s, Andrei Gromyko, as quoted in his son's memoirs, believed that the international situation was 'heating up': 'The US is trying to challenge the status of the Soviet Union as the great power.' To demonstrate this, the Soviet minister repeated the mantra of official Soviet accusations, citing Reagan's invasion of Grenada and the 'attacks' on Nicaragua, Ethiopia, Angola and Mozambique; the US was also attempting to undermine the solidity of the socialist community by profiting from the internal difficulties in Poland. From Anatoli Gromyko's memoirs it can be seen that Soviet leaders of that time were quite impressed by the bellicose ideological rhetoric of the US President, whose speeches frequently included expressions such as the 'crusade against communism' or a promise to throw it on the 'scrap heap of history'.[22] One of the top Soviet diplomatic experts, Oleg Grinevsky, who used to meet Gromyko quite often, quotes the Soviet minister from the conversation he had with him in January 1984: 'I think to read Reagan and his team, they are trying to destroy us and we really have to do something against it,' said Gromyko, continuing: 'This is fascism. There is fascism beginning in the United States.'[23]

Yet according to Georgi Shakhnazarov (the former deputy head of the Socialist Countries Department of the Central Committee and future political adviser to Mikhail Gorbachev), his conversations with various members of Politburo suggested that it was not the danger of US aggression against the Soviet Union that was influencing the Soviet leadership's foreign policy of the early 1980s; rather it was the quest to enlarge Soviet control over the 'no man's land' of the third world. Success here would serve not a strategic but rather an internal political purpose: 'It would provide compensation for the shortcomings of the failing system and at the same time would offer new-found hope that the communist project could regain its historic perspective.'[24]

This perverse expression of a survival instinct by a dying system, wrapped in the formulas of political and ideological 'renaissance', had the effect of pushing the Soviet leadership to finance its 'family' of clients in Asia, Africa and Latin America despite the tremendous cost of economic and military support already being provided to the other 'socialist countries' and 'progressive' regimes.[25] Since most Soviet clients in the 'third world' were governed by economically inefficient authoritarian or dictatorial regimes, there was usually little hope that credits or loans would be repaid to the generous donor. This situation not only put additional stress on the already anaemic economy, it also meant that Soviet foreign policy became the hostage of virtually any 'third world' leader who declared his 'socialist orientation'. Striking examples of this self-imposed dependency would include the cases of Angola and Afghanistan, where the Soviet Union was compelled to act under the pressure of events it had neither instigated nor anticipated and where it was forced to respond to *faits accomplis* which in the longer run ran counter to its own strategic interests.

In Angola, for example (according to the testimony of Gromyko's first deputy, Georgi Kornienko), the Soviet leadership was obliged to react to Fidel Castro's largely impulsive decision to send Cuban troops to fight on the side of the MPLA. The Soviet Union was faced with a difficult choice: either publicly to distance itself from the maverick Cuban leader or comply with Fidel's demands, supplying transport planes for his troops and getting involved in the whole adventure. In the end the Soviets reluctantly followed Fidel.[26]

As for Afghanistan, different sources in the then Soviet leadership (again Georgi Kornienko and the former KGB

Chairman, Vladimir Kryuchkov, who at the end of the 1970s was the head of Soviet External Intelligence) claim that from 1976 the Soviet leadership used KGB channels to communicate with Nur Muhammed Taraki and his colleagues in the Khalk, one of the two main Marxist parties in Afghanistan, urging him against any violent attempt to seize political power. However, in April 1978, the leftist officers connected with the Khalk staged a military coup against the government of Prime Minister Mohammed Daoud without a preliminary consultation with Moscow.[27]

Apparently despite their initial hesitation, the Soviet leaders could not resist the temptation to profit from the chance that was offered to the USSR – an unexpected opportunity to project its strategic influence into the sensitive zone to the south of its borders, allowing the possibility of counterbalancing the US presence in Iran. As Marshal Ustinov declared during one of the Politburo meetings (referring to Afghanistan): 'Why shouldn't we be entitled to act in the proximity of our borders as the US are doing in their Latin American backyard?'[28]

The reasoning of the Minister of Defence resembled the logic that almost twenty years earlier had pushed Nikita Khrushchev to launch an adventurous attempt to install Soviet nuclear missiles in Cuba in order to 'match' the deployment of US missiles at their bases in Turkey and Italy. In 1962 Khrushchev's decision, and particularly the covert nature of the whole operation, resulted in the most dramatic and dangerous crisis ever experienced in US–Soviet relations, bringing the world to the verge of nuclear catastrophe. Marshal Ustinov was certainly conscious of the lessons of the Cuban crisis and was not proposing to threaten the vital security interests of the USA by deploying nuclear warheads. In any case, he was not the General Secretary, just a 'hawkish' Minister of Defence. Yet his remark makes it clear that in the late 1970s some of the most powerful members of the Soviet leadership were convinced that the strategic balance in the world was changing in favour of the Soviet Union; this in turn meant that the rules of the strategic game between the superpowers had to be changed accordingly, especially with regard to Soviet behaviour in the 'third world'.

The date 12 December 1979 will forever remain a fatal anniversary in the annals of Soviet foreign policy, a symbol of the political dead end into which the country had been led by the 'old political thinkers'. It was on this day that the Politburo decided to render 'internationalist assistance' to the pro-Soviet regime in Afghanistan. And on the very same day the leaders of the NATO countries formally decided to deploy American 'Pershing II' and cruise missiles in Western Europe in response to the deployment of SS-20s by the Soviet Union. Not only did this decision finally destroy Moscow's hopes of splitting the Western alliance over the question of the American 'euro-missiles' on European soil, it also foreshadowed a future deterioration of the Soviet Union's strategic position on the international scene.

The Ustinov–Gromyko stamp on Soviet foreign policy in the late 1970s served to drive the USSR to a position of confrontation, not only *vis-à-vis* its long-time strategic rival, the United States, but also in relation to other countries, including China, large parts of the Muslim world (alienated by the Soviet invasion of Afghanistan) and most of the states of Western Europe. Furthermore, this policy, which was used as an instrument to prop up the decaying political regime and justify new programmes of military spending, not only placed an additional burden on the exhausted national economy but also had a crippling effect on the internal structure of Soviet society, subordinating it to the purposes of military production. The whole country was thus sentenced to become a giant war machine, and a militarized camp.

## 'Moles' in the Corridors of Power

The imperial foreign policy pursued by an ailing leadership totally cut off from the reality of the country was bound to inspire a rise in symbolic protest actions by political dissidents (ultimately rather limited in scope and easily suppressed by the totalitarian regime), but it also provoked concern and even resentment within the Soviet political elite. The expression of this growing unease ranged from the hardly audible sceptical murmur of political and military experts who were obliged to prepare draft speeches and documents with which they disagreed, up to more or less open manifestations of doubt or indirect criticism coming from the liberals within the Party's advisory community and academic circles. Concerned by the evolution of Soviet foreign policy in an expansionist direction, some sort of 'communist imperialism', many of them were above all troubled by the regime's apparent drift toward neo-Stalinist positions in domestic policy. The deepening international isolation of the Soviet Union signified the destruction of their last hopes for the modernization of the country's economy, while the widening gap separating the country from the Western world meant the indefinite postponement of the chance for a democratic renovation of the system.

Shared by only a tiny fraction of the political elite, views of this kind in no way amounted to a questioning of the original ideological foundations of the regime or, even less, a real challenge to the dominant system. Yet they reflected the emergence of a kind of *alternative political culture* distinct from the official one. Although rarely in an overt form, a growing number of members of the Soviet political establishment were ready to question the traditional ideological approach to foreign policy.

The first to express their reservations and doubts about the rationality of Soviet engagement in the unrestrained arms race with the West, already quite soon after Stalin's death, were the Soviet scientists associated with the creation of arms of mass destruction. Their position was quite close to that of some of their Western colleagues, from whom they were in most cases totally separated by a screen of secrecy and the almost absolute ban on travel abroad. Needless to say they had no possibility of public expression due to the strict secrecy measures, which had not changed much since the days of Stalin, when their professional activity was put under the supervision of the MVD (Ministry of Internal Affairs) headed by Lavrenti Beria – Stalin's chief of the secret police. Yet during the Khrushchev years, academician Andrei Sakharov addressed a letter to the Soviet Politburo in 1962 in which he defended intellectual freedom as the necessary condition for the progress of Soviet society, and he was not the only one to voice his concerns.[29] There were also several other prominent Soviet scientists (Nikolai Vernardsky, Lev Landau, Yuli Khariton, Petr Kapitsa) who did not hesitate to express ideas similar to those formulated in the Russell–Einstein Manifesto during private meetings with members of the political leadership.

In the course of the 1970s, the range of the Soviet academics who ventured to suggest less ideological approaches for Soviet foreign policy expanded considerably. The suppression of the 'Prague Spring' by Warsaw Pact armies had aroused considerable dismay, while at the same time the spirit of *détente*, accompanied by a certain development of international contacts and scientific exchanges with the West, had an encouraging effect. It was no longer just a question of nuclear physicists or other 'technical' specialists, who had limited possibilities of communication with the world outside their laboratories and in practical terms could not exercise serious influence on the political leadership. Now it was prominent figures from the official Soviet *nomenklatura* who were involved, the directors and leading experts of prestigious academic institutes with direct access to the highest levels of the political hierarchy.

Among them one should mention the directors of the official 'think-tank' of the Party Central Committee – the IMEMO – the Institute of World Economy and International Relations: academicians Anushavan Arzumanian and Nikolai Inozemtsev; the chief editors of the *World Marxist Review* published in Prague under the supervision of the International Department: Yuri Frantsev and Alexei Rumiantsev; and also the directors of other academic institutes directly supervised by the Central Committee: Georgi Arbatov for the Institute of USA and Canada Studies and Oleg Bogomolov for the Institute of the Socialist System. They were surrounded by teams of bright experts and consultants such as Fedor Burlatsky, Georgi Shakhnazarov, Anatoli Chernyaev, Aleksander Bovin, Nikolai Shishlin and others who in the following years served as speechwriters for Brezhnev and Andropov and later formed the base of an intellectual reserve for Gorbachev.

Some of these 'Party intellectuals' (Inozemtsev, Arbatov, Chernyaev, Shakhnazarov, Yakovlev) belonged, like Brezhnev and Andropov, to the 'war generation'. Having themselves fought at the front during the Second World War, they were politically more 'protected' by their veterans' past than were their younger colleagues. A kind of common political denominator for most of them was the fact that they had served as young officers in the army during the hardest years of the battle against the Nazis, with the Western democracies as allies in that fight. They emerged from this ordeal with profound hopes for the renovation and liberalization of Soviet society.

This explains why in most cases they enthusiastically supported Khrushchev's de-Stalinization policy announced at the 20th Party Congress in February 1956. In fact they represented a new reform-orientated Soviet political generation that was trying to combine romantic socialist ideals with the pragmatism of Party *apparatchiki*. Experts in Russian history might compare them to the illustrious 'Decembrists' – liberally minded young officers from the Russian aristocracy inspired by the ideas of the French Revolution who, having returned home after the victorious campaign against Napoleon, staged a first political revolt against Tsar Nicholas I in 1825, demanding the introduction of a constitutional monarchy.

Like the Decembrists, the Soviet *'frontoviki'*, the generation of intellectuals who had fought on the 'right side' against fascism hand in hand with the armies of the Allied powers, nourished hopes that the community of goals established between the USSR and the Western democracies during the war against fascism could be maintained after it was over. For those who chose international relations as their profession, their involvement in foreign policy analysis was often motivated by the intention to assist their country's progress toward democracy, which necessarily involved cooperation with the West.

Obliged for evident reasons to wait for Stalin's death, at the first signs of Khrushchev's 'thaw' they joined his camp, hoping that their country would reunite with the outside world. This also explains why many of these men experienced the Soviet invasion of Czechoslovakia and later of Afghanistan, signalling a new edition of the Cold War, not merely as political setbacks but also as a profound personal drama.

In terms of Soviet internal political vocabulary, this was what came to be called the generation of *'shestidesyatniki'* ('people of the sixties') – intellectuals who continued to believe in the possibility of merging the Russian communist project in its true 'Leninist' version, 'cleansed' of Stalinism, with Western-type democracy. Mikhail Gorbachev was referring to them when he wrote:

> All of them were children of their time. Starting with their first steps and then in their school years, they absorbed the basics of official ideology. All of them were deeply shaken by the revelations of Stalin's crimes in Khrushchev's report to the 20th Party Congress. Yet during the fifties their liberation from ideological chains was not yet complete. The internal struggle within their own consciousness involved a long process of self-liberation that had just begun.[30]

In reality, beyond the occasional contact with Party leaders who liked to list these reputed intellectuals among their circle of advisers (according to Shakhnazarov, Andropov treated him like an intellectual 'punching-ball'), their possibilities for influencing the formulation of foreign policy were quite limited. First, their own sources of information were rather accidental and depended to a large extent on their personal contacts abroad, while information from diplomatic, military and KGB channels was generally beyond their reach. And secondly, under the conditions of the communist regime, not only were the publications of academic institutions subject to severe ideological censorship and control, even internal discussions on sensitive political or diplomatic issues were strictly supervised by political watchdogs and Party 'commissars' who were charged by the Central Committee's Propaganda and Science Departments to ensure the orthodoxy of all the scientific debates. 'Yet they were a social group . . . of great intellectual and cultural strength . . . unorganized but numerous and fairly united in spirit,' wrote Aleksandr Yakovlev.[31]

In an attempt to loosen the political control of the Party *'instances'*, the directors of the most important institutes (IMEMO, the Institutes of USA and Canada Studies, the Institute of the Socialist System, the Institute of Oriental Studies, etc.) – started creating various 'safe havens' inside their institutions in the form of 'closed' sections and departments that were meant to produce a genuine picture of the USSR's international and strategic situation and to analyse in non-ideological terms relations with the West, China and also allies within the Warsaw Pact. Quite often researchers were recruited among retired experts of the General Staff or the KGB, who could provide them with a reliable network of contacts and sources of information.

The 'products' of such studies were naturally not books, academic papers, articles or scientific reports for public debate but various 'zapiski' – internal working papers for limited circulation that the directors of institutes submitted to the 'higher instance', the Party Central Committee. Another way of attracting the attention of political leadership to their activity were the so-called 'situatsionnye analyzy' – reports coming out of 'brainstorming' sessions on sensitive political or strategic issues that gathered specialists from academic institutions, the MID, KGB, Ministry of Defence and Central Committee experts from the International Department around the same table.

Since the directors of institutes were not suspected of political disloyalty, they could themselves rise to relatively high official positions within the nomenklatura. Thus, the most prominent figures in this category, academicians Nikolai Inozemtsev and Georgi Arbatov, having obtained the status of the Central Committee membership, could then assure for their institutes a kind of protection screen that would allow their collaborators an additional possibility freely to express their opinions on sensitive subjects. (Yet even the status of full Central Committee member did not save academician Inozemtsev from the ideological witch-hunt campaign launched against his institute, IMEMO, by the Moscow City Committee leader Victor Grishin, which after a short while led to his death in 1982 from a heart attack. Arbatov, who had also to fight tough battles with Party and KGB controllers in defence of his liberal-minded researchers, himself became their target when the publication of the report of the Olaf Palme Commission, of which he was a member, provoked the ire of Mikhail Suslov, chief party ideologist at that time.[32])

Despite the fact that they were confidential, the real practical effect of the position papers prepared by the institutes and submitted to senior political leaders remained insignificant. This, for example, was the fate of a zapiska submitted in January 1980 by the head of the Institute of the Socialist System, academician Oleg Bogomolov, who, using rather sharp language, predicted the grave political and strategic consequences of the Soviet invasion in Afghanistan that had just begun.[33]

When a highly placed member of the advisory community profiting from direct access to Party bosses tried to insist on a position that contradicted official policy or the views of the most powerful members of the Politburo (particularly Gromyko, Andropov or Ustinov), at best he would be advised to try himself to persuade the concerned member of the Politburo (according to the memoirs of Shakhnazarov, Brutents, Chernyaev and Falin.[34]) (This, for example, is how Brezhnev and Kosygin reacted when Arbatov and Falin suggested setting 'reasonable' limits to the deployment of SS-20s.)[35] In worst case scenarios, there could be a warning or severe reprimand for interference in spheres beyond the competence of the individual who had offered unwelcome advice.[36] This situation reduced the role of academic advisers to the status of marginal lobbyists who could only seek to limit the damage of decisions they considered counterproductive.

The situation began to change only when Mikhail Gorbachev became a member of the Politburo in 1979. Gorbachev started regularly to invite academics to his office in the Central Committee (Georgi Arbatov, Evgeny Primakov, Evgeny Velikhov, Roald Sagdeev, Tatyana Zaslavskaya, Abel Aganbegyan) to brief him on matters related to foreign policy, the world economy or the Soviet strategic situation, trying to build a kind of informal intellectual 'think-tank', which in the hypothetical future could play the role of his 'shadow' advisory cabinet.[37]

\* \* \*

Academicians were also closely associated with the other group of experts on foreign policy matters that belonged to the core of Party *nomenklatura*, the Consultants of the International Department (ID) of the Central Committee. They constituted a highly privileged autonomous group directly subordinate to the heads of the International Department and the Socialist Countries Department, respectively Boris Ponomarev and Yuri Andropov (later replaced by Konstantin Katushev and after him by Konstantin Rusakov).

ID Consultants' groups represented a kind of internal intellectual elite inside the *apparat* of the Central Committee and had a rather specific status.[38] The particularity of the Consultants' status was assured first of all by the criteria of cadres selection. In contrast to the rest of the Central Committee *apparatchiki*, the Consultants were not recruited on the basis of absolute loyalty to superiors, normally the main factor for selection, but according to their expert professional qualities: there had to be knowledge of foreign languages, expertise with regard to the country or region for which they would be 'responsible', or experience of work abroad. Already these elementary requirements were transforming the *'mezhdunarodniki'* (collaborators of the International Department) into a kind of separate caste within an otherwise homogeneous *nomenklatura* family. The contrast was accentuated also by one specific character of their professional activity – broader access to information: this included foreign press and wires coming from the embassies and KGB sources as well as frequent travel abroad accompanying various Party and 'social organization' officials. Chernyaev stresses the point: 'We high-level cadres were particularly sensitive to the worsening international position and loss of authority of the Soviet Union since we were in a position of better access to information.'[39]

The privileged status of the ID's Consultants was also secured by the fact that quite often they were summoned by senior Party bosses, including the General Secretary, to join the working groups of personal aides drafting the most important political texts: political reports to Party congresses, Plenary meetings of the Central Committee or other public speeches by the party leaders. This gave them direct access both to the intimate circle of assistants of the General Secretary and to the top leader himself. Since their mission on these occasions was to submit not just propaganda pieces but political texts that would stand up as 'competitive products' on the international scene, they were encouraged while drafting their texts to suggest new 'fresh' ideas or even to 'tell the truth'. Since their bold, often heretical, ideas were strictly limited to 'internal circulation', in contrast to the contributions of scholars in the academic institutes, they were able to feel protected against ideological persecution from the Ideological Department and could operate outside daily KGB control. In the conditions of closed Soviet society this privileged status not only gave rise to jealousy among Party functionaries from other departments but also exposed the ID's Consultants to severe criticism for their 'estrangement' from the 'reality' of their country.[40]

Despite their apparent integration into the ruling political elite, many of these political advisers shared the views and feelings of the open-minded intellectuals of their own generation. Some of them maintained close relations with liberal and even dissident elements of the Moscow intelligentsia (in their memoirs, Chernyaev, Shakhnazarov and Arbatov cite among their close friends the theatre producers Yuri Lyubimov and Oleg Efremov as well as the poets Evgeny Yevtushenko and Andrei Voznesensky, who were publicly criticized by the official Party censors) and often tried to use their access to the Party bosses in order to lobby on behalf of these friends, trying to ease ideological censorship or get permissions for travel abroad.

Belonging to the privileged caste meant a greater feeling of protection compared to the situation of their friends, but at the same time it involved a sense of moral responsibility for the oppressive character of the regime; for many this often led to feelings of deep frustration or even psychological crisis. Chernyaev describes how his colleague on the *International Marxist Review* in Prague, Aleksandr Bovin, who was one of Brezhnev's favourite speechwriters, wept during the night of the Soviet invasion of Czechoslovakia in 1968 while contributing to the official text justifying the operation. Chernyaev himself confessed that on a number of occasions, because of growing psychological frustration and emotional stress, he was on the verge of resigning from his already important position within the Party apparatus, ready to abandon his political career.[41]

Without challenging the basic goal – consolidation of the Soviet state's position in its historic dispute with the capitalist world – many experts, and particularly those who were directly associated with the ruling elite, believed that socialism could become 'competitive' on the international scene once it had been reformed, modernized and democratized. It would then no longer be obliged to depend on the coercion and repression inside the country or have a need to use military threat as a tool in its foreign relations in order to assure its own survival. According to Evgeny Primakov, many of his colleagues shared his wish to put an end to the arms race 'not because they assumed it would be impossible for the Soviet economy to keep up with the United States in this competition, but simply in the hope of making better use of national wealth'.[42]

In general most of those who constituted the Soviet foreign policy expert elite, irrespective of their official positions, represented a rather homogeneous group from the point of view of their education and political orientation: in a majority of cases they were graduates of the same institute – MGIMO (one of the most liberal educational institutions of postwar Moscow, for many years directed by Yuri Frantsev, who later was appointed chief editor of the *World Marxist Review* in Prague). As Robert English rightly observes, 'By the mid-to-late 1960s the various reformist critiques [inside the Soviet political elite] were coalescing into a single coherent and vigorous intellectual current. . . . All sought similar liberalization in economic, social, and political life. Moreover, most were united by an increasingly Western orientation in foreign policy.'[43]

Shocked by the 1979 invasion of Afghanistan, many members of the 'advisers' community' interpreted it as a sign of the potential transformation of the Soviet Union into a neocolonial power. The invasion destroyed their remaining illusions about the possibility of transforming Party and state policy in a positive rational direction. It was at this time that the whole system began to lose its remaining ideological justification in the eyes of the idealistically motivated portion of intellectual elite.

Yet it would be a serious exaggeration to describe most of its members as 'Western-orientated'. It is true that for a fraction of the political elite, the largely idealized image of the Western democracies served as a reference point and an example to be followed. Yet they were a minority. Two other groups constituted a much more important part of the potential for dissent within the elite. One was the classic *shestidesyatniki* – still sincere believers in the capacity of the Soviet socialist model, once reformed and modernized, to 'converge' with an appropriately 'socialized' Western world. The other was made up of those top-level professional bureaucrats who were competent enough to detect the signs of the approaching collapse of the existing regime and were convinced that the only way to save the Soviet state and secure its international position was to modernize its political system.

Whatever their motivation, a considerable number of the foreign policy experts hardly expected to witness any radical change at the top political level in their own lifetime. If they refrained from joining the isolated community of dissidents, it was not only a question of conformism or a lack of personal courage (although these considerations did play a role), but because they simply did not believe in the political efficacy of such action. Yet although condemned to an existence of hibernation, they constituted a kind of professional political army awaiting its leader. 'We could write a lot of memos and speeches for our leaders that stated all these [new thinking] points, but it didn't matter until a leader appeared in the General Secretary's chair who came with these ideas beforehand,' noted Georgi Shakhnazarov.[44]

## Cracks in the Monolith

Two other fractions of the 'advisers' community' – experts of the Ministry of Foreign Affairs and the Ministry of Defence working under the direct orders of the main protagonists of the official Soviet line, Gromyko and Ustinov – were evidently in a different situation. The undisputed monopoly position of their institutions in the field of diplomacy and state defence policy certainly increased the prestige of those who belonged to the experts' teams of the two ministers, and this certainly did not encourage dissenting behaviour. Yet even within these families of professionals one also could detect signs of scepticism and frustration characteristic of the *mezhdunarodniki* from the academic institutions and International Departments of the Central Committee. The difference was a question of motivation. While in the International Departments the prevailing reasons for hidden dissent were mostly ideological, the reservations of the diplomatic and military experts were largely based on their professional appraisal of the evolution of the Soviet foreign policy.

It would be unrealistic to expect that within these two rigid structures organized on the principle of strict subordination and discipline one would discover any signs of overt challenge to the positions of the two all-powerful minister-bosses. Both Gromyko and Ustinov were in the habit of governing their subordinates with well-known severity and neither was inclined to encourage more open discussions. Yet even within these institutions, a number of highly placed experts and functionaries during internal debates would occasionally question the justification for certain foreign policy decisions, arguing that their implementation might bring about grave political and strategic consequences. Naturally this kind of bureaucratic dissent was usually wrapped up in expressions of desire to assure greater effectiveness for official state policy and was mostly limited to a discussion of better *means* while never challenging the *goals*. Still, even the MID bureaucrats were often painfully aware of the growing international isolation of the Soviet Union and the decline of its popularity. 'Wherever we went with official delegations, we were greeted by demonstrations condemning the violations of human rights in the Soviet Union. That was quite depressing,' comments Sergei Tarasenko, who later became one of the two closest aides of Edward Shevardnadze.[45]

Only a limited number of highly placed experts inside the MID and Defence Ministry dared to distance themselves from the hard-line position of their two bosses. To do this they had to be assured of the direct encouragement or personal protection of the General Secretary. The experience of at least two high-ranking Soviet diplomats – Valentin Falin and Anatoli Kovalev – is illuminating. Falin, in his function as the head of the 3rd European Directorate of the MID (before being dispatched as the Soviet Ambassador to Bonn) assumed the role of principal Soviet 'sherpa' during the preparation of the Soviet–FRG state treaty (1970); he did not hesitate to question Gromyko's negotiating tactics during the precarious stage of the formulation and ratification of the Moscow Treaty and could only have done this having obtained an assurance of personal support and encouragement from Brezhnev and Kosygin.

As for Kovalev, the Deputy Foreign Minister in charge of drafting the Final Act of the Helsinki Conference, he found a different roundabout way to ease the pressure of Gromyko's heavy hand while working in Geneva on the text of the Final Act. He obtained Brezhnev's permission to get his directives on the sensitive matter of human rights directly from the head of the KGB, Yuri Andropov, whose position paradoxically was more 'liberal' than Gromyko's.[46] As Brezhnev weakened, Falin and Kovalev could no longer rely on his protection and were rather rudely pushed aside by Gromyko, happily at a time when both could be invited by Gorbachev to join his 'shadow' foreign policy team.

For evident reasons one could hardly find any members of the unofficial fraternity of MGIMO graduates among Soviet Defence ministry officials or experts of the government's Military-Industrial Commission (VPK). Yet here too there is a record of at least one case of a widely known clash between Dimitri Ustinov and his First Deputy Chief of the General Staff, Nikolai Ogarkov, over the question of the future development and modernization of the Soviet armed forces. While Ustinov gave preference to an unlimited build-up of strategic nuclear weapons, Ogarkov opted for the modernization of the structure of the armed forces, suggesting that emphasis be put on the mobility of conventional army contingents.[47] Ogarkov's position apparently began to cause serious worry among Pentagon officials, as has been confirmed by Gen. Edward Rowny,[48] who admitted that one of the motives behind the SDI programme was to prevent the potential reform of Soviet military strategy in accordance with Ogarkov's ideas.[49]

While manifestations of disagreement with the official line among army commanders were practically imperceptible, scientists and technical experts directly involved in military research and production were finding ways to make known their growing hesitation about the continuation of the arms race with the USA, because it was subordinating Soviet science and technology to American priorities. They were also sensitive to the growing technological gap separating the Soviet Union from Western countries. Members of the technical intelligentsia massively involved in military production were quite capable of evaluating the genuinely monstrous dimension of the military sector within the Soviet economy; they could not remain indifferent as they observed the irrational waste of national resources, material and intellectual, even if they were personally interested in keeping their jobs and high salaries. Alongside the critical professional's judgement, these feelings of frustration reflected the civic reflexes of an important part of the Soviet educated class.

Those who occupied important positions inside the Central Committee Defence Department like Nikolai Detinov and Vitali Kataev were well placed to understand that the reason for the backwardness of the national economy lay in the burden of excessive military expenditure. None of these experts was ready to advocate dramatic cuts in the defence budget, nor would they accept the perspective of an unchallenged US military superiority over the USSR. Yet they considered it possible to achieve the same strategic and political goals with more efficient spending at considerably less cost.[50]

Similar feelings were shared by senior Soviet economic managers and top Party functionaries occupying important positions in the regional Party structures. As the ageing regime experienced conditions of progressive decay, these local leaders had to cope most of the time with a shortage of financial resources; they were obliged desperately to seek solutions for the multiple economic and social problems of the population in their regions. Few of them would be prepared to admit that the source of their daily problems lay in the general inefficiency of the prevailing system. For the majority the only acceptable explanation for the continuous deterioration of the economic situation of the country and of its evident backwardness in comparison to the prosperous Western world was the huge amount of Soviet defence spending, without which, they believed, the system would be quite competitive on the international scene.

Belonging on the whole to the new generation of the Party *nomenklatura* and too young to have taken part in the war, they did not suffer from '1941 syndrome' and consequently did not share the complexes of older generations obsessed with the fear of external invasion. For this reason they were not ready psychologically to pay any price whatsoever to protect their country against a threat that they considered to be quite hypothetical. These regional Party secretaries like Mikhail Gorbachev, Yegor Ligachev and Boris Yeltsin, as well as high-ranking economic managers such as Nikolai Ryzhkov, who later became Gorbachev's Prime Minister, formed a new echelon of political leaders who were not prepared to accept uncritically the unlimited demands of the military-industrial complex, especially at a time when it had begun to devour vital parts of the body of Soviet society.

Thus by the end of the 1970s, an impressive although extremely heterogeneous and unstructured cohort of intellectuals, political, diplomatic and military experts, as well as the new generation of high-level Party functionaries was preparing to step onto the Soviet political stage. Sharing similar concerns about the new edition of the Cold War with the West with its excessive cost for their country, for the time being its members occupied behind-the-scene positions and were not prepared to challenge the principal decision-makers openly. With no thought of establishing formal contacts, most members of this 'coalition' were nevertheless quite critical of the manner in which Soviet foreign policy was formulated and conducted by the *troika* – a 'mini Politburo' that had come to control the General Secretary.

Within the Soviet political elite there spread a growing sense of the flagrant incompatibility of current policy with the true national interests of the country and that this was undermining its real security. With the dramatic increase of the casualties produced by the Afghan war, this view began to spread across the Party apparatus (especially in the provinces), where local cadres were facing the mounting feelings of frustration and distress among growing numbers of affected families.

The growing ossification of the mechanisms of Soviet foreign policy in the late Brezhnev years limited the Kremlin's capacity to react to a changing international climate. As a result, the situation, which demanded urgent action, was passively left to rot.

By the beginning of the 1980s it became clear that the logic of superpower arrogance had left the USSR isolated and led its foreign policy into a blind alley. In theory, Brezhnev's death on 10 November 1982 could have led to a major reorientation of Soviet foreign policy. Brezhnev's disappearance from the scene and the promotion of Andropov to the position of the supreme leader obviously destroyed the balance within the Ustinov/Andropov/Gromyko 'triangle', where Ustinov had the strongest hand while Gromyko, as his closest ally, could claim to be number two.

Despite Gromyko's seemingly uncontested authority in the sphere of foreign affairs, Andropov certainly was a man capable of imposing his own will and therefore could have set his own personal seal on a new Soviet foreign policy. Besides his obvious force of character, the new General Secretary apparently did have ideas about changes he wanted to introduce. After several decades of a virtual monopoly rule over Soviet diplomacy, Gromyko was now forced to display his resources of flexibility and a capacity to accommodate to the new boss (those who witnessed Andropov presiding over sessions of Politburo report that he would cut Gromyko short in order to conclude the discussion in accordance with his own objectives).[51]

It was soon after Brezhnev's death that Chernyaev, who was a deputy of Ponomarev, drafted a list of priority foreign policy recommendations. The list included the following items:

- Withdraw from Afghanistan
- Tell Jaruzelski that we are not going to intervene in Poland under any circumstances – Draft a declaration announcing a new policy of non-interference in the internal affairs of the Warsaw Pact countries (similar to the one made by Khrushchev in 1956)
- Remove the SS-20 missiles from the European part of the Soviet Union
- Curb the VPK [Military-Industrial Commission], ignore American blackmail and reduce the Soviet army fourfold
- Let the dissidents emigrate, starting with Sakharov; the same with regard to Jews wishing to leave for Israel
- Publicly condemn anti-Semitism . . .[52]

Initially Chernyaev hoped to submit this paper personally to the General Secretary; however, because of his rapidly progressing illness, Andropov lacked the time and strength seriously to approach the subject of foreign policy changes, despite his inclination to do so.[53] Chernyaev's agenda was consigned to a drawer to await some future opportunity.

In any case, given the international political climate, it was not an auspicious time for bold innovative gestures. After the shooting down of a South Korean civil airliner by a Soviet interceptor over the Sea of Okhotsk on 1 September 1983, and the highly publicized NATO 'Able Archer' 'war scare' exercise (imitating a US nuclear strike against the Soviet Union) in November, political relations between the USSR and the US dropped to one of the lowest levels of the postwar period.[54] After a heated dialogue in Geneva in the autumn of 1983, the US Secretary of State George Shultz publicly refused to shake hands with Gromyko; this confirmed the new escalation of tension in Soviet–American relations. On 22 November the German Bundestag voted to proceed with the deployment of Pershing-IIs and the missiles began to arrive. Two days later, Moscow announced that its negotiators would not return to either the INF or START negotiations.

Andropov's death in February 1984 and the ephemeral rule of Konstantin Chernenko solidified Gromyko's political position within the Politburo, but at the same time highlighted his personal responsibility for the progressive weakening of the Soviet Union's position on the world scene. Probably it was this that pushed Gromyko to start looking for the way out of the evident political stalemate in relations with the United States. In the same period, 1983–4 – and this can hardly be seen as a coincidence – with the evident encouragement of his father, Gromyko's son Anatoli collaborated with a popular political journalist, Vladimir Lomeiko, to write and publish a book called *New Political Thinking in the Nuclear Age*; the text summarized the essential ideas on questions of war and peace that were then circulating widely in the international intellectual community while remaining inaccessible to the Soviet public except for a limited privileged circle of academics.[55]

The fact that a progressive deterioration of Soviet–US relations was almost spiralling out of control also worried members of the American 'adviser community'. Some of Reagan's aides felt embarrassed by the 'excessive ideologization' of relations between the two countries, to which the President's anti-communist rhetoric contributed in a major way. According to Robert McFarlane and Jack Matlock, shortly after the unsuccessful meeting between Gromyko and Shultz in

Geneva and the public humiliation of the Soviet Union during the debate in the UN Security Council after the shooting down of the South Korean plane, Reagan's advisers started to work on proposals directed toward the resumption of Soviet–American political dialogue and disarmament negotiations.

A number of their ideas were incorporated in the text of President Reagan's speech delivered on 16 January 1984; the basic concept motivating the speech was an intention 'to give the Soviets incentives to bring the Cold War to an end'. 'If the Soviet government wants peace, then there will be peace. Together we can strengthen peace, reduce the level of arms, and know in doing so we have helped fulfil the hopes and dreams of those we represent and, indeed, of people everywhere. Let us begin now.', said Reagan.[56] But at that time there was no real political leader in Moscow who could respond to this important message. Gromyko, in the climate of uncertainty reigning over the Kremlin with Andropov on his deathbed, preferred not to circulate the text of Reagan's speech to the other members of the Soviet political leadership. (However strange it may seem today, they did not read the Western press and had no sources of information other than the news bulletins that had been carefully distilled and edited by TASS and Soviet Embassy cables.) Chernyaev confirms that the International Department was deliberately kept in the dark (by the MID) about Ronald Reagan's speech and its political significance.[57]

Apparently at this stage Gromyko himself was looking for a way back to a resumption of the privileged superpower relationship which could re-establish his personal authority. For this reason, having previously initiated the interruption of US–Soviet arms control negotiations in 1983, he quickly agreed (on behalf of Chernenko) to their resumption.

In those days, as his future deputy Yuli Kvitsinski recalls, Gromyko 'was very nervous' and seemingly anxious to bring the unhappy page in the US–Soviet relations, for which he obviously was responsible, to a close as soon as possible.[58] In contrast to their previous encounter, Gromyko's January 1985 Geneva meeting with George Schultz progressed quite smoothly, with both sides announcing the beginning of a 'new edition' of US–Soviet arms control negotiations. According to

Gromyko's son Anatoli, it was this meeting of his father with Schultz followed by a meeting with President Reagan that launched the process of the normalization of relations, opening the way for a future summit meeting between the American President and the next leader of the Soviet Union in November of that year.[59]

For Gromyko it was crucial to seize this occasion as confirmation of his continuing role as the main manager of Soviet foreign policy, because while he was settling accounts with his US counterparts, an alternative, unofficial pole of Soviet diplomacy had emerged on the international political scene, immediately attracting the attention of Western leaders. A seemingly ordinary Soviet Parliamentary delegation that arrived in London in December 1984 was received with particular attention, and its leader spent several hours in an extremely intensive political discussion with the British Prime Minister, Margaret Thatcher. The delegation was headed by a certain Mikhail Gorbachev. At that time he was the Second Secretary of the Central Committee in charge of ideological affairs.

# 2

# AMBITIONS AND ILLUSIONS OF THE 'NEW POLITICAL THINKING'

It is practically impossible to understand the life and behaviour of people of my generation if one forgets that we were simply the children of the war years who had been given the chance to stay alive.

Mikhail Gorbachev[1]

## Training for Leadership

By the time Mikhail Gorbachev reached the position of supreme power in the Soviet Union, he was competent to deal with domestic politics but virtually unprepared when it came to handling international affairs. Despite his relatively (by Soviet political standards) young age – he celebrated his 54th birthday a week before his election to the position of General Secretary – he had already spent fifteen years governing Stavropol *krai*, one of the most important economic regions of the country (in Soviet administrative vocabulary, a *krai* was superior in status to the more common territorial subdivision, the *oblast*). This role implied substantial experience supervising a huge economic complex (largely agricultural) while directing a massive Party organization and simultaneously managing the extremely sensitive and potentially conflictual inter-ethnic situation of the North Caucasus bordering with Chechnya (at that time the Chechen–Ingush Autonomous Republic inside the Russian Republic of the USSR).

This was his first school of diplomacy, Soviet-style. But once Gorbachev moved to Moscow to take up the position of Secretary of the Central Committee responsible for agriculture, the established rules of the Soviet *nomenklatura* obliged him to limit his interests mostly to his own specific sector. His diplomatic training radically speeded up only after Brezhnev's death during the short period of Andropov's reign between November 1982 and February 1984. Although formally his official portfolio remained unchanged, within the Politburo in this period Gorbachev started to function *de facto* at Andropov's side as the 'number two', supplanting Konstantin Chernenko, the official occupant of that position, who had been a colourless Brezhnev aide.

This is confirmed by Andropov's assistant, Arkady Volsky: 'Gorbachev was the man to whom we passed most of the Politburo papers and whom we consulted on all important subjects during the increasing periods of Andropov's serious illness and absence.'[2] Volsky's testimony is corroborated by Yegor Ligachev, former regional Party Secretary from Siberia, who was chosen by Andropov on the advice of Gorbachev to direct the strategically important Organization Department of the Central Committee. According to Ligachev, Gorbachev was the real substitute for Andropov during the periods of the latter's forced absences.

> It was he who stayed at work until eight or even nine in the evening on an almost daily basis. It was with him that one could at any time discuss a whole variety of questions and it was to him that regional Party Secretaries turned when visiting Moscow, in order to share their problems and gain support in the endless process of lobbying for regional interests and needs.[3]

Yet even after having established himself as the first deputy and possible heir to Andropov, Gorbachev would not have dared to interfere in the very specific sector of foreign affairs dominated by the authoritative figure of Andrei Gromyko.

The fact that Andropov wished Gorbachev to become his heir is confirmed by an episode related by Arkady Volsky. At the end of 1983 he visited his boss in the hospital – the office had been shifted there – and received from Andropov the text of the General Secretary's report to the coming Plenary session of the Central Committee; it would have to be read to its members since Andropov himself was not well enough to appear. The draft text transmitted by Volsky to Chernenko's Secretariat had been revised by Andropov and included a phrase suggesting that in his absence Gorbachev should preside over sessions of the Politburo. But this recommendation disappeared from the final version presented to the audience.[4]

When Chernenko became General Secretary after Andropov's death in February 1984, he himself proposed to the Politburo that Gorbachev be officially nominated to be responsible for the ideology sector, a position that he had previously just occupied. In terms of unofficial status on the Party power pyramid, it was understood to be the second position in the Party hierarchy. With this title Gorbachev also inherited the supervision of the CPSU's international contacts and chairmanship of the Supreme Soviet's Commission for International Affairs. Before his formal promotion to this post, Gorbachev did not display any particular interest in matters of foreign policy. And even if he had been so inclined, it would not have been easily accepted. Since Stalin's time the Politburo functioned according to strictly observed rules according to which every member exercised oversight of a concrete sector of the Party's activity without interfering in the affairs of colleagues. The right to supervise the general situation and maintain political balance was the exclusive prerogative of the General Secretary.

As the youngest in age as well as experience, Gorbachev was obliged to abide by established procedures. Yet while avoiding any premature or open defiance of the old guard, he began to accumulate information about international affairs, anticipating the day when he might need this knowledge as the national leader. From this rather uncertain perspective, however, foreign policy questions were seen as auxiliary.

Aleksandr Yakovlev, characterizing Gorbachev's state of mind during his visit to Canada in 1983 in his capacity as the Secretary responsible for agriculture, mentioned a kind of 'obsession' with the idea of 'necessary internal change'. (At the time, Yakovlev, 'punished' by Brezhnev and Suslov for the public expression of his liberal views, was serving a kind of golden exile in Ottawa as the Soviet Ambassador.)

> Gorbachev was above all interested in talking to me about the intolerable situation at home, showing almost no interest in the agricultural programme prepared by his Canadian hosts. The only feature of the local scene that did attract his attention was the evident contrast between the advanced state of Canadian agriculture and the situation in this sector in the Soviet Union. The fact that Canada's climate and soil conditions were quite comparable to those of many regions of the USSR, including Gorbachev's Stavropol home territory, made the comparison even more striking in his eyes, since it deprived Soviet agriculture and its chief overseer of any plausible excuse.

During a visit to a Canadian private farm, Yakovlev heard Gorbachev murmuring to himself: 'Even after fifty years we will not be able to reach this level of efficiency.'[5] Reporting some time later about their discussions in Toronto, Yakovlev told his old friend Boris Pankin: 'You won't believe it, but he [Gorbachev] was attacking the system more vigorously than I would or even you.'[6]

This progressive discovery of the West on top of the experience of previous trips to Western Europe as a Party functionary (on one such visit, to Belgium, Gorbachev was accompanied by Anatoli Chernyaev, who at that time was Ponomarev's deputy) helped Gorbachev to construct his own personal vision of the 'other world' and led him to at least two key conclusions. First, the Soviet Union was clearly losing the competition with its historic capitalist rivals not only from the point of view of technological progress and economic efficiency but even with regard to the provision of more decent living conditions for the 'working masses'. Secondly, and no less crucial for the political education of the future Soviet leader: contrary to the declarations of official propaganda, the so-called 'imperialist world' represented a complex reality of different states, societies and pluralistic political families and apparently was in no way preparing to attack or invade the Soviet Union.[7]

These two 'heretical' conclusions would have been quite disturbing for someone who had been heavily indoctrinated throughout the years of his studies and initial Party career.

They were to become the first steps in forming Gorbachev's broader vision of the modern world and the place occupied in it by the Soviet Union. Two other more specific subjects of international relations were part of Gorbachev's daily concerns and were closely related to the internal situation of the country: the economic burden of the arms race and the war in Afghanistan, which had turned into a quagmire for the Soviet army. Both issues certainly threatened to hold back the radical internal reform that he was already planning. Yet at the moment of his election to the supreme political position, this project was still at a rather embryonic stage. Aleksandr Yakovlev recalls that during their first serious political discussion in Canada, Gorbachev's ideas about a future remodelling of the Soviet system could be summarized by a limited set of rather general propositions and ethical principles: 'an aversion to violence, a rejection of Stalinism in its various forms and a veneration of the law'.[8]

Chernyaev believes that before Gorbachev began to analyse and study concrete aspects of Soviet foreign policy, he had first created for himself a moral foundation on which any future political construction would be based. It reflected his conviction that it was possible to unite politics with morality, as well as his manifest aversion to violence and disbelief in the reality of an 'imperialist threat'.[9]

At the same time, during his first years as a member of the Soviet political leadership (Secretary of the Central Committee, later a candidate and then a full Politburo member), Gorbachev apparently continued to believe that the basic orientation of the Soviet foreign policy in the postwar period was correct, justified by the prevailing interests of national security and concerns for the historic destiny of world socialism. Of course it must be remembered that as a high-ranking member of the Soviet *nomenklatura*, Gorbachev would have been obliged to observe the ritual of pronouncing official, propagandistic formulas in public. It is difficult to determine now whether, for example, the statement in a 1985 interview for a Portuguese newspaper in which he said that 'a limited nuclear war in Europe remains part of Washington's plans and strategies' reflected his true conviction or was part of the obligatory liturgy. The same could be said about his passionate defence of Soviet policy banning the emigration of Soviet 'refuseniks' to Israel or the West, since they were holders of 'state secrets'.[10]

Yet it would be an over-simplification to present the young Soviet leader as a banal conformist who would not hesitate to declare something he did not believe in simply in order to further his career. As a convinced communist serving 'the Party cause' in the distant Stavropol province, Mikhail Gorbachev grew up as a sincere believer in many of the official clichés of Soviet propaganda. Thus while recognizing (in private conversations) that the Soviet invasion of Afghanistan was a mistake, at that time, as he himself has recognized, he would have made a distinction between this unjustified 'political folly' and the Soviet military interventions in Hungary (1956) and in Prague (1968), where the 'vital interests of the socialist system' had to be defended in the face of 'imperialist interference and pressure'.[11]

The same can be said about Gorbachev's initial attitude toward the existence of the Berlin Wall and, in a more general sense, the German problem. A functionary of the Central Committee who accompanied Gorbachev in his younger years (when regional Party Secretary) on a trip across West Germany recalls the latter's conversation with an elderly German serving at a petrol station who quite aggressively accused the USSR of responsibility for the partition of Germany. Gorbachev's reply, apparently a sincere one, reproduced the official Soviet position, explaining the division of Germany by the historic responsibility of the German nation for the consequences of its defeat in the war that had been started by the Nazi regime.[12]

The recapitulation above of Gorbachev's first uncertain steps in foreign policy is intended to demonstrate the tremendous distance that he managed to cover in a very short amount of time. From these uncertain beginnings, in the space of few years, he transformed himself into one of the world's greatest statesmen, who managed to achieve what many much more experienced politicians could only dream of – a world political landscape utterly transformed beyond recognition.

* * *

If Gorbachev's real interest in foreign policy issues can be traced to 1984, it was not simply because at that time he had inherited Suslov's formal functions; rather it was linked to a growing realization that domestic and foreign policy were organically connected and that favourable external conditions constituted a crucial prerequisite for any serious project of internal reform. Gorbachev's first public remarks reflecting his intensive re-evaluation of the Party/government line on international affairs go back to the two important trips he made during that year in his new capacity as chief ideologist of the Party.

The first was his visit to Italy in the summer of 1984 when he led the CPSU delegation to the funeral of the Italian Communist Party leader Enrico Berlinguer. By that time the relationship between the two 'sister Parties' was quite cool, and the gap between their respective positions was widening visibly. The Italian party, certainly the largest and most authentic in the Western world, was probably the first to openly defy the discipline of obedience to the Kremlin; it began to look for legitimacy at home as a national political party and not just as the Italian branch of the Communist International. The bilateral relations between the two parties were already gravely affected by the Warsaw Pact intervention in Czechoslovakia in August 1968, resolutely condemned by the Italian communists. They certainly suffered a new and serious blow with the Soviet invasion in Afghanistan. Reacting to the Afghan intervention, the Italian party, headed by Berlinguer, raised criticism of Soviet policy to a new level of disapproval; it was no longer a question of censuring concrete steps taken by the Soviet leadership and its Warsaw Pact allies but rather a more general and devastating critique. And one year later in December 1980, reacting to the declaration of the state of emergency in Poland by General Jaruzelski (under obvious pressure from Moscow), Berlinguer did not hesitate to announce that 'a phase of development of socialism that had started with the October revolution has lost its driving force'.[13]

In these circumstances Gorbachev's decision to lead the CPSU delegation to Berlinguer's funeral had the significance of an important political gesture. According to Vadim Zagladin, the first deputy of Ponomarev and future member of

Gorbachev's foreign affairs team who accompanied him on that trip, Gorbachev, although already familiar with the unorthodox writings of the Italian party's founder, Antonio Gramsci, 'reread his texts to prepare for the occasion'. And once in Rome, instead of giving his Italian hosts lessons in communist orthodoxy, he admitted in his conversation with Berlinguer's successor, Alessandro Natta, that the deceased leader "had good reason to criticize us".'[14] After Gorbachev's return to Moscow, the CPSU's *de facto* frozen relations with the Italian communists improved considerably. In his non-public remarks at various meetings in the Politburo, Gorbachev declared: 'We can't disregard a party like that. We have to treat it with respect.'[15] On several occasions Gorbachev used formulas borrowed from the Italian party's political analyses, in this way showing how impressed he was by their arguments, and above all by their declared determination to establish a direct connection between the communist project and the culture of political democracy.[16]

If the attention paid to the position of the Italian successors to Berlinguer could be seen as an expression of Gorbachev's own reflections about the changing nature of modern socialism, his visit to the United Kingdom as head of a Soviet parliamentary delegation in December 1984 undoubtedly turned into a dress rehearsal for his future diplomatic role. Of course the visit was not totally separated from internal political considerations. When Chernyaev met Gorbachev in a corridor of the Central Committee building, the young leader told him: 'I'll go to England . . . . This way we'll gradually erode the monopoly . . .', the meaning of the unfinished phrase was quite clear. 'Monopoly' would have referred to Gromyko's grip on the entire sphere of foreign policy.[17]

The trip to Great Britain was regarded by Gorbachev as a chance to send a signal to Western leaders, and announce the seriousness of his intentions. Britain and its reputedly conservative (in both senses) Prime Minister, Margaret Thatcher, were deliberately chosen for the purpose. Understanding that any real change in the Soviet Union's relations with the West depended on the success of the Soviet–American dialogue, Gorbachev singled out Thatcher as the shortest way to send a message to Washington. He was well aware of her reputation as a 'tough' politician, a 'hard-liner' *vis-à-vis* the Soviet Union, implacably critical of communist ideology, and he believed this to be an advantage rather than a handicap. In a conversation with a 'highly placed American politician' that took place a few weeks before his trip to Britain, Gorbachev had been advised to 'start discussing matters of nuclear disarmament with the right-wing Western politicians rather than with the left'.[18] Thatcher fitted perfectly into this category. The British Prime Minister had already been briefed by British experts on Soviet affairs about the emergence of a new star on the Soviet political horizon, and she was most interested to meet Gorbachev, the probable future Soviet leader and a man representing a new generation of the political elite, as yet an unknown quantity in the West.[19]

Gorbachev also meticulously prepared for his formal debut on the international political stage. Much thought was given both to the substance of the coming discussions and to the composition of the team of experts who would accompany him, most of whom would later form his first unofficial foreign policy 'task force': Aleksandr Yakovlev, Evgeny Velikhov Anatoli Kovalev and General Nikolai Chervov (a deputy of Sergei Akhromeev, Chief of the Soviet General Staff).[20] And Raisa Gorbachev's glamorous appearance at the side of her husband, such a contrast to the conventional dreary image of a Soviet leader's wife, turned into a most successful public relations exercise, attracting considerable attention in the British media, from the serious *Times* to the tabloids.

In his conversations with Margaret Thatcher, Gorbachev centred all his arguments on the central point: his determination to reach a real military *détente* with the West, the predominant theme of his future foreign policy agenda. To make the point, Gorbachev, having put his prepared notes aside, displayed an unprecedented and unexpected degree of transparency in front of the fireplace at Chequers when he unfolded a chart prepared by the Moscow General Staff showing the positions of both Western and Soviet strategic missiles, thus illustrating the combined East–West overkill potential. Gorbachev's intention was to stress the absurdity of the competition to accumulate arms for a confrontation that evidently both sides were inclined to avoid.[21]

However, it was not so much the charts but rather Gorbachev's apparent determination to undertake major reforms and prepare important change at home that impressed the British Prime Minister. After their meeting Margaret Thatcher not only publicly announced that she 'liked Mr. Gorbachev' and thought that the West could 'do business with him', she also decided to fly to Washington in order personally to brief the US President, Ronald Reagan, about the unusual Soviet politician who most likely would become the future leader of the USSR.

Another Western leader who had his eye on Gorbachev from the summer of 1984 was the French President, François Mitterrand. His personal friend, the former French Foreign Minister, Roland Dumas, claims to be the person who drew his attention to the new number two in the Soviet Party hierarchy on the occasion of Mitterrand's visit to Moscow in the summer of 1984. 'It was on the morning before our departure from Moscow,' recalls Dumas. 'Having learned that Gorbachev expressed a desire to have a brief talk with Mitterrand, I per-suaded the President to receive Gorbachev at his residence. Their conversation lasted for about half an hour.' On the way to the airport, Mitterrand, apparently impressed by the encounter, told Dumas: 'You were right to insist that I meet him.'[22] In October the following year, the French President was the first of Western leaders to receive Gorbachev in the West as the newly elected General Secretary of the Central Committee.

## First Exercises in Foreign Policy

Much of Gorbachev's preparation for the leadership took place during the brief reign of the ephemeral Chernenko, when it was he who assured the continuity of governance. This would explain Gorbachev's considerable assurance from the start in the handling of domestic policy when he was finally elected General Secretary on 11 March 1985.

Paradoxical as it may seem, his election to this supreme posi-tion in the Soviet political hierarchy had very little to do with his personal qualities as a man capable of formulating and directing the foreign policy of the world's number two super-power at a time when the Kremlin's relations with its principal international partners, both West (starting with the US) and East (China), were problematic, to say the least.

Some Western commentators have argued that the Politburo chose Gorbachev, the future promoter of a softer line, as a response to the hard-line posture of the Reagan administration; others, citing Gromyko's description of Gorbachev as a man with 'steel teeth', interpreted his election as a sign that the Soviet leadership had chosen a man who was young and vigorous and who would be able to stand firm against Western pressure. In my view both interpretations are equally wrong. Archie Brown was much nearer the truth when he wrote: 'Gorbachev's accession to the most senior party post was very much a product of Soviet domestic policy. . . . External pressure played no part in the decision . . . .'[23]

One could perhaps argue that by deploying SS-20s and invading Afghanistan, Brezhnev and his colleagues did have a direct effect on American political developments in the sense that they made it easier for the conservative, anti-communist Ronald Reagan to replace Jimmy Carter in the White House. It is far less plausible to suggest that the subsequent US military build-up accompanied by Reagan's hard-line rhetoric influenced the choice of a former Party secretary from Stavropol to become his main opponent. In any case, at the time of Gorbachev's election, the very fact that he was recommended by Gromyko was interpreted by many as a signal that, as in previous years (if not decades), Soviet foreign policy would continue to be supervised by the experienced Minister and patriarch of the Politburo.

Immediately after his election, however, Gorbachev was obliged to demonstrate assurance in the handling of foreign affairs. 'An interest in reaching concrete agreements' – this was the main message to be transmitted to their American counterparts by Soviet negotiators, whom Gorbachev instructed personally before the US–Soviet disarmament talks in Geneva, due to resume on 15 March. To confirm the goodwill of the Soviet side, on that day *Pravda* carried an editorial announcing that the USSR was ready to suspend the further deployment of its SS-20 missiles in Europe while awaiting the outcome of the negotiations.[24]

Still, in general, Gorbachev's initial approach toward matters of foreign policy reflected a rather traditional if not conservative position. Only a very attentive listener, someone expert in reading between the lines of Soviet political jargon, could have detected hints of future policy innovations, including a mention of the subject of human rights, preferential attention given to China and an upgrading of Europe among Moscow's most important partners.

Gorbachev's behaviour in the first weeks that followed his election could well be explained not so much as a lack of interest in foreign affairs but rather by the heavy presence of Andrei Gromyko at his side, limiting his capacity to act. The only phrase in Gorbachev's report at the April Plenum of the Central Committee – just after his election – that suggested a possible change in relations with the USA was rather banal and cautious: 'We want to express a hope that the present position of the USA will be corrected. This would open the possibility of reaching mutually acceptable agreements. From our side we are ready for it.'[25] In a way it looked like nothing more than a polite answer to US President Ronald Reagan's speech of 16 January the previous year (athough it is not at all clear that Gorbachev had read it), but its real significance was that it served to give notice that after several years of virtual limbo there was at last a man in the Kremlin who could answer telephone calls from Washington. By that time Gorbachev had accepted the invitation to have a meeting with Reagan, which had been conveyed to him by the Vice-President, George Bush, during his visit to Moscow for Chernenko's funeral.

After Gorbachev presented his political programme, a disappointed Chernyaev even commented in his diary: 'Gorbachev's speech had a dynamic domestic section . . . and a bland, standard, disappointing foreign affairs section. Either he doesn't want to be distracted by this issue just now, or – even worse – he's decided to trust Gromyko again.' Summing up his first impressions of the initial working weeks of the new leader, he comes to a quite critical conclusion: 'I don't think Gorbachev has any clear idea yet of how he is going to bring the country up to world standards.'[26]

To a large extent Gorbachev's initial foreign policy 'conservatism' or prudence reflected an observance of two sacrosanct principles of Soviet political life: 'continuity' of policy plus a manifest show of cohesion within the Politburo; these were obligatory elements of the mythological unanimity so diligently displayed to their own society and to the outside world by the Soviet leaders. As Gorbachev later confirmed, having been proposed by Gromyko and elected by a unanimous vote of Politburo members, at least initially he found himself in a paradoxical situation, more dependent than before and forced to abide by the rules of 'collective leadership'. Furthermore, at least in his first few months, the new General Secretary did not have any very clear idea about the real degree of change he would need to introduce in the conduct of foreign policy.[27]

According to the recollections of Anatoli Chernyaev, in the hours following his election to the post of General Secretary, Gorbachev noted on a sheet of paper several major foreign policy issues: 'stop the arms race, withdraw troops from Afghanistan, change the spirit of the relationship with the USA, restore cooperation with China'.[28] In a later interview Gorbachev confirmed this set of priorities, placing particular stress on the necessity of stopping the arms race: 'without that, any plans for *perestroika* would have had to remain in the realm of fiction'.[29]

It is not at all surprising that Gorbachev's initial foreign policy agenda could be summed up by several lines jotted down on a sheet of paper. Had he been asked to elaborate on any of the items, he would hardly have been able to go beyond a rather vague declaration of intent. Moreover, as long as Gromyko continued to occupy the post of Foreign Minister, there was no way Gorbachev could challenge him openly in the area that had become his exclusive territory. It was not simply a question of being indebted to Gromyko; rather the problem lay in the fact that Gromyko personally was implicated in precisely those crucial decisions of the Soviet leadership (deployment of SS-20 missiles in Europe and the invasion of Afghanistan) that Gorbachev was inclined to reconsider. But at this stage Gorbachev had to rely upon the experience of Gromyko and accept his tutelage until he had managed to build a foreign policy team of his own.

\* \* \*

The first public moves of the new Soviet leader in the field of foreign policy provided no indications to suggest that he would be initiating any kind of dramatic change aside from a change in the 'style of leadership'. On the basis of Gorbachev's reputation as a dynamic Party *apparatchik*, Western diplomats anticipated a stiffening of the Soviet position on certain subjects that were a source of conflict in relations with the West – Afghanistan, for example, or Poland – but possibly tempered by more cautious behaviour in zones less vital for Moscow's strategic interests such as Africa or Central America.[30]

Western commentators and politicians were inclined to view Gorbachev as a vigorous, aggressive young leader but hardly imagined him to be the eventual apostle of a new *détente*. The prudent scepticism of the West was shared by Soviet dissident political writers analysing his performance, whether from within the USSR or from abroad. In an interview for *Newsweek* the Soviet dissident historian Roy Medvedev was reported to say: 'I don't think he will change the current foreign policy. It will be the same policy we've had for the past two or three years'. The exiled writer Georgi Vladimov, living in West Germany, was more pessimistic: 'Since Gorbachev comes from the Party *nomenklatura* supported by Andropov's KGB, he will be obliged to build a base for himself in the third remaining pillar of the regime – the army. That is why he will be listening attentively to the generals.'[31]

Nevertheless, despite these sceptical forecasts, even in the very first weeks of his reign, Gorbachev sent some significant political signals abroad indicating his intention to change at least the tone of relations with the West, if not yet the substance. On 22 March 1985 he proposed a freeze on the development of the strategic nuclear arsenals of the two superpowers and simultaneous suspension of the deployment of Soviet and American middle-range missiles in Europe. Several days later, on 7 April, apparently impatient to launch his own 'peace offensive', he took a further step: he declared a unilateral moratorium on the deployment of SS-20s and expressed readiness to consider a 25 per cent cut in Soviet strategic forces in exchange for the abandonment by the US of President Reagan's Strategic Defense Initiative. On 6 August, with the evident intention of raising pressure on the US, Gorbachev proclaimed a unilateral moratorium on the Soviet nuclear tests. The moratorium was subsequently prolonged four times and lasted until 26 February 1987.

But although these rather chaotic political moves did not in fact signify a real departure from the typical Soviet Gromyko–Ponomarev style of 'public diplomacy', they should not be interpreted merely as banal propagandistic gestures. For Gorbachev they represented genuine attempts to announce to the West his intention to do 'real business' in foreign policy. Yet, surrounded by the old Politburo, he could hardly have allowed any unorthodox statements even if he had in fact already formulated a new foreign policy programme. However, at that time this certainly was not the case; the philosophy of the 'new thinking' had not yet been drafted and even its vocabulary did not yet exist. For the time being, Gorbachev's vision of desired change in the Soviet Union's relations with the West was limited to a general and vague set of intentions. 'We reformers dreamt of ending . . . the division between East and West, of halting the insanity of the arms race and ending the "Cold War",' wrote Aleksandr Yakovlev in 1994.[32]

Well schooled in the corridors of Soviet power, Gorbachev realized that had to impose his authority as soon as possible in order not to remain hostage to the majority of the Politburo inherited from Brezhnev. He needed to change the political balance within the Politburo and create his own team of foreign policy experts. A solution to the first question was also an equally urgent political priority with regard to the issues of internal reform. For a provincial newcomer to Moscow like Gorbachev who had not spent enough time in the capital to form a cohort of supporters, it was crucial to start building a base of his own. In April 1985, at the first Plenary session of the Central Committee following his election, Gorbachev obtained the promotion of his several allies to the status of full Politburo membership: Yegor Ligachev, Nikolai Ryzhkov (the future Prime Minister) and Viktor Chebrikov (chairman of the KGB). All three were rewarded for the crucial role they had played in March, mobilizing the majority of the local Party secretaries in favour of Gorbachev's candidacy while neutralizing his potential rivals. The upgrading of Ligachev, Ryzhkov and Chebrikov not only guaranteed support for Gorbachev in the coming battle for change on the domestic front, but also strengthened his chances to accomplish one of his most crucial goals related to foreign policy – a radical reduction of defence spending. (The most important possible opponent to this, Marshal Ustinov, had died in December 1984.)

Additional new members of the Politburo (Eduard Shevardnadze) and the Secretariat (Lev Zaikov and Boris Yeltsin) were elected in July 1985. Simultaneously two of Gorbachev's closest allies were promoted to direct key departments of the Central Committee – Propaganda (Aleksandr Yakovlev) and General Affairs (Anatoli Lukyanov).

## Building the New Team

Despite all the ambiguity of his position during the months he had spent 'in the shadow' of Chernenko, Gorbachev even before his election managed to gather around him an important group of specialists on various subjects. Among them: academicians Tatyana Zaslavskaya and Abel Aganbegyan, working in a Siberian institute, who had produced an extremely candid report on the state of the Soviet economy; young bright physicists Evgeny Velikhov and Roald Sagdeyev; as well as professional experts on international affairs and political science Aleksandr Yakovlev, Evgeny Primakov and Georgi Arbatov, directors of the most important Soviet 'think-tanks'. Several members of the group – Velikhov, Yakovlev, as well as one of Gromyko's deputies, Anatoli Kovalev, accompanied Gorbachev on his December 1984 visit to Great Britain that marked his entrance on the world political scene. It was they who formed the nucleus of the future foreign affairs team.

In July 1985 Gorbachev managed to solve the delicate problem of replacing Andrei Gromyko, who had occupied the post of Foreign Minister since 1957. (Obviously, having served four previous Soviet General Secretaries, Gromyko was reluctant to continue in the same role on behalf of a much younger new leader, and was eager to upgrade his status, accepting the post of the Chairman of the Praesidium of the Supreme Soviet.)

Presumably, given his uncontested political weight and particularly in view of the role he had played in Gorbachev's elevation, Gromyko envisaged himself as the political tutor of the General Secretary. He was convinced that his authority in matters of foreign policy would certainly mean that he could continue supervising activity in this sphere, *de facto* running the Ministry of Foreign Affairs from his new office in the Kremlin. With this scenario in mind, he had already selected a successor for the post of Foreign Minister, his first deputy, Georgi Kornienko, and went so far as to congratulate him in advance.[33]

But to Gromyko's great surprise Gorbachev disregarded his recommendation and made a totally unexpected choice – a Party Secretary from Georgia who was also his close friend, Eduard Shevardnadze. 'When I mentioned Shevardnadze, Gromyko's first reaction was close to shock,' writes Gorbachev in his memoirs.[34] The fact that he ignored Gromyko's advice provided a clear political signal intended to show that the new General Secretary would not accept patronage when it came to questions of political importance; from that time onward, foreign policy would bear his own personal stamp.

Gorbachev's unexpected choice of Shevardnadze – someone ostensibly competent in any sphere of Party or state activity except diplomacy – was proof of his determination to recruit a Foreign Minister who would conduct no policy other than that of the General Secretary. When the bewildered Shevardnadze received the phone call from Gorbachev offering him the job, he expressed hesitation, alluding to his lack of experience and his 'non-Russian origins'. Gorbachev waved these objections away: 'As to your nationality, it's true you are Georgian but you are above all a Soviet man! No experience? Perhaps in this case it's a good thing. Our foreign policy is in need of a fresh approach, it needs courage, dynamism, and innovation.'[35]

Curiously enough *Newsweek*'s comment that 'the most important of Shevardnadze's virtues in Gorbachev's eyes may well be his lack of diplomatic experience'[36] was shared by various long-time MID professionals such as Gromyko's deputy, Anatoli Kovalev, or the then Soviet Ambassador to France, Yuli Vorontsov. According to Vorontsov, the choice of somebody completely new to the profession was a happy decision by Gorbachev, since 'anyone in the job who had spent his professional lifetime in Gromyko's MID, starting certainly with Kornienko, would find it personally and psychologically difficult to come out from under Gromyko's shadow and follow Gorbachev in a completely new direction, not to mention the question of "the new political thinking"'.[37] Anatoli Kovalev was even more enthusiastic about Shevardnadze, whom he compared to one of the greatest Foreign Ministers of Russian history, Aleksandr Gorchakov.[38]

Yet despite the designation of the new Foreign Minister, at least for a certain period Gorbachev was obliged to reckon with the presence of Gromyko, who was still an authoritative senior member of the Politburo. This explains why Gorbachev found it necessary to ensure that preparations for his first major diplomatic moves toward the West were conducted outside the traditional circuits of the MID, including his visit to France and subsequently to Geneva for the summit meeting with President Reagan.

Anatoli Chernyaev, who at that time had not yet replaced Aleksandrov-Agentov as Gorbachev's official foreign policy assistant and continued to work as Ponomarev's deputy, wrote in his personal diary: 'More and more often he [Gorbachev] puts Ponomarev in charge of various foreign issues – not because he thinks so highly of Ponomarev, but in order to let Gromyko know that there's a group in the Central Committee capable of giving the General Secretary a "second opinion". It was another hint that Gromyko's monopoly has ended.'[39]

* * *

The choice of France to be the first Western country visited by the new General Secretary was partly inspired by an intention to reinforce his political position before the crucial summit meeting with his American counterpart (a move of this kind would have been perfectly in accordance with the traditional style of Soviet diplomacy); but it also was a manoeuvre that reflected a hidden political struggle taking place between the Ministry of Foreign Affairs and the Central Committee's International Department over the priorities of Soviet foreign policy. Gromyko focused almost entirely on the United States, which was seen as the principal strategic adversary of the Soviet Union and consequently also its privileged diplomatic partner, while the International Department paid greater attention to Western Europe. According to the analysis of Ponomarev and his team, this was where the Soviet Union could find and count on important political allies, which would also be helpful in the strategic confrontation with the United States. They included not only governments such as those in France or Germany, considered to be considerably 'softer on Moscow' than Washington tended to be, as well as the traditional forces of the left (communists and social democrats), but also the trade unions and other mass movements regarded to be 'progressive', 'anti-imperialist' and 'peace loving'.

During the period of Gromyko's alliance with the two other strong men of the late Brezhnev regime, Ustinov and Andropov, alternative positions devised by the ID were formulated in a rather timid manner and hardly noticed. Nevertheless liberally minded 'Europeanists' within the International Department often succeeded in softening the rigid superpower approach of their MID colleagues, due to the fact that the Department was, after all, an organic element of the highest political 'instance'. It had direct access to the aides of Brezhnev and also profited from the patronage of Mikhail Suslov, who jealously resisted Gromyko's intrusion into the sphere of global political issues, which he considered to be his domain. With the change of leadership at the top, the 'Europeanists' and liberals inside the ID found themselves in a much stronger position.

During the period of Chernenko's reign, Gorbachev discovered that

> two lines were affecting the elaboration of the Soviet foreign policy. One could be traced via Andrei Aleksandrov-Agentov [Brezhnev's foreign policy assistant] back to the International Department of the Central Committee; the other came from the MID. The first suggested negotiations, research about possible agreements, liberalization and the improvement of relations; the second [that of Gromyko] was much more rigid, constructed, one could say, out of concrete.[40]

This explains why Gorbachev's first official trip to the West – to France in October 1985 – was prepared mostly by the International Department.

## Summits in Paris and Geneva

The French President, François Mitterrand, who had not forgotten his first meeting with Gorbachev in Moscow in the summer of 1984, regarded the change of leader in Moscow as a promising development. Much like Margaret Thatcher, he was impressed by Gorbachev's unusual candour and openness. Claude Estier, the French senator who had accompanied Mitterrand on that early visit, recalled: 'Gorbachev arrived with some delay to the official reception in the Kremlin. When he sat down at our table he apologized, saying that he had been busy trying to solve some urgent problem of the agricultural sector. I asked when the problem had arisen, and he replied with a sly smile: "In 1917".'[41]

With Gorbachev at the summit of political power in the Kremlin, Mitterrand wanted to make sure that he was still determined to carry into effect the far-reaching plans which he had outlined during their meeting in Moscow. Roland Dumas confirms: 'We had noticed the small phrase about Europe in one of Gorbachev's first speeches and were curious to get from him directly a broader presentation of his vision of foreign policy.'[42]

Commenting on the atmosphere in which these tactical priorities were discussed in the Kremlin, Vadim Zagladin said:

> We knew that we would not be able to move ahead in a major way without the USA. Yet since we were living in hard times in our relations with the Americans, our main political partner in the West was Europe. That is why we chose France as the place where the new Soviet approach could be presented to the world. In any case, even though the US–Soviet summit in Geneva had already been announced, we could not know in advance how things would turn out – Reagan's reaction was unpredictable. Strengthening our relations with Europe could also be useful as an element that might influence the Americans.[43]

According to Eduard Shevardnadze, 'the idea of a kind of a circuitous route towards Washington was put forward: attention to Europe plus an activization of our relations and contacts with other countries of the world'.[44]

This approach, largely inspired by the traditions of Soviet diplomacy, did not prove to be very efficient. Gorbachev's highly publicized 'European peace initiative' and his appeal for a 'common European home', repeated in Paris,[45] received only polite, lukewarm applause in the salons of the National Assembly (despite Gorbachev's expressed desire, he was not invited to make an official address to the French Parliament). He proposed a simultaneous 50 per cent cut in Soviet and American strategic nuclear forces in exchange for the US abandonment of the Strategic Defense Initiative and repeated a call for a US–Soviet moratorium on the further deployment of the 'euro-missiles', but his proposals were practically ignored by the West and in particular by the US administration.

At that point neither the US nor its European allies were ready to trade their precarious consensus on the question of the deployment of American missiles in Europe for a vague promise of a radical change in Soviet foreign policy by a still completely unknown new leader in Moscow. From the point of view of West European leaders, he still had to pass his main test during the US–Soviet summit due to take place a month later in Geneva.

Like Thatcher before him, Mitterrand immediately communicated his optimistic assessment of the character and intentions of the new Soviet leader to the US President and it was attentively received by the White House. By that time Ronald Reagan (encouraged by his wife, Nancy) was looking for an opportunity finally to turn the page and shift the atmosphere of confrontation between the United States and the Soviet Union, convinced that his administration had repaired the damage caused to America's strategic position by Jimmy Carter's 'soft on Moscow' policy.[46]

The US–Soviet summit took place in Geneva on 19–21 November 1985. Gorbachev was accompanied by an impressive team of new advisers – Aleksandr Yakovlev, Georgi Arbatov, Evgeny Velikhov, Roald Sagdeev – who de facto marginalized the military experts and especially the MID officials represented in Geneva by the still low-profile Eduard Shevardnadze, veteran Soviet Ambassador to the US Anatoli Dobrynin and particularly Georgi Kornienko, who had accepted the difficult task of representing Gromyko's line at the first such summit to be held in the absence of his former boss.

There was a certain asymmetry of objectives between the two leaders: Gorbachev was intending to play the card of personal diplomacy in order to impress the American President, hoping to obtain a radical change of climate in US–Soviet relations, while Reagan simply wanted to get his own idea of the new Soviet General Secretary and to check out the favourable impressions reported by Margaret Thatcher and François Mitterrand. Unsurprisingly, therefore, their first meeting produced little practical result. After the initial reconnaissance *tête-à-tête*, which lasted over an hour instead of the scheduled fifteen minutes (the Americans wanted to minimize the first exposure of their ageing leader to the pressure of his pushy Soviet counterpart), Gorbachev was obviously upset and during the pause complained to his team: 'The man does not seem to hear what I am trying to say. He's deep in his memos prepared by the advisers. He's a real dinosaur.'[47]

Nevertheless Gorbachev had no other choice but to continue his 'charm offensive', strictly following the directive for the negotiations that he himself had submitted for approval to the Politburo. The spirit of the mandate was 'not to leave Geneva without obtaining sizable results'. According to Chernyaev, there was a basic recommendation to 'try not to anger Reagan, thereby increasing the danger of war and playing into the hands of the US "hawks" '.[48]

At the next stage, however, things did improve. After the famous 'fireplace conversation' improvised by the two leaders in the outbuilding housing the swimming pool of the villa Fleur d'Eau, which served as residence for the Reagans, their initially icy relations began to thaw. Although there was no real progress toward practical agreements – the Soviet side continued to demand that the US abandon SDI before there could be an eventual 50 per cent mutual reduction of strategic potential – Gorbachev and Reagan did exchange invitations for official visits and instructed their experts to draft a final document announcing the renewal of political dialogue as well as the resumption of Aeroflot flights to the USA, which had been suspended after the South Korean Boeing had been shot down by the Soviets in September 1983.

Despite the mandate they received, during the night the experts' teams reached an impasse in the preparation of the final documents, largely because of a hard-line position adopted by Kornienko (talking to Arbatov about it afterwards, Gorbachev called Gromyko's deputy a 'political cave-man'[49]). The summit could have ended in a spectacular failure had not Gorbachev in the presence of Reagan given unequivocal instructions to Kornienko urgently to find a compromise. He could hardly have allowed his first serious negotiations to be seen as a fiasco.

The final outcome of the Geneva summit did not live up to Gorbachev's initial hopes; all it amounted to was a solemn statement by the two superpowers declaring that 'a nuclear war cannot be won and must never be fought', and with a promise from both sides to refrain from seeking to gain military superiority over the other.[50] Yet it played an important role in Gorbachev's continuing education in diplomacy.

First of all, it liberated the Soviet leader from the illusion that ending the Cold War between East and West would be an easy enterprise where merely his statement of best intentions would be enough. He was also forced to accept the fact that exposing the absurdity of the arms race (as he did when talking to Thatcher in December 1984) was not enough to bring it to an end, and that the barrier of mistrust separating East and West was probably even more solid than the 'iron curtain' dividing Europe. Yet it was of crucial importance that Gorbachev escaped the trap of blaming the American 'dinosaur' for the failure, as he began to realize that a real breakthrough in the Soviet Union's relations with its Western partners would demand the elaboration of a major long-term strategy.

Gorbachev reached another important conclusion as a result of the Geneva summit: he now understood that the establishment of a new type of East–West relations after the decades of the Cold War depended on confidence building – a process that implied not only a new level of the exchange of information about the other side's intentions but also the need for internal political guarantees in support of official policy statements. It thus became clear for Gorbachev that there was an unavoidable interconnection between the new image he sought for

Soviet foreign policy and the internal reform he was planning to undertake within the country.

\* \* \*

'We cannot remain a major power in world affairs unless we put our domestic house in order,' declared Gorbachev in December at a reception in Moscow for a group of Belgian parliamentarians.[51] The reverse logic also applied to the project for political change: 'When we started *perestroika,*' he wrote with hindsight in his book *Razmyshlenia o proshlom i buduschem (Reflections about the Past and the Future),* 'we understood that without changes in the international position of our country, nothing would come out of our plans for internal reform.'[52]

In his memoirs Gorbachev summed up the conclusion he reached at the end of his first year in power: '*Perestroika* started to advance simultaneously internally and externally. Success in one direction encouraged movement in the other, while any failure in either had the effect of retarding general progress.'[53] But the new leader had yet to discover the fact that the interrelation between the internal and external aspects of his reform plan could not be reduced merely to the synchronization of his actions in both spheres; rather it was a question of an organic political connection that implied a major revision of the established model of Soviet foreign policy. According to Anatoli Chernyaev, at first Gorbachev was not yet fully aware of the nature of this link and proceeded from the belief 'that he could end the Cold War solely by proposing to cut weapons'.[54] This probably would explain Gorbachev's unexpected move two months after the Geneva summit when on 15th January 1986 he announced a 'program for the definitive and universal elimination of nuclear armaments by the year 2000'.

## A 'Tail' of Soviet Diplomacy?

The limited success of the first US–Soviet summit left the impatient Gorbachev dissatisfied. Since his frontal attack on 'fortress Reagan' had not brought about immediate results, he started to reflect on a possible next move. Intuitively he was conscious of the fact that he must not relinquish the political initiative, and as a freshman in diplomacy (Soviet-style) he believed that he could achieve the desired results simply by increasing political and propaganda pressure on his Western counterparts. As in all bureaucracies, the apparatus that he had inherited from his predecessors was certainly ready to react to impulses from the new boss, but not much inclined to propose any real innovation.

Thus when Gorbachev sent a directive to the sections of the Ministries of Defence and Foreign Affairs in charge of 'political planning', demanding that they come up with a new 'bold political initiative', they produced a typical Soviet-style document suitable for public diplomacy. The intended innovative charge of Gorbachev's message, announcing for the first time Moscow's readiness to pay a real price for the proposed reductions of strategic weapons, was wrapped in the envelope of a traditional Soviet 'peace programme'.

And yet in contrast to his predecessors, this time, at least personally, Gorbachev really meant 'business'. This explains why he decided to accept the American logic for disarmament talks and, in addition to the embarrassing 'euro-missiles', agreed to put the most impressive Soviet trump card on the table: land-based strategic missiles. Since for obvious internal political reasons he could not publicly overnight disavow the previous official Soviet position, Gorbachev could only break away by fleeing into the future, concealing his 'defection' within solemn formulas of another global 'peace offensive' so familiar to the ears of Soviet citizens and *nomenklatura* alike.

Traditional Soviet form thus represented the obligatory price that had to be paid for the insertion of new content. The only way in which Gorbachev ventured to break with tradition was his refusal to incorporate his new 'historic' proposal within the General Secretary's report to the Party Congress, the usual way in which major political initiatives customarily were announced. (According to established tradition, on these occasions the Soviet leadership was always expected to proclaim impressive 'peace initiatives' destined to embarrass the imperialist camp.) As Gorbachev writes in his memoirs,

the programme for the abolition of all nuclear arms by the year 2000 was initially meant to be incorporated into the General

Secretary's report to the coming XXVIIth Party Congress. But since this option represented a stereotype of the past, after careful consideration we decided that the incorporation of this initiative in the text of the report would undermine its significance as an autonomous political act.[55]

The Soviet programme for a nuclear-free world was announced on 15 January 1986. The proposal was intended to be 'revolutionary' enough to satisfy the ambitions of the new young Party leader while unrealistic enough to be rejected by the West, thus allowing the Soviet propaganda machine to put all the blame on the adversary for obstructing the achievement of practical results. Pavel Palazhchenko, a former Foreign Ministry disarmament expert who later became Gorbachev's preferred English-language interpreter, agrees that the new leader's widely publicized 'historic peace initiative' essentially represented 'the tail of the traditional Soviet foreign policy from which Gorbachev had not yet managed to extricate himself'.[56]

General Nikolai Chervov, who was then deputy to the Head of the General Staff, Sergei Akhromeev, confirms that the conception of a staged mutual abolition of nuclear armaments was elaborated inside the Ministry of Defence's directorate responsible for the arms limitation talks, 'naturally without any hope of seeing it implemented'.[57] General Viktor Starodubov, who had been one of the chief Soviet negotiators at the Space Arms Limitation Talks, confirms that the idea of spectacular cuts in nuclear weapons – the so-called 'big zero' – came from Akhromeev:

> He was just looking for an impressive reply to Ronald Reagan's 'zero option' proposal for euro-missiles. The logic of his reasoning was simple. If by chance the Americans accept the idea, the Soviet side will be able to make full use of its advantage in conventional weapons. Yet since the chances of leading the US into this rather evident trap were quite slender, the General Staff was hoping to make propagandistic use of their refusal. The detailed proposal for the 'big zero' was stored in Akhromeev's safe before the 1985 US–Soviet summit in Geneva but the Marshal did not want to 'offer' it to Gorbachev for his first exploratory meeting with the American President with its uncertain chances for success, for fear that the idea might be wasted. When after Geneva Gorbachev insistently demanded that the military

suggest 'something new', Akhromeev pulled the cork out of the sealed bottle.[58]

(In fairness to the top members of the Soviet *nomenklatura*, one has to be reminded that in the years of the Cold War confrontation they were not alone in following such logic. During the 1998 conference at Brown University, Douglas McEachin, a former Soviet specialist in the CIA, who from 1984 to 1989 was director of that agency's office of Soviet analysis, told the story of the origin of Ronald Reagan's 1981 'zero option' solution to the 'euro-missiles' problem: 'I do know from first-hand knowledge that some of the people who designed our zero solution to INF designed it believing they had come up with a proposal which would not get a yes from the Soviets, which would therefore make it possible to deploy the missiles, and we could still say we're not being aggressive.'[59])

Kornienko and Akhromeev thought they had good reason to be satisfied with their work. What they did not understand was that this time their boss was not merely interested in propaganda. Gorbachev's real intention behind the 15 January declaration was to send a message to his Western partners announcing the seriousness of his determination to engage a process of deep cuts in armaments as well as his readiness to make new and important concessions to the West, retreating from traditional Soviet positions.

In reality Gorbachev reversed the trap designed by the General Staff for the West, turning it against his own military establishment. First of all, on the basis of the proposed document, he had trapped them into formally accepting the idea of cutting the Soviet strategic offensive potential by half, apparently without prejudice to the national defence. Later, by adding conventional arms to the list of potential bargaining subjects, he transformed the predominantly propaganda intention behind the initiative, thus turning it into a practical offer. During the discussion of the subject with his aides on 20 March 1986, Gorbachev was frank about his reasoning:

> We sincerely want to achieve *détente* and disarmament. Foul play is no longer possible. In any case neither party can dupe the other. As an answer to our proposal on nuclear disarmament we

get a counterargument raising the issue of conventional weapons. OK, we are ready to discuss this question as well. We are in favour of a balance in all types of armaments, including the conventional.[60]

With a certain degree of hindsight, Gorbachev admits that there might have been a degree of ambiguity in the presentation of his nuclear disarmament programme to the public, both Soviet and international. He acknowledges the likelihood that among members of Soviet leadership who approved it and the experts who drafted it 'There may have been cynics whose reasoning was as follows: it's still a long time until the year 2000, all methods are useful in the Cold War, a certain amount of demagogy won't do any harm.' Yet he defends the whole political gesture, claiming that it accomplished its aim. 'Quite soon,' according to Gorbachev, 'we started to move ahead in practice along the basic lines of the disarmament process indicated by the statement of 15 January, starting with the abolition of a whole class of medium-range missiles. If the Soviet Union had continued to exist,' he concludes, implying also that he would have stayed in the Kremlin, 'we could have moved further in the direction of the goal we announced in this visionary document, which perhaps was simply ahead of its time.'[61]

## 'New Thinking' or Ideology Revisited?

The two key individuals who in the first months of 1986 helped Gorbachev shape the new foreign policy line that would become an organic part of his internal reform project were Aleksandr Yakovlev and Anatoli Chernyaev. The former was charged by Gorbachev to prepare the foreign policy section of his Political Report for the next Party Congress. The latter, who became Gorbachev's foreign policy aide on 1 February, finally replacing the long-serving Aleksandrov-Agentov, prepared the draft of Gorbachev's speech at the Ministry of Foreign Affairs in May 1986 – the event that Gorbachev himself characterized as 'a meeting that became the starting point for the full-scale implementation of the policy of "new political thinking" '.[62]

As usual the preparations for the Party Congress started several months in advance. Traditionally a major event in the Soviet political calendar, in the particular circumstances of the winter of 1985–6 this Congress had additional significance: it would be the first Congress of the Gorbachev era and was intended to offer the new General Secretary an opportunity to address his country and the world, announcing his long-term intentions. Gorbachev's closest allies were put in charge of the elaboration of different sections of the Political Report. With regard to the foreign policy section, Gorbachev was clear about what was needed: 'What is "new thinking"? We have to give it a substantial definition.'[63]

Aleksandr Yakovlev, who from the summer of 1985 was in charge of the Propaganda Department of the Central Committee (although not yet formally an elected member of this body), was given the responsibility of preparing the international section opening the report. According to established routine he was supposed to collect working papers submitted for this occasion by various Party and state bodies – the International Department, MID and the Ministry of Defence – as well as the relevant academic institutions, and then draft a text integrating the various submissions.

In fact Yakovlev hated collective authorship and had a well-known penchant for writing things himself; he invited only two people to join him in preparing this strategically important text: Nikolai Kosolapov, who before becoming his assistant in IMEMO and later on the Central Committee had for several years worked for Nikolai Inozemtsev, the former director of this powerful, most prestigious 'think-tank'; and Valentin Falin, who had served as Soviet Ambassador to West Germany and after that was First Deputy to Leonid Zamiatin, the head of the Central Committee's Department of International Information.[64]

Falin recalls:

Yakovlev invited me to come to his office in the Central Committee building and explained that Gorbachev wanted a section in his Report that would present a 'fresh' vision of the international scene along with the constructive role that the Soviet Union was prepared to play in it under its new leadership. He said, 'Papers presented by the MID and International Department are too traditional, too conservative and banal. Try to put the best of yourself into it.'[65]

The other member of Yakovlev's team, Nikolai Kosolapov, said that when he was asked to prepare the first draft of the future report, he mainly used various informal papers along with ideas that had been discussed with his former boss Nikolai Inozemtsev. 'Aleksandr Nikolaevich [Yakovlev] said that this was the time to include in the text most of the ideas we had dreamt of and talked about between ourselves in the past, that we had to use the chance that we were offered.'[66]

The text submitted by Yakovlev to Gorbachev for the first time presented the philosophy behind what would be later called the 'new political thinking'; it turned out to be the only section of the General Secretary's political report to be accepted by Gorbachev without major changes. As a result of their first fundamental discussions in Canada and many subsequent meetings, Yakovlev was probably the person who best understood what the new Soviet leader had in mind.

The paper produced by this *troika* of 'new thinkers' in fact represented a certain set of ideas and opinions that were characteristic of a whole stratum of the Soviet intellectual elite. 'The ranks of the new thinkers', remarks Robert D. English in his study *Russia and the Idea of the West*, 'were not limited to a narrow group of security specialists but comprised a broad cohort of social and natural scientists, students of culture and the humanities, ranging from academics to *apparatchiki*.'[67] This comment is both relevant and accurate, since in many cases there was no strict borderline between academics and members of the *apparat*; quite often the former, especially on the level of the directors of the academic institutes, were recruited from the latter.

It is certainly true that many members of the Soviet academic community in the early 1980s were engaged in active contact with their Western colleagues and participated in a process of intensive intellectual inquiry in an attempt to find alternative policies that could provide a new basis for assuring world stability and security.[68] One could certainly describe various concepts and even such terms as 'sufficient security', which began to appear in their joint reports and statements as ideas borrowed from Western colleagues and transmitted, via these privileged representatives of the Soviet political elite, into the closed world of the ruling *nomenklatura*. Rather paradoxically, on the Western side the appearance of these same ideas was often interpreted by political leaders in an opposite manner, that is, as an example of the efficiency of Soviet 'subversive' tactics which allowed Moscow to recruit respected Western intellectuals into the ranks of 'peace-loving forces', thus undermining and isolating the anti-Soviet 'hawks'.

Ultimately it is a futile debate. When speaking about the roots of 'new thinking', Gorbachev does not hesitate to list Albert Einstein or Bertrand Russell among those whose ideas influenced his intellectual evolution.[69] For the first time since 1917 the supreme leader of the Communist Party and Soviet state abandoned the 'class approach', condemning not only national societies but the entire world to antagonistic confrontation, and declared 'the real dialectics' of modern development to be a combination of 'the competition and struggle between the two systems with a growing tendency for interdependence among the states forming the world community'.[70]

Another important innovation of the Report was the abandonment of what had been the cornerstone of all political programmes periodically proclaimed by the Soviet leaders from the tribune of the Party Congress: the promise to do away with world imperialism and send it to the 'scrap heap of history'. Even when softened by Khrushchev, who rejected Stalin's dictum on the inevitability of war with capitalism and advocated peaceful coexistence between states with different social systems, communist ideology formally never departed from the idea of the final victory of communism as the inevitable culmination of history. (In a way one can say that the Soviet propagandists had invented the formula of the 'end of history' a long time before Francis Fukuyama.) In his report to the Congress, for the first time Gorbachev refused to repeat this mantra or even make reference to it as a form of ritualized propaganda. 'Gorbachev's "new thinking" is fundamentally different from Khrushchev's peaceful coexistence', declares Chernyaev, 'precisely due to the fact that it envisages the compatibility of different social systems on the basis of common norms and criteria or, even "worse" than that, the possibility of convergence.'[71]

At the same time, this apparently low-profile approach toward the immediate tasks of practical foreign policy did not mean that the new Soviet leadership had renounced the great ambitions associated with *perestroika*, which at times seemed to take on a messianic quality. As Gorbachev wrote in his book *Perestroika and New Political Thinking for Our Country and the World*, first published in the autumn of 1987 in the United States and only after that in the Soviet Union, he viewed *perestroika* as a kind of a universal lever capable of transforming not only Soviet reality but also the world situation in general. The draft of the book was prepared by a group of his advisers headed by Yakovlev's deputy Nikolai Shishlin on the basis of Gorbachev's notes, statements and replies to questions during discussions in the Politburo. It was reviewed and largely rewritten by Gorbachev assisted by Yakovlev and provides a true image of the thoughts of the initiators of *perestroika* in its first, euphoric stage.

In those first years (1985–7), which Yakovlev called the 'silver age' of *perestroika*, the ambition and enthusiasm of Soviet communist reformers led them to believe that they had found universal solutions to most of the complex problems of the new times in which they lived. In reality, while retreating from old-fashioned communist dogmas and proclaiming a new Soviet foreign policy free of ideology, Gorbachev and his supporters were *de facto* replacing one ideology with another, no longer based, it is true, on Marxist postulates of class struggle or historic determinism but on 'universal democratic values', which curiously enough were supposed to bring about the same result as the apparently discredited and failed theory of world revolution: an assured and honourable place for the Soviet Union in the vanguard of world history.

As Yakovlev claims, the philosophical foundation of the new foreign policy was presented to the ruling *nomenklatura* and Soviet public in a particular ideological form, largely owing to the obligatory pragmatism of its authors: it was necessary to camouflage the abandonment of the original Bolshevik ambition to build an alternative universe and impose its rules worldwide. It was also necessary at this stage to provide reassurance to the Soviet Union's loyal allies; otherwise 'the sister parties' might suspect the new Soviet leadership of defection from the 'class approach' to international relations.

Yet even though Gorbachev's new political discourse involved considerable use of inventive political tactics, it was not at all a question of hypocrisy. There is good reason to believe that at the initial stage of their project, Gorbachev and the people around him, including convinced reformers like Yakovlev, sincerely believed that they were formulating a new political philosophy with all the potential to become a universal humanitarian ideology – a kind of political religion – that would mean not the abandonment of the communist dream but its modernization. As Jacques Lévesque justly remarks, 'the ideology of "new thinking" . . . reflected a shift from Marxism-Leninism toward social-democracy, though this was not, as such, a conscious goal. It sought an entirely new form of socialism for the USSR and the future world order, a new "synthesis" of socialism and democracy based on "universal values".' On the other hand, what remained of Leninism in this project was the messianic imprint of it. Gorbachev and his team were convinced that they had understood, if not discovered, 'the basic trends in an emerging new world order'.[72]

'In his heart Gorbachev had already rejected "victory over imperialism" by means of the arms race, and he realized that unless it was halted we could not solve any of our domestic problems. But he was optimistic that *perestroika* could give the socialist world a second wind,'[73] notes Chernyaev. Believing that the 'new thinking' was necessary to save the world, Gorbachev was still convinced that it also could save the Soviet version of socialism.

## From Philosophy to Politics

Once the conception of the new policy was elaborated and announced *urbi et orbi* from the tribune of the 27th Party Congress it was then the turn of practical politics to start the process of realization. This task required not romantic political writers like Yakovlev but foreign policy professionals. The

Party Congress gave Gorbachev the opportunity to complete the formation of his foreign policy team. Gromyko may have remained a member of the Politburo, but his possibility to supervise the functioning of the MID was considerably reduced. With a new Politburo loyal to Gorbachev elected by the Congress, this sent a signal that the times when Gromyko's opinion on foreign policy issues could not be challenged were definitely over. The fact that his long-time rival in the Politburo, Boris Ponomarev (Secretary of the Central Committee and head of the International Department), was sent to retirement provided him with little consolation. Ponomarev was replaced by Anatoli Dobrynin, the veteran Soviet diplomat whom Gromyko kept away from Moscow for more than twenty-five years as Soviet Ambassador in Washington, precisely because he was one of the very few who could challenge Gromyko's authority professionally.

Two other nominations that did not require approval by the Congress proved in the long run to be even more important for the transition from solemn statement to practical action. First came the transfer of Georgi Kornienko from the MID, where he had continued to serve as first deputy to the new Foreign Minister, to the Central Committee's International Department as deputy to Dobrynin. The departure of the last guardian of Gromyko-style diplomacy certainly freed the hands of Shevardnadze, who by this time had accumulated a sufficient degree of confidence in his new role. The other nomination was that of Anatoli Chernyaev to replace the long-serving Brezhnev aide Andrei Aleksandrov-Agentov as Gorbachev's foreign policy assistant.

Gorbachev's choice of Chernyaev for this key position was actively supported (and perhaps had been suggested) by Yakovlev and Arbatov. Yet Gorbachev must have taken the decision on the basis of his own recollections of their various trips abroad together. Chernyaev's role, both in training Gorbachev for international statesmanship and in translating his general intentions and philosophy into practical political action, can hardly be overestimated. From February 1986 he seemed practically inseparable from Gorbachev, advising him not only on foreign policy subjects but also on the crucial political decisions he was obliged to take in the domestic arena. Largely due to Chernyaev's tutelage, the process of Gorbachev's transformation into a professional world states-man speeded up considerably. 'In the spring 1986', writes Chernyaev, 'Gorbachev began meeting with various foreign dignitaries. I believe this played a big role in shaping him as a leader of world caliber. In his talks and arguments with people of totally different intellectual traditions and political culture his "new thinking" was refined.'[74]

Chernyaev accompanied Gorbachev on practically all his official visits abroad, participated in most of his boss's meetings with foreign leaders in the Kremlin, and it was he who prepared working memos and draft speeches for Gorbachev, including the famous speech at the UN General Assembly in December 1988; he also edited all official reports of Gorbachev's conver-sations with his foreign counterparts for the press, contributing in this way to the shaping of Gorbachev's public image.

In August 1991, as one of the small number of assistants who used to accompany Gorbachev during his vacations, Chernyaev was detained at the summer residence of the General Secretary in the Crimean resort of Foros by the putschists with his boss and family, expecting to share with the President his as yet unknown fate. Several weeks before his resignation during a last official visit to Spain, Gorbachev in the presence of the author introduced Chernyaev to the Spanish Prime Minister, Felipe Gonzales, as his 'alter ego'.

\* \* \*

By the beginning of spring 1986, a year after his election to the position of General Secretary, with Shevardnadze finally in full control over the MID, Dobrynin assuming the direction of the International Department and Chernyaev having replaced Aleksandrov-Agentov as adviser, Gorbachev had at last com-pleted the formation of his own foreign policy team. The 27th Party Congress had just approved the 'new political thinking' as the ideological basis of his diplomacy, thus providing him with a clear political mandate. What he now needed were some practical results from the new foreign policy, so essential for the advance of his internal reform.

It was probably also around this time that Gorbachev realized how much easier it was to free himself from certain

specific individuals than to overcome the inertia and stereotypes of Soviet foreign policy traditions. He was impatient to
start diminishing the burden of the arms race, to begin the
withdrawal of Soviet troops from Afghanistan and to draw
Western capital into the Soviet economy to provide necessary
financial assistance for his political reform. Yet he could
not start moving ahead in any of these directions without a
qualitative shift in his relations with his Western partners.

The Geneva summit meeting with Reagan, despite all his
hopes, did not bring about the desired change in US–Soviet
relations. On the contrary, as if trying to test Gorbachev's real
intentions (or the degree to which the new Soviet leader would
be willing to retreat from his predecessors' positions), in the
months that followed Geneva, the Reagan administration
assumed a 'tough stand' on Gorbachev.

First came the announcement by Washington of its unwillingness to observe the restrictions imposed by the still not yet
ratified SALT II (Strategic Arms Limitation Talks) treaty on the
ceiling levels for strategic bombers. (Awaiting ratification,
both sides had agreed informally to behave in accordance
with its clauses.) Next came the decision of the US government, taken without seeking the approval of the UN Security
Council, to bomb Tripoli in reprisal for the presumed personal
involvement of Lybian President Gaddafi in the explosion of
a Boeing passenger plane over Lockerbie. The two incidents
provoked heated debates in the Politburo. In both cases
Gorbachev reacted to Washington's unilateral decisions with
overt, calculated anger, which no doubt was quite genuine, since these unexpected confrontational gestures by the
Reagan administration meant for him internal political complications that could risk the destruction of the fragile consensus he had just managed to build for his new approach to
foreign policy.

Another reason for his disappointment was the lukewarm
reception he had received in the West following his 15 January
proposal to start building a nuclear-free world. This reaction
made it clear to Gorbachev that after the decades of accumulated mutual mistrust, despite all his personal capacities of per-
suasion and resources of political imagination, he would not be
able to obtain the desired breakthrough in Soviet–Western

relations by words alone. It was probably at this moment that Gorbachev started to realize that in order to overcome Western scepticism he would have to pay a much higher price – his promises and announcement of intentions had to be confirmed, first, by concrete actions on the international scene and, secondly, by the introduction of heralded changes in the functioning of the Soviet political system.

Conscious of the fact that he would be judged in the West not simply on the basis of the changes of personal style or the more flexible approach to matters of military security, Gorbachev proceeded to make a series of spectacular gestures with regard to sensitive issues of human rights. In February 1986 Anatoli Sharansky, the famous Jewish activist condemned on charges of 'spying', was freed from imprisonment and sent into exile to the West. Yet the foreign policy of *perestroika* had not only to be proclaimed but supported with a coherent strategy. This was also true for the solemnly proclaimed doctrine of 'new thinking', which would have to be completed by a manual of practical policy. This was the first task assigned by Gorbachev to his new assistant on foreign policy questions, Anatoli Chernyaev. The fruit of his efforts, a text rewritten several times on the basis of Gorbachev's remarks and corrections, took the form of a new 'road map' for Soviet diplomacy and was presented on 23 May in the MID skyscraper on Smolenskaya Square to those who were supposed to implement it. It was the first time in Soviet history that the CPSU General Secretary had come to that building to address an audience of ambassadors and high dignitaries of the Soviet political elite.

Gorbachev's unpublished speech (it appeared in the *Vestnik MIDa*, the information bulletin of the Ministry of Foreign Affairs, only three years later), which sounded quite revolutionary and contrasted even with the opening remarks of the new Foreign Minister, was based on a couple of apparently simple ideas. First, the revision of Soviet foreign policy based on the ideas of 'new political thinking' was meant to become the instrument of a major internal political project: a reform of the system that was vital to assure its competitiveness on the international scene. Second, the national security of the USSR preferably would be assured by political means rather than the concentration of society's military, economic and human resources on the preparation for a hypothetical and highly improbable military conflict with some potential aggressor.

'The strategy based on the assumption that the Soviet Union should be as strong as any possible coalition of states that might oppose it was portrayed by Mikhail Sergeevich Gorbachev as totally erroneous. Trying to follow it meant acting contrary to the national interest,' commented Shevardnadze in his memoirs.[75] Gorbachev himself regarded the speech as the real 'starting point for the full-scale implementation of the "new thinking"'.[76] One year after his accession to power, it served as an announcement that the new General Secretary felt himself finally ready to launch a foreign policy of his own.


## Reykjavik – 'the Failed Summit'?


One of the main practical conclusions of the newly formulated strategy was a decision to make another attempt to establish fundamentally different relations with the US administration. By April 1986 (the time he was working on the contents of his speech in the MID), Gorbachev placed his stake on a direct dialogue with the American leadership. Having analysed the meagre results of the Geneva summit, the poor response to his 15 January Declaration and the limits of his attempts to exercise pressure on Washington via its European allies, Gorbachev came to the conclusion that a new bilateral meeting with Reagan was necessary.

But April turned out to be a fatal month for the new Soviet leader. On 26 April one of the nuclear reactors at the Chernobyl power station exploded. The shock of the explosion with its dramatic human and economic cost was tremendous. In one month the cost of neutralizing the reactor and evacuating the population rose to 3 billion roubles.[77] But this unprecedented catastrophe also had its international dimension and deeply affected Gorbachev, strengthening his anti-nuclear feelings and forcing him to make a psychological leap in the direction of transparency. One can say that it marked the border between two Gorbachevs: one before, the other after 26 April. In a way

Chernobyl became for him the equivalent of his personal Cuban missile crisis.

Before 26 April his intention to propose a curb on the arms race along with a radical reduction of nuclear weapons was mostly based on economic and security concerns, while after Chernobyl his attitude towards nuclear weapons transformed into a psychological aversion, a moral rejection (bringing him in this respect closer to Reagan). The fight for a non-nuclear world (formulated in his Declaration of 15 January) became a personal challenge. Already two weeks after the Chernobyl disaster during the Politburo session on 8 May 1986 he had established a direct connection to the process of nuclear disarmament:

> We need negotiations. Even with this 'gang' [use of this term alluded to the US administration's challenging actions on the international scene, obviously part of his effort to keep the Politburo members 'on board'] we need to negotiate. If not, what remains? Look at the Chernobyl catastrophe. Just a puff and we can all feel what nuclear war would be like.[78]

For several months Chernobyl must have become his obsession. A month later in the Politburo session on 13 June, while discussing another subject – the results of the meeting of Warsaw Pact leaders in Budapest – Gorbachev exclaimed: 'I spoke there about Chernobyl. Everybody was shocked. Imagine what a nuclear war would mean for Europe with its concentration of population!'[79]

But Chernobyl became for him not only a security nightmare. It also provided a political challenge. Addressing the Politburo on 3 July, he said:

> What has happened [in Chernobyl] is an extraordinary event bordering on the use of a nuclear weapon. . . . Consequently we bear an enormous responsibility to evaluate the consequences, draw conclusions and prescribe further actions. . . . Our behaviour will be scrutinized not only by our own people but by the entire world. We owe them all the full information on what has happened. A cowardly position – would be unworthy politics.

And insisting on adding an international dimension to the decision that was to be taken, he continued: 'We have frankly to inform our friends in socialist countries, the International Atomic Energy Agency, world public opinion. There should be no tricks. Secrecy on this matter would be harmful for ourselves.'[80]

It was in this context that the conception of Reykjavik found its origin. Gorbachev says that the idea of suggesting a new US–Soviet summit occurred to him in the Crimea after receiving a rather banal letter from the American President to which the Ministry of Foreign Affairs had prepared a routine reply.

> After Chernyaev gave it to me to sign and I started to read it, I realized that it was a mere continuation of the banal exchange of polite words and nothing else. We were steadily retreating from Geneva's results and commitments. I could see we were just going round in circles. That might suit them [the US] but not us. At the same time I understood that we were the only ones who could change gear and speed up the process. A completely new approach was needed. I thought it imperative to meet Reagan and straighten things out with him. And I had the feeling that it could work.[81]

Proposing the new US–Soviet summit, Gorbachev was not only guided by the personal 'feeling' of Reagan he had built for himself since their meeting in Geneva. The idea that a candid talk between the two leaders could bring about the desired breakthrough was suggested to Gorbachev by François Mitterrand. Reacting to Gorbachev's complaints about Washington's behaviour, his fears that the influence of the American 'military lobby' was responsible for a 'fading' of the spirit of Geneva, Mitterrand argued that it would be a mistake to identify the goals of the US military-industrial complex with the policies of the Washington administration or the personal intentions of Reagan. 'In contrast to other American politicians, Reagan is not an automaton. He is a human being,' remarked the French President. 'This is extremely important,' Gorbachev replied, 'and I am taking special note of it.'[82] Thus it was the French President who prompted to Gorbachev to seek that crucial tête-à-tête with Reagan which eventually led to results that seriously angered the French and the British governments.

Having tested the idea of an extraordinary summit on Chernyaev, Gorbachev called the members of his 'inner circle'

– Shevardnadze, Ryzhkov, Ligachev and also Gromyko – to get their backing for his idea '*to force Reagan to agree to the summit that was necessary for one vital goal of perestroika – the easing of the military burden*'.[83] Unlike the year before, this time, when preparing for a new US–Soviet summit, he realized that to obtain the desired result he would have to pay a substantial price.

Speaking before the Politburo, first on 22 September and again on 8 October, as well as when discussing the conception of the summit with his assistants, Gorbachev presented his approach that basically meant only one thing: make to the American President 'an offer that he cannot refuse'.

> We certainly cannot propose to the Americans something that is sure to provoke a refusal. That is not politics. . . . Let's put strategic weapons first, not nuclear tests. Everybody is worried about them. The leitmotiv should be the liquidation of the nuclear weapons, about which we spoke with the President in Geneva. And let's show a political approach and not the arithmetical . . . always keeping in mind our priority: kick the 'Pershing-II' out of Europe. It's a revolver put to our temple. . . . If Reagan refuses to react positively, we shall make everything public. This is the design.[84]

To make his proposal attractive for the Americans, Gorbachev was prepared to incorporate certain points borrowed from the American position that the Soviets until then had rejected as unacceptable. This included a readiness to cut by half the most threatening and efficient part of the Soviet strategic triad – the land-based intercontinental ballistic missile; also an acceptance of the 'zero option' for the 'euromissiles' proposed by Reagan for Europe and an abandonment of the traditional Soviet demand to include the British and French nuclear potential in the general East–West balance during the SALT negotiations. As a reserve position, in further negotiations Gorbachev was ready to include Soviet middle-range missiles in Asia and even the nuclear artillery.

In fact in return for this sensational, lateral slashing of the previously monolithic Soviet negotiating position, Gorbachev was demanding much less than a 100 per cent acceptance of his proposal; he sought 'just' an American promise to honour the

Anti-Ballistic Missile Treaty for the next ten years while confining SDI to laboratory testing. Having realized he had no real means of persuading or forcing Washington to abandon SDI, Gorbachev was hoping to ransom its slow-down from Ronald Reagan by offering a maximum price. Commenting on the reasons for the evident Soviet overreaction to Reagan's 'Star Wars' project, Gorbachev claims that it was not the fear of losing the competition with America from the point of view of security.

> We were not afraid of SDI, first of all, because our experts were convinced that this project was unrealizable, and secondly, we would know how to neutralize it. When I said that to the US President I was not bluffing. We did in fact have the possibility of an eventual response, a terrible one – I can confirm it now – although more efficient and less costly than the SDI. It was not out of fear that we were objecting, but because of the destabilizing effect. So for us it was not a question of fear but of responsibility.[85]

Gorbachev was less elusive when 'selling' his position to the Politburo, explaining that the true danger coming from the SDI was not a security threat but the economic challenge:

> Our super-goal is to avoid a new round of the arms race. Which would force us to face the modernization of the strategic weapons. 'Tridents', 'Minutemen', arms in space . . . It would mean the deterioration of our ecological, strategic and political security, the loss everywhere, but above all exhausting our economy. And this is not acceptable. That is why we need not sacrifice the important things for the details . . . .[86]

If this in fact was the real explanation for Soviet opposition to SDI, then the political and propaganda tactics chosen by Moscow to 'kill' it were probably not the most efficient. As the former US State Secretary George Shultz argues, it was precisely the Soviet obsessive opposition to SDI that in his view was transforming SDI into 'the propellant that would lead the Soviets to agree to deep reductions'.[87] Apparently it was this kind of reasoning (in addition to Reagan's obsession with the idea of a 'defensive shield in space') that proved to be the main explanation for the eventual refusal of the US side in Reykjavik to trade a continuation of a highly hypothetical 'Star Wars' project for a real reduction of the Soviet offensive potential on conditions most favourable for the Americans.[88]

For his part, having put his personal authority and reputation at stake within the Politburo, Gorbachev could not return to Moscow empty-handed. According to the directives he received from the Politburo (which of course he had himself formulated), in case of failure to reach an agreement he was supposed publicly to put all the responsibility for the lack of success on the United States, making maximum propaganda use of the impasse. It was in fact on this condition that he obtained the agreement of his colleagues to the package of unprecedented proposals he was bringing to Reykjavik.[89]

This logic was not after all very different from the typical Soviet way of challenging its strategic adversary: 'Either you accept our peace-loving proposals, or we address world public opinion and reveal your true aggressive nature.' (The major difference signalling a break with traditional Soviet methods was that, previously, new proposals coming from Moscow were usually only conceived in order to be rejected, i.e. solely for propaganda purposes, whereas now Gorbachev was ready to take the American position as the basis for genuine negotiation.) Yet one can say that the first real leap into the practice of 'new thinking', Gorbachev's true rupture with the legacy of the past, came not only in the offer of an authentic deal, but also in his refusal to exploit the rejection politically, to use it for propaganda purposes, thus *de facto* disregarding the mandate he had brought from Moscow.

The failure 'was transformed into a ray of hope by Gorbachev just twenty minutes after his parting handshake with Reagan. . . . Everyone saw that agreement was possible. . . . Indeed before, we were talking about limitations on nuclear arms. Now we were talking about their reduction and elimination', writes Chernyaev.[90] Eduard Shevardnadze was less sympathetic in his evaluation of the results of the summit (perhaps because he was less involved than Chernyaev in working out the strategy for the meeting). According to his interpretation, 'the two leaders just could not handle the ball that they had thrown too high. In the end perhaps it was good that the meeting in Reykjavik ended the way it did.'[91]

Chernyaev, on the contrary, regards the 'failed summit' as the crucial turning point in the further evolution of Gorbachev's approach not only to Soviet–American relations but also to foreign policy issues in general. In his view the principal result of the Reykjavik summit was more a question of a psychological shift in the minds of the two superpower leaders rather than any concrete progress on agreements, including the strategic arms and 'euro-missile' agreements that eventually were signed in the months that followed. This further progress would never have been possible without the new level of confidence and understanding reached in the Hofdi house. 'It was then, in Reykjavik, that Gorbachev became convinced that he and Reagan could "do real business" together after all. A spark of understanding was born between them as if they had winked at each other about the future. . . . After Reykjavik [Gorbachev] never again spoke about Reagan in his inner circle the way that he had before.'[92]

In a more general sense Reykjavik marked for Gorbachev the end of the superpower 'game', a futile exercise in political and propaganda point-scoring over the adversary, while disregarding the continuing slide of humankind towards the danger of apocalyptic confrontation. 'After Reykjavik Gorbachev was no longer playing games with the Americans, despite the fact that he clearly saw through their tricks. . . . Gorbachev began his march towards the main goal, intending to reach it by means of confidence building and the easing of military confrontation.'[93]

## 'New Political Thinking': Rules and Tools

To prepare for Reykjavik, for the first time Gorbachev put into action the new mechanism for the implementation of foreign policy that he had created. His report to the Party Congress and his speech at the MID signalled the determination to assume personal control over this sector of the state's activity. Having spent almost a year in office, he had gathered important experience and discovered the autonomous value of foreign policy not only as an auxiliary instrument to support internal change but also as an efficient lever for spreading the reformist impulse of *perestroika* on the world political scene.

Formally the relationship between government and Party bodies involved in the elaboration and execution of Soviet foreign policy had not changed. The Ministry of Foreign Affairs formulated proposals concerning all important foreign policy issues and submitted them to the Politburo for consideration 'on the political level'; it would then be responsible for carrying out the decisions and directives adopted by the Party leadership. As in previous years, it remained the principal official representative of the Soviet state in its contacts abroad. Yet though it was supposed to coordinate the activity of other ministries and agencies operating in the field of foreign policy, it was no longer fulfilling the same supervisory function as it had in Gromyko's time, when the MID commanded a monopoly of control over the entire spectrum of Soviet foreign policy.

The new political dynamics of *perestroika* explain why the MID obviously was losing an essential part of its former privileges (for example, neither Shevardnadze nor his top advisers were involved in the preparation of the international section of Gorbachev's report to the 27th Party Congress or his May speech in the MID building). Still, largely thanks to Shevardnadze's privileged personal relations with Gorbachev, the Ministry managed to maintain its leading role in the execution of foreign policy.

Together with Yakovlev, Shevardnadze belonged to the intimate circle of the General Secretary's closest companions. Yet despite his closeness to Gorbachev, the new Minister knew that he would be judged on a daily basis by his foreign partners and also by his subordinates, according to his level of competence. This explains why this former provincial Party functionary, freshly recruited to diplomacy and always a workaholic, made an enormous effort to become an irreproachable foreign policy expert. Even on normal days Shevardnadze would rarely leave his desk before ten o'clock in the evening, carrying home piles of documents for the night's reading and occasionally staying overnight in the office, using the bed in an adjacent room. He would spend hours listening attentively to the reports of the Soviet negotiators, asking numerous questions and making notes so as to be able on the next day freely to conduct the discussion with his foreign colleague without having to look at his papers or demand a figure from an expert.[94]

Understandably, once he set foot in the MID building, Shevardnadze undertook a post-Gromyko 'clean-up' that was not limited to the traditional replacement of the former Minister's acolytes, such as Kornienko, by his own. He promoted some bright young diplomats to key posts in the Ministry or to ambassadorial positions. New departments headed by deputy-ministers were created: one, a special department on questions related to the disarmament process directed by Viktor Karpov, the other, a department on humanitarian problems under the direction of Anatoli Adamishin.

Although Shevardnadze never tried to emulate the arrogance of Gromyko and had the external appearance of a rather mild, generous, well-mannered Caucasian nobleman, in his contacts with colleagues from other state and Party bodies he displayed a considerable degree of 'Georgian self respect and pride'– in Gorbachev's words – so much so that few would dare to challenge the MID's role as gate-keeper in matters of foreign policy. According to Gorbachev, it was largely Shevardnadze's 'wounded pride after my decision to involve Primakov in the search for a peaceful outcome of the Gulf crisis' that pushed him to his unexpected announcement of resignation in December 1990.[95]

At the same time Shevardnadze seemed to accept without much resistance the primary role played by Gorbachev's assistants and particularly by Chernyaev in the strategic planning and formulation of foreign policy priorities. The reason for this was not only Chernyaev's closeness to Gorbachev but rather the fact that, unlike Primakov, Chernyaev had never displayed any personal political ambition and was content to remain behind the scenes; he could therefore hardly be seen as a rival nor did he in any way publicly undermine Shevardnadze's authority.

Paradoxically the traditionally adversarial relations between the MID and the International Department of the Central Committee, quite tense at the time of the duels between Gromyko and Ponomarev, did not settle down after key positions in the Department's leadership were occupied by the two MID veterans, Dobrynin and Kornienko. On the contrary, continuing rivalry brought further proof of the rule that corporate interests and personal ambition tend to prevail over the professional background of a functionary in any bureaucratic system. Another apparent paradox was related to the fact that the two International Departments that had supplied a significant number of their members to Gorbachev's closest circle of advisers (Chernyaev, Zagladin, Shakhnazarov, Shishlin), or perhaps exactly for this reason, rapidly lost their former reputation as the informal 'think-tanks' of the General Secretary.

One further reason for the rise of Shevardnadze's authority in the articulation of foreign policy had to do with the fact that he was not as constrained as Gromyko had been by the need to coordinate his strategic moves with a powerful Minister of Defence like Ustinov. With the course for disarmament and *détente* with the West set by the political leadership, the military lobby lost much of its previous weight. Additionally, the prestige of the Ministry of Defence suffered a severe blow in May 1987 at the time of the forced resignation of Marshal Sokolov, who had to pay the price for the humiliating failure of the Soviet anti-aircraft defence that allowed a German amateur pilot, Mathias Rust, to land on Red Square in Moscow.

The decision to dismiss Sokolov was taken by Gorbachev after he heard the shocking news on the plane returning from a visit to the GDR, largely under the influence of Shevardnadze.[96] His particularly harsh reaction (together with the Minister a number of high-ranking military commanders also were fired), not normally typical Gorbachev behaviour, was a calculated political move intended to curtail the excessive political role that the military had acquired in the Soviet political hierarchy.

Sokolov was replaced by his deputy, the unimpressive Dimitri Yazov (one of the future putschists in August 1991), who would not evidence much ambition to interfere in the political debate, even over aspects of foreign policy that directly affected the strategic situation of the USSR. Here he mainly relied on his Chief of Staff, Marshal Akhromeev, who looked after the preservation of the interests of the military in the disarmament process. The Minister would rarely express his disagreement or reservations during the meetings of the 'Zaikov Commission', the so-called *bolshaya piaterka* ('the big five'), even when he personally was not convinced of the correctness of proposed solutions. Yazov usually accepted the compromises imposed on him by the majority of the Commission, justifying them by the pressure of 'political choices' taken by the General Secretary', confirms Akhromeev's deputy, General Nikolai Chervov.[97]

Conscious of the professional and psychological problems that these 'political choices' were creating for the military, Gorbachev tended to use the structure the 'Zaikov Commission' as a shock absorber. It was an assemblage that brought together the heads of the MID, the Ministry of Defence, the KGB, the VPK Commission and the Party's International Department. Its task, on the basis of inter-agency consultation, was to work out recommendations for the Politburo on the Soviet position at various disarmament talks and to submit draft directives for the Soviet negotiating teams.

The 'big five' members were assisted by the 'small five' (*malaya piaterka*), a working group which consisted of deputy heads of ministries and agencies and of experts on specific problems which did the necessary preparatory work before the meetings of the bosses. Since the participants in the 'big five' were also members of the Politburo, unlikely to pay much attention to complex technical details, in the majority of cases real agreements usually were reached at the lower level. This working group, in reality not a gathering of five but of up to approximately forty or fifty functionaries and experts, was usually convened by the deputy head of the General Staff and 'worked in an atmosphere of free and often heated debate searching to reach consensus'.[98]

The *piaterka* mechanism had been created and was smoothly functioning long before Gorbachev came to power. From the late Brezhnev years its working mode reflected the Gromyko–Ustinov condominium established in the sphere of foreign policy and national security. Draft papers prepared jointly by the Kornienko and Akhromeev teams were usually adopted without great debate by the others. Things started to change radically after the election of Gorbachev and his appointment of Shevardnadze, a much closer friend of the General Secretary than of the new Minister of Defence. Positions of the MID and of the General Staff were increasingly less synchronized. In these circumstances the functioning of the Commission, which embodied the authority of the superior political *instance*, the Politburo, regained its initial function and purpose. Gorbachev put at the head of the 'big five' someone in whom he had confidence – Lev Zaikov, a Party secretary from Leningrad. Previously Zaikov had worked in the military industry, hence he was quite familiar with the specific features of the defence sector.

Zaikov managed to preside over the sessions of the Commission with great skill, even at times when opinions sharply diverged. 'Usually he succeeded in finding reasonable compromise formulas acceptable for everybody and only then forwarded the common position to the General Secretary. Gorbachev practically never challenged the consensus agreements. He usually submitted them for the formal approval of the Politburo, but there was practically never any open debate on these issues.'[99] This consensus style of directing the functioning of the Commission started to change after Reykjavik. 'The first lively debate of a paper submitted by the Zaikov Comission was in connection with the expected signing of the INF Treaty in Washington in December 1987,' testifies Vitali Kataev, assistant to Lev Zaikov.[100]

According to Zaikov, Gorbachev himself – at least until 1989 – never formulated any specific directives in advance, trusting Zaikov's competence and mastery of the art of compromise; he was prepared to leave it to the members of the Commission to find consensus formulas. With the development of tension in the relations between the military and the MID (which started to take the form of open and sharp disputes between Shevardnadze and Akhromeev), he was increasingly obliged to take sides, which usually resulted in his unofficial backing of Shevardnadze. Lev Zaikov was then charged to work on the wording of directives for the Soviet negotiators, in conformity with the position agreed upon with Shevardnadze.[101]

Gorbachev confirms that he continued to receive written directives from the Politburo in his capacity of the General Secretary until he was elected President of the USSR in 1990. 'It is a nonsense to maintain that there was any kind of improvisation. The mechanism and the procedures leading to the elaboration of the positions were well defined.'[102] This whole mechanism continued to function rather smoothly until the implosion of the internal political foundation of the Soviet Party-state in the spring of 1990, with the abrogation of Article 6 of the Soviet Constitution, which formally attributed the monopoly of state political power to the Communist Party.

# 3

# BREAKING THE ICE

I've made my choice and will not retreat whatever the price or the end that awaits me. I want democracy and freedom and I am determined to free my country from a terrible past. Let the people judge me the way they choose. I am ready to pursue this path even if many of my contemporaries are not ready to understand me.

Mikhail Gorbachev[1]

## Untying the Reykjavik 'Package'

After Reykjavik, Gorbachev was faced with a difficult choice. His first 'cavalry attack' on the foreign policy front apparently had failed. It had been launched with the intention of gaining the territory and reserves necessary for internal reform without sacrificing strategic parity with the US, and particularly without any open recognition of the dramatic miscalculations and political errors of his predecessors. He was now obliged to choose between returning to the traditional Soviet-style policy, seeking to salvage the image of a powerful Soviet Union for internal purposes, or daring a genuine break with the past by embarking on a principally new approach to foreign policy. In practice it would mean unilaterally starting to apply the declared principles of the 'new thinking' in his own daily practical activity even without guaranteed reciprocity from his Western partners.

The two basic considerations behind Gorbachev's pressing attempt to persuade Reagan to retreat from his position on SDI at Reykjavik, even if only symbolically, were not based on military considerations. Gorbachev claims that the Soviet leadership at no time seriously believed that this programme posed a potential danger for the security of the USSR, at least in the foreseeable future.[2] (Gorbachev's statement is supported by academician Evgeny Velikhov, who presided over the joint team of scientific and military experts created by Andropov to evaluate the 'feasibility of the SDI'. According to Velikhov, the practically unanimous conclusion of his Commission was that in its announced model this programme 'will not work'.[3])

The reasons for Gorbachev's insistence were different. One was political. He had paid dearly for the Politburo's approval of his offer of a historic deal with the United States: to agree to a 50 per cent reduction of the strategic offensive potential of each of the superpowers – something that was very close to the initial US proposal. He could not return to Moscow empty-handed. If that were to be the case, he would be exposing himself to accusations of making unjustified unilateral concessions and of selling out the interests of national security.

Of course stopping the arms race with the West and consequently having the possibility of starting to reduce Soviet defence expenditure represented one of his priorities at a time when he was preparing the overall restructuring of the Soviet system. Yet he felt that above all he was in need of political arguments in debates with his own military-industrial complex since even the 'asymmetric response' to SDI proposed by Soviet generals and weapons manufacturers envisaged 117 scientific and 86 research projects and 165 experimental programmes with approximate spending during the ten-year period amounting to between 40 and 50 billion roubles.[4] In the absence of any compromise with Washington, Gorbachev certainly would have had additional problems persuading his entourage to abandon these plans and to accept a move in the direction of unilateral disarmament.

Yet he could not allow his reform project to become hostage to securing a concession on SDI. The imperatives of the situation inside the country left Gorbachev no choice other than to start treating disarmament issues on a piecemeal basis, untying the Reykjavik package. According to Chernyaev, a decisive role in his personal decision to move in that direction was the fact that during this second summit meeting with Reagan, for the first time Gorbachev internally came to the conclusion that the US government was not preparing an attack against the Soviet Union. Reykjavik convinced Gorbachev that he would be able to cooperate successfully with the American President, who had a sincere and deep-seated conviction of the need to relieve the world of the nuclear threat. It was the first time that Gorbachev perceived Reagan not as a 'representative of US imperialism' but as a trustworthy partner, who shared similar hopes and ideas. During the coming months and even years, this 'revelation' became the solid psychological foundation for his position during the difficult domestic debates with the leadership of the Soviet Defence Ministry and the General Staff. 'At the moment when discussions would start to heat up,' writes Chernyaev, 'Gorbachev did not hesitate to ask the generals publicly: "Are you really planning to go to war with the Americans? I'm not!"'[5]

A renowned Soviet writer from Byelorussia, Ales Adamovich, elected during the *perestroika* years to the new Soviet Parliament, characterized in these words Gorbachev's internal 'transformation' brought about by the double effect of Chernobyl and the Reykjavik summit: 'Gorbachev's devotion to peace is more than politics or even a system of thinking, it's his nature. Had it not been so he wouldn't have successfully resisted the obstinate opposition to his efforts coming from the two militarized structures – ours [Soviet] and theirs [American] – ossified and deadened in their mutual mistrust.'[6]

For various reasons the first most urgent issue on his disarmament agenda was the question of the 'euro-missiles'. Even prior to Reykjavik, Gorbachev had obtained a green light from the Politburo for an 'asymmetric' reduction with the objective of totally eliminating this whole class of intermediate- and small-range Soviet and American nuclear missiles (which would require the USSR to destroy twice as many nuclear warheads as the Americans). After Reykjavik a number of new factors complicated the previous debate. Even if formally the decision to deploy new SS-20 missiles had been collectively approved by the Politburo, first in the European and later in the Asian part of the Soviet Union, it was well known that personal responsibility for this decision was shared by three members of the Soviet leadership: Brezhnev, Ustinov and Gromyko. With Gorbachev and his new team replacing the old Soviet leadership, the situation radically changed. The political logic and the priorities of *perestroika* moved to the front line of Soviet state interests, forcing the arms producers and the generals to adjust their own positions. Yet one of the psychological barriers they had to overcome was the realization that in order to repair the damage caused by the deployment of the 'euro-missiles', the Soviet Union would have to accept an asymmetric formula of missile reduction.

For former war veterans like Sokolov, brought up in the conviction that there can be no such thing as an excessive amount of weaponry, the very idea that the Soviet Union might be obliged to destroy a whole class of new weapons sounded like heresy, if not high treason. 'This is a state crime!' Marshal Sokolov would exclaim without hesitation in the lobby of the Central Committee building, trying to get support for his reservations.

> The army cannot participate. We all remember Khrushchev's improvisations that cost our country the destruction of the navy and of aviation. How can one ignore the army's position in these matters? It's the army and not the Ministry of Foreign Affairs that is charged to look after the security of the state and it knows better what kind of arms we need and in what quantities in order to fulfil this task.[7]

It was only after the deadlock at Reykjavik, where Gorbachev evidently went as far as he could on the basis of the position approved by the Politburo without obtaining any concession on the question of SDI from Reagan, that he could flatly demand from his colleagues in the Politburo and the military that they consider what to do next. At one of the Politburo sessions after Reykjavik he said: 'If we do not want to lose the dynamic impulse of our new policy and if we really care about the credibility of our position, we have seriously to start considering the proposals coming from NATO circles.'[8]

Aware of the hesitation of the Americans after Reykjavik while simultaneously trying to neutralize the residual opposition of his own opponents among the military, Gorbachev resorted to the escalation tactic, suggesting the addition of a 'third zero' to Reagan's initial formula: the elimination of all tactical Soviet and American nuclear missiles with a range of 500 km or more (i.e. down from 5,000 km), thus widening the latitude of the vectors concerned. This gesture, even at the cost of further increasing the asymmetry of figures for eliminated missiles in favour of the US, benefited Gorbachev politically since it provided him with the possibility of 'selling' his 'peace initiative' to his domestic public opinion as a confirmation of the active character of Soviet foreign policy.

The sudden radical change of Moscow's position, offering the Americans a shift from sterile bargaining over secondary aspects of the continuing arms race to the real business of nuclear disarmament, even embarrassed the American side, since Reagan's 'double zero' proposal had itself been elaborated according to the old rules of the superpower game and made public with the assumption that the Soviet side would never accept it. It was not only the 'Gorby-sceptics' who were concerned that there could be an eventual 'decoupling' of the security connection between the United States and Western Europe in the event of a withdrawal of Pershing-II and cruise missiles; others also expressed their reservations.

In reply to the unexpected Soviet offer, Washington raised the stakes and put forward a 'modernized zero option', first adding the Soviet SS-20s based in Asia to the proposed arms cuts and then insisting on the very eve of the signing of the treaty that a shorter-range 'Oka' (SS-23) missile be included in the list of the Soviet reductions. This move demonstrated Washington's intention to subject Gorbachev to a difficult test: he could either accept to pay a higher price for the treaty or refuse to sign it. Either of these variants would raise the political cost of the decision for Gorbachev at home.

Forced to recognize the strategic imbalance in favour of the West produced by the deployment of the American Pershing-II missiles and cruise missiles in Europe, and facing the prospect of the possible modernization of the tactical Pershing-I missiles in Germany, the Soviet General Staff under Gorbachev's pressure reluctantly agreed to accept an extremely asymmetrical total elimination of all intermediate-range nuclear missiles. On 26 February 1987 the Soviet Politburo approved Gorbachev's proposal along these lines. After he convinced the Politburo, on 1 March in a television speech Gorbachev announced the 'untying' of the Reykjavik 'package' and the decision to single out the issue of the SS-20 missiles from the general strategic nuclear weapons package; he proposed the urgent conclusion of a separate agreement on this issue.

Defending his position against critics who accused him of making a bad bargain, Gorbachev explains:

> We just had to bury them all [the American missiles]. Everything else was a matter of tactics. It is true the initial proposal was to keep 100 missiles on each side. And that suited the US. They, too, were interested in keeping production possibilities and maintaining research in this field. But I insisted that we go up to zero. First they started to object, but we told them, look, it's your own proposal. So we finally obtained the three zeros. It was important because they had the tactical Pershing-I and the Lance that with a slight modernization could be substituted for the destroyed ones. While our intention was to end this problem completely.[9]

In his memoirs Shevardnadze confirms Gorbachev's evaluation of the significance of the INF Treaty, stressing that the General Secretary considered its signing in Washington on 8 December 1987 to be a 'major contribution to the strengthening of the security of the Soviet Union because it pushed the American nuclear presence away from the Soviet borders'.[10]

However, this was not the unanimous verdict on the Treaty within Gorbachev's entourage. Not only the military but also a number of senior Party functionaries felt 'betrayed' by Gorbachev and Shevardnadze's decision to sacrifice an essential part of the Soviet threat potential. One of the 'hawks', the Secretary of the Central Committee in charge of the defence industry, Oleg Baklanov, himself a former director of one of the huge military-industrial enterprises, did not hesitate to send a memorandum to Gorbachev emphasizing his disagreement with the proposed formulas of 'unjustified' Soviet arms reductions and insisting that as a result the strategic parity between the USSR and the West would be fatally broken.[11]

It was not only the quantitative imbalance of the INF Treaty that aroused an allergic reaction within the military lobby, but also the extremely detailed character of various oversight measures, which included unprecedented possibilities of access by the other side's inspectors in order to supervise all stages of the destruction of the missiles as stipulated. Opponents of the elimination of middle-range missiles then tried to use the argument of inspections in order to question the expediency of the Treaty in general. Yet what emerged during the discussion in the Politburo was that their main fear was not so much a revelation of military secrets but that the actual state of the Soviet military would be exposed – the miserable conditions and poor internal discipline that prevailed in Soviet army units was indeed a well-protected state secret. Only when Gorbachev, extremely dissatisfied with this type of reasoning, sarcastically suggested to the head of the General Staff that he would invite more of the American inspectors since this apparently could help improve the situation in the army did the Defence Ministry withdraw its last objections.[12]

In the case of inspection measures, as in a number of other situations, for example on the question of human rights, Gorbachev developed specific tactics to turn the former defensive Soviet position into an offensive one. By doing so he intended not only to seize the political initiative in the course of negotiations, but also to reassure his own public, schooled by official propaganda to believe that the Soviet leadership never submits to the views of the adversary but, on the contrary, imposes its own position on the rest of the world. Thus on 10 December 1987 in Washington, when presenting the results of the US–Soviet summit to the press, Gorbachev proudly announced that the INF Treaty 'establishes unprecedented standards of openness and *glasnost*. . . . In this way concrete action confirms the position that we have expressed more than once: when both sides actually start talking about real control over disarmament, we'll be the most determined champions of the strictest, most efficient inspection system.'[13]

The signing of the Treaty was endangered when a row took place with indignant Soviet generals, angered by Gorbachev's last-minute concessions to the Americans. During his conversation with US State Secretary George Shultz in October

1987, Gorbachev had agreed to include the shorter-range 'Oka' (SS-23) missile in the list of weapons subject to elimination, although according to the official Soviet stance this missile was not capable of operating at a range of 500 km. What infuriated the military was the fact that for the first time Gorbachev took a decision of this kind without formally asking for the views of the General Staff or waiting for its consent. Marshal Sergei Akhromeev, who was supposed to attend Gorbachev's meeting with Shultz, later explained that by the time he joined their conversation Gorbachev had already yielded the 'Oka' to the Americans. He felt so humiliated by Gorbachev and Shevardnadze that he nearly resigned his post as Chief of the General Staff.[14]

It was inconceivable that this could have happened when Ustinov was Minister of Defence. Yet even in a new, apparently more comfortable political situation, Gorbachev remained reluctant to antagonize the grumbling generals, and in order to avoid direct confrontation between the Ministry of Defence and the MID, he usually used the Zaikov Commission as a shock absorber. It served both as a security valve and as a place for the elaboration of useful compromises between the diplomats and the military.

This situation did not prevail for long, however. With the accumulation of problems along the bumpy road of *perestroika*, the General Secretary more and more often was confronted with situations which required him to take an increasing number of decisions himself in order to assure the progress of the disarmament process. His growing loneliness reflected his conscious choice to be a reformer determined to forge ahead despite the increasing political risk. Increasingly isolated, he knew that he could not very much count on the support of his ever more sceptical colleagues or his foreign partners.

## Withdrawing from Afghanistan and Retiring from the 'Third World'

Another concern as high on the list of Gorbachev top priorities as the 'euro-missiles' was the war in Afghanistan. Much more than the missile issue, it exemplified the combination of acute domestic and foreign problems facing the new Soviet leadership. Even inside Brezhnev's Politburo, a reappraisal of the decision to send troops to Afghanistan began almost immediately after the start of military action, as soon as it became clear that the initial scenario of a 'lightning operation' followed by the rapid withdrawal of a 'limited contingent' was unrealistic.[15] In February 1980, just two months after the invasion, Brezhnev himself (certainly under the pressure of his aides) raised the question of troop withdrawal in the Politburo. But it was too late – the trap had already closed, and the Soviet Union was mired in a regional conflict on its borders that bore all the characteristics of a colonial war.

Under the double pressure of the danger of military fiasco along with growing international isolation, the Soviet leadership reluctantly agreed to the beginning of negotiations on a political solution of the Afghan conflict. Talks between Afghanistan and Pakistan started in Geneva on 16 June 1982 under the patronage and mediation of the United Nations with the Soviet Union and the United States as potential guarantors of an agreement. The negotiations seemed to be doomed to mark time without any real breakthrough, with Moscow and its Afghan protégés totally excluding any discussion of regime change while the Americans and the Pakistanis demanded the announcement of a precise timetable for the withdrawal of Soviet troops and the transfer of power to the opposition, as a preliminary condition.[16]

Concerned with the need to find a way out of the stalemate, Andropov used the opportunity offered by Brezhnev's death in November 1982; as the newly elected General Secretary he signalled to Pakistan's President Zia, who came to Moscow for Brezhnev's funeral, that he would withdraw the Soviet troops on condition that Pakistan stopped its military support for the Islamic opposition.[17] But the serious illness that intensified in the summer of 1983 and led to Andropov's death in February 1984 left too little time for the new Soviet leader to demonstrate whether or not his intentions were serious.

For Gorbachev, elected to the supreme position in the Soviet leadership after five and a half years of a futile war, the main question was not whether or not to pull out the Soviet troops but *how* to prepare, announce and execute this decision. It had become obvious, not only for him but also for the majority of members of the Politburo, that the Soviet Union could no longer afford to go on indefinitely paying such a heavy price for its Afghan adventure – in casualties, expenditure and dramatic isolation on the international scene.[18]

Yet even if Gorbachev had no need to fear opposition within the Politburo to a policy of troop withdrawal as the long-term objective, he faced understandable opposition within the Soviet army leadership, unwilling to acknowledge the reality of its ignominious failure. The local Afghan government headed by Babrak Karmal strongly rejected withdrawal, fearful of losing crucial Soviet military protection. Later, in response to the criticism of those who accused him of having taken too much time before announcing the formal decision to withdraw, Gorbachev justified his behaviour: 'It took us a year and a half to persuade Babrak Karmal, who categorically opposed the troop withdrawal, and to overcome the resistance of our own military.'[19]

Yet he was not wasting time. Already in the summer of 1985 Gorbachev sent General Zaitsev on a mission to Kabul to explore the chances for a military resolution of the conflict. The conclusion brought back to Moscow by Zaitsev was that the only hope of ending the war on Soviet terms lay in hermetically sealing the Afghan borders with Pakistan and Iran in order to prevent the shipments of weapons and ammunition to the opposition from abroad. But this was totally unrealistic.[20]

Gorbachev's next step was to inform Babrak Karmal that there was only a limited amount of time left to profit from the Soviet presence to prepare his own political survival. During a secret encounter with Karmal in October 1985 Gorbachev advised him to abandon slogans of socialist construction in his backward country and to return instead to the Islamic values of Afghan national culture, while at the same time offering broad opportunities for independent entrepreneurs and the private sector in the economy. On the political level, the Soviet leader recommended that the leaders of the communist regime get ready for power sharing with the opposition, including not only exiled politicians but also the armed *mujahideen* fighters. Karmal was 'dumbfounded'. As Gorbachev reported to the

Politburo, 'he had expected anything but this from us, he was sure we needed Afghanistan even more than we did, he's been counting on us to stay there for a long time – if not forever'.[21] Yet as further developments showed, Karmal, a megalomaniac and by that time a heavy drinker, either did not believe Gorbachev, having heard similar statements from Soviet leaders on previous occasions, or was simply not capable of realizing the gravity of the situation.

By autumn 1985 Gorbachev had accumulated strong enough arguments to suggest that the Politburo take a decision in principle on the necessity of ending the war. During the meeting of 17 October he obtained unanimous support and a mandate from Politburo to start elaborating the strategy of troop withdrawal. Yet probably the most difficult interlocutor for Gorbachev was the Soviet public. It was not so much that people were convinced of the necessity of continuing the war, but official propaganda had been quite effective in concealing the truth about the real human price that had been paid.[22]

In February 1986 in his political report to the 27th Party Congress, for the first time Gorbachev described the war in Afghanistan as a 'bleeding wound'.[23] Yet what was necessary was not just to lift the taboo imposed on this particular subject; the whole system of ideological argument justifying the Soviet Union's involvement in third world conflicts had to be reversed. Since apparently there was no chance of seeing socialism winning in Afghanistan, even assisted by the Soviet army, in order to avoid the impression of a humiliating historic defeat, it would be necessary to replace the previous ideological dogmas used to justify the invasion with new formulas that would prepare the public for the inevitable withdrawal.

One of the functions of the philosophy of the 'new thinking' was to build a psychological bridge between the traditional communist doctrine that had been used for seven decades to brainwash the minds of several generations of Soviet citizens and the new pragmatic needs of Gorbachev's foreign policy. To fulfil this mission the new ideology was obliged to sacrifice the presentation of conflicts in the third world as an integral component of a world revolution. Already an apparently semantic change had been introduced in Gorbachev's report to the Party

Congress – the replacement of the term 'national liberation movements' by the ideologically neutral 'regional conflicts' – served to eliminate the moral contrast or opposition between 'progressive' and 'reactionary' forces and in this way released the Soviet Union from its historic bondage, including the obligation to support self-proclaimed 'revolutionaries' across the globe. The new de-ideologized presentation of conflicts in the third world provided Soviet foreign policy with a salutary way out – inevitable setbacks in this area would no longer have to be interpreted as u-turns of the course of history.

'The chief issue now for Gorbachev was how to resolve these conflicts [in the "third world"] with minimum damage to the interests, and above all the image, prestige and credibility of the Soviet Union as a global player,' wrote Jiří Valenta in *Gorbachev's New Thinking and Third World Conflicts*.[24] This radical change in the Soviet approach toward national liberation movements, previously presented in traditional Soviet ideological jargon as the 'natural allies' of the socialist camp and the world communist movement, signalled the impending abandonment of world revolution as an officially proclaimed strategic goal; on the level of practical policy it would mean renunciation of any ambition to conquer new territory on the map. In this way, whatever the personal beliefs of Mikhail Gorbachev at that time, his newly formulated philosophy served to perform the function of an ideological cover-up for the Soviet state's enforced retreat from its initial ambitions as proclaimed by Lenin in 1917.

Defining the new overtly pragmatic and modest goals of Soviet foreign policy, Gorbachev explained to the Politburo on 13 November 1986: 'We don't seek socialism there [in Afghanistan]. Our objective is to have a friendly neutral neighbour so that we can get out. What we don't want is the Americans with their troops and bases. If there are no US airfields or military camps, anything else they can decide on their own.'[25]

Quite soon Gorbachev realized that Babrak Karmal was hopeless as a partner in any withdrawal strategy. The initial decision on the necessity of replacing Karmal in the posts of Party and state leader was taken in Moscow in March 1986, and by May of that year Dr Najibullah, formerly responsible for the Afghan secret service KHAD and a representative of the younger generation of the Parcham wing of the ruling Party, was elected its General Secretary. Yet perhaps to avoid unfortunate associations with the way in which the December 1979 'election' of Karmal had been arranged by the Soviet military after the removal of Hafizullah Amin, Gorbachev insisted on a 'smoothly' staged scenario for Karmal's removal from power that would take several months to carry out.

In his July 1986 speech in Vladivostok, Gorbachev publicly anticipated the prospect of Soviet troop withdrawal and announced the first symbolic reduction of a 'limited contingent' of six regiments. This would commence on 15 October. Since the Soviet high command had only just sent 15,000 new troops to Afghanistan, the international community was not impressed, and on 5 November the UN General Assembly by an overwhelming majority reiterated a demand for a total Soviet troop withdrawal from Afghanistan. October 1986 was not chosen by chance as the time to signal the Soviet side's intention to begin an effective evacuation of Afghanistan. Gorbachev wanted in this way to create a positive atmosphere on the eve of his Reykjavik meeting with Reagan, hoping that this gesture would encourage American reciprocity. Yet as in the case of his 15 January Declaration or other unilateral moves such as the nuclear test moratorium, Gorbachev's American partner remained unimpressed and continued to suspect the Soviet leader of resorting to a show of traditional Soviet-type propaganda; much more was expected from him than verbal statements or symbolic gestures.

The US Defense Secretary, Caspar Weinberger, depicted the Soviet move as 'a farce', which also reflected his personal distrust of the Soviet leader; apparently it had not diminished since his openly expressed opposition to the resumption of top-level US–Soviet dialogue on the eve of the Geneva summit the year before.[26] Nor were other members of the US administration or Reagan himself in any way inclined to offer political gifts to Gorbachev or to pardon the errors and miscalculations of his predecessors. 'Although the US had a compelling interest in the resolution of regional conflicts, it did not have a collateral interest in resolving conflicts in a manner that preserves or enhances the global power credentials of the Soviet Union,' observed Valenta.[27]

Gorbachev returned to Moscow from Reykjavik conscious of the fact that with regard to a solution of the Afghan crisis, at this stage he had nothing to expect from his American partners, yet had no time to lose. On 13 November 1986, he opened a general Politburo debate on the situation in Afghanistan with unusually harsh language:

> Six years have gone by and we are still waging a war in Afghanistan. If we don't change our approach we'll be in a state of war for another 20–30 years. . . . To sum up, I would say we have not found any key to the solution of this problem. Should that mean that we are condemned to continue the war indefinitely, bearing in mind the fact that our troops cannot cope with the situation?[28]

Gorbachev's resolute stand at the Politburo meeting looked like a show of strength and was indeed the behaviour of a political strongman. Nikolai Detinov speaks of a 'personal authoritative decision'.[29] Yet behind this posture lurked the despair of a leader who had tried all solutions that would be politically less costly but had come to the conclusion that he had no choice other than to accept total responsibility for an action that could be interpreted as a recognition of defeat.

Immediately after the Politburo ratified his position, Gorbachev moved into the next gear. On 20 November 1986 he gave the green light for the formal transfer of political power in Kabul from Babrak Karmal to Najibullah. Several days later, Najibullah used the opportunity of a visit to Moscow publicly to mark a principal shift of political orientation with the announcement of a policy of national reconciliation, suggested by Gorbachev several months earlier in his speech in Vladivostok at the end of July.[30] Upon his return from Moscow, Najibullah declared that neither he nor the Party over which he presided were any longer representatives of Marxist-Leninist or communist ideology and that the construction of socialism in Afghanistan was no longer their political goal.

During his meeting with the new Afghan leader in Moscow on 12 December 1986, Gorbachev formally informed Najibullah that Soviet troops would leave his country within one and a half to two years. In Moscow a special Politburo Commission on Afghanistan was set up chaired by Shevardnadze and on 5–7

January 1987 a Soviet delegation including Shevardnadze and Dobrynin went to Kabul to discuss the basis of the political settlement and the preparations for Soviet troop withdrawal. The fact that this delegation was headed by the Minister of Foreign Affairs provided a signal that in the attempt to find a solution for the Afghan problem, the accent had shifted from the military to the political. Reporting to the Politburo on the results of his mission, Shevardnadze said:

> I am not going to give my judgement now about the justification of our entry there [in Afghanistan]. But what is obvious is that we did it totally ignoring the psychology of this people and the real state of affairs there. And everything that we have been and are doing in Afghanistan is incompatible with the moral image of our country.[31]

Throughout the whole of 1987 Gorbachev was trying to speed up the process toward the ultimate goal he had announced. Commenting on the evolution of the situation in Afghanistan at the Politburo meeting in May, in a show of pragmatism he suggested: 'We have to bring the country back to its natural state. And we know that Afghanistan cannot exist without Islam. Why not try to invite the *mujahideen* representatives to participate in local administration.'[32] Apparently at that stage Gorbachev was convinced that just by changing the title of the ruling Party, abandoning socialist goals, adding some Islamic decorative features and offering the armed opposition several important positions in the coalition government – all of this accompanied by a Soviet military withdrawal – it might be possible to achieve a 'smooth' transition from the Soviet occupation of the country to the *status quo ante* – a situation that existed not just before December 1979 but even earlier, before the 'April revolution' seizure of power by left-wing officers headed by Taraki – without paying any substantial price for Moscow's political and strategic error.

To reach this rather utopian goal the strategic planners in Moscow were even ready to bring back the Afghan king, Zahir Shah, who had been deposed by his cousin Mohammed Daoud in July 1973. Yet the contacts with the monarch exiled in Italy initiated by the Soviet representatives led nowhere. The radical Islamist opposition, hoping to emerge triumphant after the withdrawal of Soviet troops, was not prepared to share power with anybody; certainly there was no question of accepting a national role for the king, who was considered to be responsible for the persecution of Islamic radicals during his reign and also too tolerant towards pro-Soviet leftist forces.

Another player that refused to perform its designated role in the ideal scenario drafted by Moscow was Washington. Despite his failure to impress Reagan in Geneva and Reykjavik, Gorbachev continued to hope that the goodwill he had demonstrated on the question of the Soviet retreat from Afghanistan would end up convincing the US administration to support him in the elaboration of a formula for the gradual transition of Afghanistan from war to peace, thus avoiding major civil conflict. Gorbachev's new great moment of hope was linked to the Washington summit of December 1987. In the euphoric atmosphere that surrounded the signing of the INF Treaty, for which he believed he had paid an extremely high price, Gorbachev felt that he had passed the test of being a reliable partner and could anticipate a perspective of working hand in hand with Washington for the solution of remaining world problems.

Yet even if Reagan seemed to show an increasingly open affection for Gorbachev, having realized that the Soviet leader could be trusted and deserved assistance, apparently this was not the attitude of everyone in his administration. Observing the evolution of the situation in Afghanistan and convinced that time was on the side of the radical Islamists they had supported, United States officials felt no urgency to support Gorbachev's plan, which would provide international legitimacy to the pro-Soviet formation headed by Najibullah.[33] It was rather the opposite line that prevailed: 'We thought that by giving them [the *mujahideen*] a greater capability to resist, this would give the Soviet Union more incentive to get out,' confirms Jack Matlock.[34]

In these conditions Gorbachev decided to go ahead with the withdrawal schedule that had been ratified by the Politburo, 'with the Americans or without them'. On 8 February 1988, two months after his return from Washington, he solemnly declared that the Soviet government was ready to start withdrawing its troops from Afghanistan and that the process would be completed within a period of nine months. On 7 May

1988, addressing newspaper editors and writers in the Central Committee, Gorbachev said: 'We already lost 13,000 killed and 43,000 wounded. Over one million people have lived through a nightmare. Not to mention the economy: we spent 5 billion a year. We should get out of that country from any point of view, human or economic. Just think of whom we have been fighting. The people!'[35]

It was at this point that the US side made it known that Washington would not in fact stop providing assistance to the armed Islamic opposition after the Soviet withdrawal unless Moscow stopped all programmes of military support to the Kabul government. To help the US administration escape from signing the draft that had been prepared in Geneva with the participation of American representatives, on 29 February the US Senate approved a resolution proposed by Senator Gordon Humphrey. The text equalized the status of the official government in Kabul with the Islamic opposition. For Gorbachev, this was a signal that the Americans were not ready to help him turn the page of the conflict by simply accepting the Soviet retreat; rather they wanted him to pay for the political sins of his predecessors even at the risk of perpetuating the civil war.[36]

Clearly Washington's position was inspired by its confidence in a guaranteed rapid victory of the Islamists over the government forces of Kabul in the absence of the Soviet troops. To the great surprise of many observers, this forecast proved to be unfounded. Once deprived of the unifying inspiration provided by the Soviet intruder, the alliance of the Islamic parties based in Peshawar met with growing internal division, while the government in Kabul, fighting for its survival, succeeded in consolidating its positions and during three years did not yield any important city to the assaults of the opposition.[37]

The Geneva agreements were finally signed on 14 April 1988. Soviet withdrawal began as promised by Gorbachev on 15 May and was completed ahead of the announced schedule on 15 February 1989. To close the 'Afghan chapter' Gorbachev needed to demonstrate remarkable strength of character, since the dramatic pleas from Kabul supported by advocates of Najibullah in Moscow (including Shevardnadze) continued to arrive almost as often as they had in 1979. For example, when reporting to the Politburo on 18 April 1988 about the Geneva agreements that stipulated the total withdrawal of Soviet troops, Shevardnadze, who felt personally tied by the promises he had given to the Afghan leader, advocated keeping 10–15,000 troops in Afghanistan 'for a while' in order to help 'our Afghan friends, who will not pardon us if we leave them without support'.

Gorbachev reacted to this in an unusually harsh way.

> We have relieved our foreign policy, our economy and the situation of the country in general of a heavy burden. . . . While taking responsibility for the legacy of the foreign and domestic policy of the past, we have done everything we could in order to minimize the unfortunate consequences of the war in Afghanistan. . . . Important aspects of the search for a solution have included our cooperation with the US side in working out the Geneva agreements along with the association of the UN; permanent contacts with the Indian leadership as well as with the governments of several Muslim states; and at the final stage, direct contact with the Islamic rebels. . . . The solution of the Afghan problem is thus an important and probably key moment in the application of the 'new political thinking'.[38]

For Gorbachev the Afghan page had been turned once and for all, and at no moment did he seriously admit the possibility of reconsidering this decision. Ten months ahead of the tenth anniversary of the invasion of Afghanistan, the 'bleeding wound' of Soviet–Afghan relations as well as of domestic Soviet political life was finally closed, even if not immediately healed.

\* \* \*

Although it was an extremely painful (both for Soviet and Afghan societies) and most sensitive international issue, the conflict in Afghanistan was, after all, just one of many controversial subjects of contention between the Soviet Union and the United States in their strategic competition across the globe. Given the realities of the nuclear age and particularly after the horrifying precedent of the Cuban missile crisis of 1962, both superpowers clearly chose to exercise extreme caution in their bilateral relations, seeking to avoid the risk of direct confrontation – above all in Europe; however, both sides felt free to settle their accounts in other parts of the globe: Asia, Africa and Latin America. Thus an important part of super-power covert activity and skirmishes over the establishment of a new power equilibrium was shifted to the troubled waters of the third world.

It was largely on the US setbacks in this area of the world (and the successes of the Soviet allies and clients) in the late 1960s and 1970s that the Kremlin based its conclusion about the historic shift in the world's balance of power to its advantage, and consequently it was Soviet behaviour regarding the regional conflicts that was chosen by the US administration as the 'critical proving ground for Soviet new thinking'.[39]

With global military conflict between East and West practically excluded (or at least highly improbable), various local conflicts depicted either as 'national liberation wars' or 'conflicts of low intensity' (depending on the ideological jargon) were not only tolerated but de facto encouraged by each of the two blocs; clashes between respective allies and clients were constantly refuelled with financial aid and supplies of arms. Out of all the territories that were regarded by Moscow and Washington as potential trophies, the African continent represented a special case.

While regional conflicts in Asia (Afghanistan) and Latin America (Nicaragua and San Salvador) were largely influenced by the proximity and direct involvement of one of the two super-powers, in Africa, probably because geography placed this continent almost equally distant from each bloc, their indirect confrontation took the form of symbolic conflicts and an almost obligatory competition for prestige. Yet since this strategic rivalry was not aggravated by the direct military presence of either of the two superpowers – with the exception of the Cuban army troops that with good reason were regarded by the Americans as a Soviet 'foreign legion' – the ground was potentially adapted to be rather easily manoeuvred by political means.

At every US–Soviet summit, the American administration raised the issue of 'regional conflicts' with almost the same regularity as the subject of human rights violations within the Soviet Union; for Gorbachev this represented another embarrassing legacy inherited from the former Soviet leadership from which he wanted to free himself as soon as possible. First of all, he knew that enormous financial and material resources were being spent abroad in a futile manner only to uphold the image and status of the Soviet Union as the world's second superpower. Secondly, in accordance with the philosophy of the 'new thinking', having abandoned the goal of constructing an alternative social-political model opposed to and hostile toward Western capitalist society, Gorbachev also renounced the ambition of his predecessors to mobilize and launch a heterogeneous army of the world's 'progressive forces' against his Western rival.

This ideological *volte-face* (the theses prepared by Yakovlev for the 27th Party Congress were its main source) had as one of its logical consequences the relegation of most former 'liberation struggles' to the category of 'local conflicts', opening the way for negotiated solutions on the basis of pragmatic and, it was hoped, constructive cooperation with the West, a perspective unthinkable in the atmosphere of heated antagonistic ideological confrontation just several years before.

This type of 'technocratic' ideology-free approach could not immediately be applied in situations where the sudden and radical change of the Soviet Union's position would be perceived as an act of betrayal by long-term close political allies (such as Cuba and North Korea) or in cases where the ideological formula of support for the 'anti-imperialist struggle' had been used to mask the great-power reflexes of the Soviet state, anxious to maintain its strategic positions (as in the Middle East). Elsewhere, when it was just a matter of reducing the overstretched global reach of Soviet foreign policy appetites to more modest proportions, Gorbachev would not hesitate to proceed quickly and unsentimentally, despite the fact that in most of these cases (Angola, Mozambique and Nicaragua) the Soviet Union had the material capability to continue its economic and military support of its friends.[40]

Anatoli Adamishin, a deputy of Shevardnadze 'in charge' of this part of the world, summarized the 'extremely loose' mandate he received from his boss and from Gorbachev:

I was told to 'assure the smooth progress of Namibia towards its independence on the basis of cooperation with the West, put an end to the civil war in Angola, and establish constructive dialogue with South Africa in order to assist the process of ending apartheid.' It was not an easy assignment, since on the one hand we had to get the Cubans out of Africa as they no longer had anything to do there. On the other, I had problems convincing the Americans that our talk about ending confrontation was serious and had to reassure the South Africans, explaining that we had no intention of dragging communism to their part of the world and that we were absolutely inclined to let them choose their own way of life.[41]

Rather rapid progress was achieved in the resolution of the long-standing problem of South Africa, a country tainted by an image of chronic malaise; to a large extent this was made possible by the constructive cooperation established between the Soviet and American emissaries, Anatoli Adamishin and Chester Croker, who at times behaved as if they were on a joint mission. Following the December 1988 Agreement jointly brokered by the Soviet Deputy Foreign Minister and his American counterpart, Cuba agreed to withdraw its troops from Angola. And a year later in November 1989, South Africa withdrew its troops from Namibia, ending the occupation of seventy-five years and opening the road to Namibian independence. In South Africa itself the newly elected President F.W. de Klerk, whom his Minister of Foreign Affairs, R.F. Botha, likened to Gorbachev, agreed to meet with the imprisoned Nelson Mandela, who was subsequently released on 11 February 1990 after twenty-seven years of incarceration. It was hoped that these successes would confirm, in principle, the possibility of a common US–Soviet diplomatic front focusing on the normalization of potentially dangerous hotbeds of conflict throughout the world.

*Détente* between the United States and the Soviet Union deprived a number of other regional conflicts of the petrol that had been provided during the days of superpower confrontation; some could then be extinguished with the way opened to the solution of others. 'This was the time when all hopes were allowed. It was indeed the dawn of a new world. The Cold War was over and with it the bipolar order,' said Amr Moussa, Secretary General of the League of Arab States, speaking at the opening of the conference 'Madrid Fifteen Years Later:

Towards Peace in the Middle East' (10–12 January 2007).[42] Yet elsewhere in the world, where Soviet and American political goals and interests diverged more sharply than in rather remote regions, the harmony of close cooperation between these two former irreconcilable enemies was never reproduced in the same way.

## 'Abandoning' Eastern Europe

Following the practice of his predecessors, upon his election to the post of General Secretary, Mikhail Gorbachev proclaimed the development of relations with the 'sister socialist countries' (referring, of course, to the Soviet Union's allies in Eastern Europe) to be a priority goal of his foreign policy. It soon became evident that for Gorbachev this statement represented more a repetition of obligatory ritual than a declaration of his true intentions. Neither the relevant countries nor the general problems of the Warsaw Pact were mentioned in the ten-point list of major foreign policy concerns drafted by the new General Secretary in the first days after his election. The explanation was simple: in the eyes of Moscow's leaders, relations with the other members of the Warsaw Pact appeared to be absolutely solid, at the time and in the foreseeable future; occasional political crises such as Hungary in '56, Prague in '68, or even the more recent Solidarność rebellion in Poland, showed that internal crises of this kind could be dealt with 'within the socialist family' without becoming critical international issues.

The apparent tranquillity of the East European scene suggested that, at least in the near future, there would be no unpleasant surprises for the new Soviet leader. Therefore, having received formal expressions of loyalty from his East European colleagues in the course of the recent state funerals, Gorbachev had good reason to place the whole subject of the Soviet Union's relations with its devoted friends on the back burner. Certain formal gestures on Gorbachev's part – such as the announcement of his intention to resume regular meetings with the First Secretaries of the Warsaw Pact countries on a bilateral basis and also in the form of the collective 'Crimean summits' that had been suspended during the last Brezhnev years – could be interpreted as the natural desire of the young leader to indicate difference from his elderly predecessors.

The minimal initial interest in the problems of Eastern Europe proved, in the long run, to have explosive consequences. In his previous positions, Gorbachev had only rarely been involved in the ritual, largely ceremonial meetings between the leaders, and with one or two exceptions had not developed actual personal relations with any of his new colleagues, the majority of whom came from the previous generation. This lack of rapport would sometimes result in friction. Georgi Shakhnazarov, who became one of Gorbachev's closest aides and was responsible for relations with the socialist countries, has described an early clash between Gorbachev and the powerful Bulgarian leader, Todor Zhivkov, who was known to have a close relationship with Brezhnev. At the time, Gorbachev was only a relatively junior Secretary of the Central Committee responsible for agriculture, but he did not hesitate to oppose the continuation of privileged access to the Soviet food market for Bulgarian agricultural products, which in his opinion was against the interests of Soviet *kolkhoz* (collective) farmers. Despite the fact that raising this question meant challenging the system of political relations with the Soviet Union's strategic allies, a matter normally the exclusive preserve of the top leadership, Gorbachev did finally succeed in getting a change of policy. This may well provide an additional clue to Zhivkov's attitude. Even after Gorbachev became the 'number one' in the Soviet hierarchy, Zhivkov made no attempt to conceal his personal dislike.[43]

This example shows that Gorbachev's initial approach toward the problems of the socialist community was mostly economic. Intent on modernization, once he started to draw a balance sheet of the strengths and weaknesses of the Soviet economy he could hardly disregard the tremendous price the Soviet Union was paying to assure the loyalty of its East European allies; in order to buy political reliability and guarantee minimum internal stability, the Soviet Union was subsidizing a standard of living largely superior to that of the majority of the Soviet population.

The permanently increasing cost for Moscow rulers of maintaining their East European dominions rose sharply with every internal political crisis; each trauma produced by heavy-handed repressive action against a local opposition or dissident elements had to be healed afterwards with additional programmes of economic assistance. According to Valeri Musatov, the former First Deputy Head of the Central Committee International Department, the economic cost of ensuring stability in the countries of Eastern Europe amounted to some five to ten billion dollars annually (a figure that did not take into account the annual 'cost of Cuba' for the Soviet economy).[44]

Therefore, while the primary foreign policy concerns of Gorbachev embraced problems in need of urgent solution (Afghanistan, the arms race with the West, tension with China), the complicated and delicate relations with East European allies represented an economic burden that had to be eased. Gorbachev's initial approach to a reappraisal of the relationship with the socialist countries was quite different from that of Khrushchev in 1956 in the aftermath of the 20th Party Congress, and certainly very different from Brezhnev, who gave his name to the unfortunate 'Brezhnev Doctrine', which implied the 'right' of the Soviet Union to intervene in the internal affairs of the Warsaw Pact countries. In one of the first debates about Moscow's relations with the East European countries in July 1986, Gorbachev stated: 'It's impossible to proceed as before. The methods that were applied with regard to Czechoslovakia [in 1968] and Hungary [in 1956] are unacceptable. . . . What is important now is the economy. It's here that we have an important hindrance to coordination and integration.'[45] Consequently, instead of attempting to formulate like Khrushchev a new solemn 'declaration of principles' (which several weeks later would not have been able to withstand popular revolts in Poland and Hungary), he sought to prepare a profound transformation of the whole system of economic relations between the USSR and its East European allies through a reform of COMECON.[46]

Vadim Medvedev, a former member of the Politburo and Secretary of the Central Committee responsible for the relations with the socialist countries, recalls that the general idea behind this reform project was an attempt to abandon the traditional pattern of economic exchange that meant a flow of cheap raw materials from the Soviet Union toward Eastern Europe and the delivery of manufactured goods in the opposite direction.

> We believed that economic relations should develop on three levels: interstate, inter-branch and directly between enterprises. The idea was to move gradually in the direction of the third type of direct economic contacts with the prospect of abandoning centralized control over prices. This long-term strategy was first announced by Gorbachev in 1986 at a summit meeting of the Party leaders and later during a session of COMECON.[47]

This Soviet initiative, although unanimously (as usual) approved by the COMECON members, was never put into practice since quite naturally neither the political leaders nor the bureaucratic apparatus of the East European regimes was keen to abandon the established formula, and they did their best to sabotage the declared reforms. Faithful to his vision of the 'socialist community' as a consolidated organic family, Gorbachev tried to suggest to the members of COMECON the same economic recipes he was prescribing for the Soviet economy: an accelerated development of modern technology and advanced scientific research. This idea took the form of a common high-tech programme intended to become an Eastern version of the West European 'Eureka' programme proposed by the French President, François Mitterrand. By December 1985 a general project of this kind was drafted, but it was quickly forgotten following the fiasco of analogous programmes in the Soviet Union.

Such improvised and somewhat chaotic gestures make it clear that at least at the first stage of his project when the real contours of economic reform remained unclear, Gorbachev did not make any political distinction between Eastern Europe and the Soviet Union; he certainly did not envisage the possibility of some autonomous political evolution independent of the elder brother. When in the weeks following his election Gorbachev was faced with the need to extend the term of the Warsaw Pact since it was soon due to expire, he arranged this in the traditional Soviet manner, avoiding any serious debate about the future role or possible reform of the alliance, practically ignoring the reservations voiced by the Romanian President, Nicolae Ceauşescu.

Yet at one point Gorbachev was provoked into defining his vision of the political principles that were meant to be observed in relations between the members of the socialist community, albeit in a rather general form. In July 1985 the official Party newspaper, *Pravda*, published an article by the then First Deputy Head of the Central Committee Department responsible for the relations with the socialist countries, Oleg Rakhmanin.[48] The author severely criticized attempts to introduce innovation and reform in East European countries and openly proclaimed a neo-Stalinist heavy-handed political course, based on a 're-established discipline' among Warsaw Pact members. The fact that the piece was signed not with its author's name but with the anonymous pseudonym Kovalyov gave it additional weight, since it then appeared to be the official announcement of a 'tougher' line by the new Kremlin leader, addressed to the whole socialist camp. The article, which in fact was written entirely on the personal initiative of a hard-line *apparatchik*, gave rise to an uneasy and embarrassed reaction within political elites across Eastern Europe; Gorbachev was forced immediately to send personal messages to the leaders of these countries repudiating the spirit of the article and assuring them of his determination to treat every country (and its national political leadership) with due respect. The author of the article shortly after this incident was sent into retirement.[49]

At that time, however, these reassuring messages still did not indicate any coherent new conception or revision of policy. It was only toward the end of 1986, when Gorbachev's project of *perestroika* within the Soviet Union began to acquire political dimensions, that he first formulated the principles that were to determine future relations between the Soviet Union and its allies in Eastern Europe. In November 1986 Gorbachev convened a secret 'working meeting' in Moscow for all the leaders of the COMECON member countries, which included ten full members.

Admission to this 'hermetically sealed' gathering held in the Kremlin was limited to the single top leader of each country, with only the Soviet Union having two representives: Gorbachev and the Prime Minister, Nikolai Ryzhkov. The plan was to have an extremely frank and open exchange of opinions where for the first time Gorbachev would present to his allies a new Soviet policy, a kind of 'Gorbachev Doctrine'. The main message that the Soviet leader wanted to convey was an advance warning – in the future each national party and its leadership would be totally accountable to its own population without the possibility of relying on the protection of the Soviet presence or military might in order to maintain power.

> Declaring that the epoch of paternalism was over and that in the future each Party would be accountable to its own population and domestic public opinion, Gorbachev tried to present this in a positive light for the whole socialist community. He referred to the reality of uneven development and of the different levels of economic progress achieved, not only with reference to the European and Asian members of COMECON (plus Cuba), but also among the East Europeans themselves, and suggested that the less developed members be assisted.[50]

According to Shakhnazarov, the main purpose of this meeting for Gorbachev was to warn the leaders of the communist bloc about the revolutionary political changes he was planning to introduce inside the Soviet system – by that time preparations were well under way for the crucial January 1987 Plenary meeting of the Central Committee that would mark the real launching of Gorbachev's political reforms. In the near future, Warsaw Pact leaders would not only have to forget the former client–patron relations with their big brother protector in Moscow, but they would also be dealing with a totally new political reality inside the Soviet Union.[51]

Although the sense of his message was evident – Gorbachev's desire to provide an advance warning in order to give the satellite regimes sufficient time to adjust to the uncomfortable future – the reaction among the political leaders present at the meeting was confused. Some, including representatives of the old Brezhnev guard, Erich Honecker of the GDR and Todor Zhivkov of Bulgaria, listened to the presentation of their young Soviet patron with barely concealed scepticism, not really believing that he would go ahead with the promised reforms or that he would be allowed to do so by the Party *nomenklatura*. Others, like János Kádár of Hungary, interpreted it as a green light to accelerate the policy of opening to the West which they had already initiated in covert form.

Yet perhaps the aspect of Gorbachev's message which caused the greatest concern among the Soviet Union's allies at that time was less its political message than its economic implications. In November 1986 Gorbachev surprised them all when he proposed that economic relations between the socialist countries be built on a mutually beneficial basis and under real market conditions. With hindsight this decision may be seen as the first step that would not only kill COMECON but also lead to the demise of the whole Soviet empire; its political significance could be compared to the withdrawal of Soviet troops from Eastern Europe. The leaders of the socialist community suddenly realized that the days of a comfortable existence under the protection of guaranteed Soviet credits with cheap oil and gas supplies was probably coming to an end; they were each therefore invited to seek the means of ensuring economic stability by reorientating their economies to the West. According to Valentin Falin, the real disintegration of the socialist camp started with the dismantling of COMECON which preceded the collapse of the Warsaw Pact.[52] Valeri Musatov also believes that the first impetus to move in the direction of the West was given to its East European allies by Moscow's announcement of the imminent reform of COMECON.[53]

At that time understandably not one of the East European leaders could have foreseen the possibility that their regimes would not only be deprived of their economic security blanket but that Gorbachev would also dismantle the two other pillars of Soviet strategic control over Eastern Europe, its military presence and its control of the Party apparatus, leaving them 'naked' to face the complex realities of their own countries. Ironically this conviction was shared, as remarked by Gaddis, by most of the West's politicians.[54]

Having warned the other communist leaders about his intentions, Gorbachev went public at the beginning of 1987. The famous 'freedom of choice' proclaimed to be a basic tenet of the 'new thinking' philosophy, if applied to the countries of Eastern Europe, could only mean that the 'choice' of

Soviet-type socialism by these countries in the aftermath of the Second World War was in fact reversible. Thus, the ' choice' of socialism, which until then was presented as the fulfilment of historical destiny, was downgraded to become a conventional political question which, taken away from the hands of history, was to be entrusted to the decision of ordinary people.

'Universal security in our time,' wrote Gorbachev in his 1987 book *Perestroika and New Political Thinking for Our Country and the World*, 'rests upon the recognition of the right of every nation to choose its own path of social development. A nation may choose either capitalism or socialism. This is its sovereign right. Nations cannot and should not pattern their life either after the USA or the Soviet Union. . . . It is up to history to judge the merits of each particular system.'[55]

In the following year, on the occasion of the 19th Party Conference he was even more explicit: 'A key factor in the "new thinking" is the concept of freedom of choice. . . . The imposition of a social system, a way of life, or policies from outside by any means, let alone military force, are dangerous trappings of the past.'[56] A statement of this kind, issued by a Moscow leader from the highest official tribune, was of course analysed most attentively by both the political elite and the public in the countries of Eastern Europe; it was nevertheless taken to be further elaborate rhetoric coming from the Kremlin rather than an announcement of principled changes in Soviet foreign policy. At the same time for Gorbachev, the organic relationship between profound democratic changes at home and the introduction of genuine equality in relations with allied socialist countries was becoming increasingly obvious. 'Having initiated *perestroika*, from the very first steps we realized that we had to put an end to intervention in the internal affairs of our allies, something that was called "the Brezhnev Doctrine". . . . Having set for ourselves the course of freedom, we could not deny it to the others.'[57]

Does this mean that Gorbachev was already prepared at that time to accept all the eventual consequences brought about by the radical change of Soviet policy toward a region which did, after all, represent for the USSR a sphere of vital strategic interest? Or had he fallen into the trap of abstract political formulas, a prisoner of his ambition to offer the world a new utopian ideology? Could he (or anyone else at that moment) conceivably have foreseen the possible results of the attempt to start applying the tenets of 'new thinking' in this specific part of the globe, a terrain so sensitively connected to the international status of the Soviet Union? Evidently there are no definitive answers to these hypothetical questions. What is nevertheless clear is that at the moment of real choice, faced with the unexpected chain reaction of political turmoil in Eastern Europe largely provoked by his own actions, Gorbachev behaved in accordance with the principles he had formulated at a time when he still believed that he would be able to control the course of events.

It is evident, though, that when proclaiming his new philosophy of international relations, Gorbachev was pursuing a quite different goal. With regard to Eastern Europe, he believed that the driving force of *perestroika* in the Soviet Union would provide an inspiring example for its allies and result in a new unity of the socialist community, this time with common action founded on mutual interest rather than coercive pressure. 'We shall keep the initiative without depending on force but rather on our intellectual activity and mutually advantageous comradely dialogue.' This was the perspective he presented to the members of the Soviet Politburo at the time of the preparation for the 19th Party Conference in the early spring of 1988.[58]

Yet this quasi-religious belief in the omnipotence of *perestroika*, a conviction that its triumph would transform not only the Soviet Union, but also the rather different circumstances of the other socialist countries, in the long run did him a disservice. It nourished a feeling of false security at the top of the Soviet political leadership, based on the assumption that the East European allies of the USSR had no alternative other than to follow the leader, especially one who was pointing the way to freedom and democracy. However, for anyone closely observing the internal evolution of the East European countries during the preceding months, it was evident that the practical implementation of the principle of 'freedom of choice' proclaimed by Gorbachev in his United Nations speech, in the absence of any vigorous Soviet counteraction, would result in their political defection to the West.

This feeling of safety perhaps explains Gorbachev's almost total transfer of attention to what he considered at that time to be his real priorities: relations with the United States and with Western Europe. Western leaders, starting with Reagan but especially Thatcher, Mitterrand and Kohl, were impressed by what was going on in Moscow, centred their attention on Gorbachev, and even consciously limited their activity in Eastern Europe; their first concern was to avoid undermining Gorbachev's endeavour. However, Gorbachev's own almost absolute belief in the principles of 'new thinking' and the final goals of *perestroika*, his conviction that success was guaranteed, served as an alibi for inaction in Eastern Europe; it allowed him to escape the necessity of settling political accounts with the past or working out a concrete programme in order to apply the new general principles to the specific conditions and complex reality of Eastern Europe.

Unlike the West, where the Soviet General Secretary's surprising conversion to the values of democracy was, after some initial hesitation, generally applauded, in Eastern Europe, even if Gorbachev and his policies were welcomed by the public, as the leader of the Soviet state he had to deal with certain unpleasant legacies. Furthermore, in most places (probably with the exception of Hungary and Poland), his preaching of the merits of democracy and *perestroika* was received with considerable reserve by the ruling elites and the Party *nomenklatura*.

At the same time his essential character as a man of consensus and compromise led Gorbachev to avoid radical moves or categorical statements that could embarrass existing political leaders and might be interpreted as a new form of Soviet interference in its allies' internal affairs (a kind of Brezhnev Doctrine in reverse).[59] This inevitably added a degree of ambiguity to his position, projecting abroad the image of a hesitant and indecisive leader.

On a number of key issues associated with traumatic experiences of the past – such as the Katyn massacre of Polish officers in 1940 by Stalin's secret police, the NKVD, the suppression of the 1956 Hungarian revolution by Soviet tanks, and of course the events of the Prague Spring in 1968 – Gorbachev's reluctance to express clear political views and his unwillingness to open the archives in order to establish historical truth were interpreted as signs of political duplicity and used against him by his critics from the opposite end of the political spectrum.

Gorbachev usually explained his hesitant behaviour on delicate political issues by saying that he was reluctant to create additional political problems for the existing leaders with a new type of Soviet intervention; he preferred leaving it to 'the peoples themselves and the natural course of history' to define the proper moment for the resolution of such questions.[60] This, evidently, was a rather weak argument since in most of these incidents the Soviet Union had been an active participant if not the main source of trouble. Each instance of equivocation proved to be politically counterproductive. 'Instead of profiting from a timely denunciation of the Soviet interventions in Hungary and Czechoslovakia for which he clearly bore no responsibility, by delaying his evaluation of these events, Gorbachev yielded ground to others. When he finally dared to make his formal statements it was already too late and passed almost unnoticed.'[61]

Another aspect of the story is purely subjective: according to Valeri Musatov, Gorbachev 'personally despised' most of his East European colleagues (with the exception of Kádár and Poland's General Jaruzelski); for him they personified the Brezhnev era. 'Observing Gorbachev and listening to his opinions, I sensed that he was unenthusiastic about contacts with socialist leaders.'[62] Chernyaev, himself a long time expert of the Central Committee on the communist parties of Western Europe, considered the ritual of obligatory hearty relations with the leaders of Eastern Europe to be the 'ballast' for the new foreign policy of *perestroika*. Yet perhaps particularly for this reason, Gorbachev was concerned to avoid the suspicion that he was personally conspiring against any one of them.

This feature of Gorbachev's character – an aversion to personal conflict and quarrels, a reluctance to take or announce harsh decisions or punitive measures in his position as head of state – had already caused him a number of serious political problems. It took him too much time to distance himself from people who were once close but subsequently became opponents or open political enemies. (Ligachev, Ryzhkov and even Yeltsin are just a few examples, not to speak of the members of the August 1991 *putsch*.) One could hardly imagine Gorbachev engaging in a sharp public debate with an aggressive tone, even with someone with whom he was in total disagreement. Out of all his numerous meetings with the leaders of East European countries, only one private evening meeting with the Romanian leader Nicolae Ceauşescu ended in a real row, but it should be remembered that the two leaders were accompanied by their wives, whose presence could have added considerable emotion to the debate.[63]

Whatever the explanations, the results were obvious: contrary to the hopes or, indeed, the political calculations of Gorbachev, the dramatic political upheaval in the East European countries produced by his domestic policies and behaviour on the international scene took the form of radical revolutionary change, even when softened by a 'velvet' façade. In 1989, the forces and leading protagonists who replaced Soviet stooges as a rule did not represent a local breed of Gorbachev-type reformers but rather the hard-line political opposition, exposing the 'father of *perestroika*' to accusations from his local conservative opponents that he had 'lost' Eastern Europe and had abandoned or even 'sold' the Soviet Union's most devoted allies to the West. As J.F. Brown noted in his *Surge to Freedom: The End of Communist Rule in Eastern Europe*: 'one of the ironies of 1989 and after was the way reform in Eastern Europe, made possible by Gorbachev, interacted with Soviet developments much to his embarrassment and political disadvantage'.[64]

After decades of Soviet domination there were in fact many who felt 'abandoned' by their Soviet patrons. Among them were not only the local Party apparatus and the countless secret service agents intimately tied to their Soviet counterparts and mentors; there were also disinterested friends of the Soviet Union, including communist reformers, enthusiastic supporters of Gorbachev's *perestroika* and, among them, survivors of the 'Prague spring' generation who had failed in their own earlier attempt to democratize and humanize state socialism. According to one of the most active participants in the Czech communist reform movement, Jiří Pelikan, some of them praised Gorbachev, since 'after almost twenty years of broken political careers and suppressed hopes they felt rehabilitated by *perestroika* and *glasnost* in Moscow'.[65] Others were convinced that any real change in Eastern Europe could only come from the East (meaning the Soviet Union). None of these precocious reformers could convincingly claim that with more 'muscled' support from Gorbachev they might have succeeded in making a political comeback. Yet many have expressed bitter disappointment over Gorbachev's 'indifference', believing that they had not been given their chance.

In fact the 'velvet' landslide of Eastern Europe somewhat unexpectedly marked a transition from the triumphant advance of Gorbachev's diplomacy to the stage where he apparently was no longer the master of the processes he had unleashed. The origin of the process can be traced back to the end of 1988 with Gorbachev's real international triumph, a standing ovation at the UN General Assembly after his historic speech envisaging a new harmonious world built on the ruins of the Cold War and governed by the principles of the 'new political thinking'. World public opinion was quite rightly impressed by the superb performance of the leader of the second superpower, who proclaimed his determination to exclude the use of force or even the threat of its use in international relations; he made a formal, solemn commitment to this effect on behalf of the Soviet government and in a token of goodwill announced unprecedented measures of unilateral disarmament and a reduction of offensive military potential.

Yet while the world praised Gorbachev's declaration as a courageous initiative that could offer the international political scene an as yet unclear but inspiring perspective, in the countries of Eastern Europe his speech was interpreted above all as the announcement of a historic opportunity to be seized, a confirmation that the new Soviet leadership was in fact ready to ease its grip on this region. The proof came not so much from Gorbachev's formal confirmation of every people's sovereign 'right to choose' the path of its historic development, but with his announcement of a future unilateral withdrawal of approximately half a million troops stationed in Eastern Europe. As has justly been suggested by the former Polish Foreign Minister, Marian Orzechowski, for the peoples and politicians of Eastern Europe, 'the end of the [Brezhnev] doctrine was not a matter of declarations but of policies'.[66]

For Gorbachev himself, as confirmed by Anatoli Chernyaev, a main speechwriter at that time, the main addressee of this unexpected step was certainly the West; conscious of the huge (although officially denied) Soviet preponderance over NATO in troops and conventional arms, Gorbachev was preparing the ground for the imminent talks on conventional arms and troop reduction in Europe. 'We shall announce 500,000 but in fact will reduce by 600,000, including construction troops,' declared Gorbachev in the Politburo session on 24 November 1988 during the discussion of the draft of his speech to the UN.[67] Apparently neither Chernyaev nor his boss imagined that in the countries of Eastern Europe, the announcement of this measure by Moscow would be interpreted as a clear signal that the Soviet Union was preparing a retreat from the region and that, unlike in the past, its military presence would not be used to suppress or block their internal political evolution.

Anatoli Chernyaev could sincerely believe that 'in general Gorbachev had no intention of pushing perestroika throughout the whole socialist world. . . . He only hoped that they [the socialist countries] would understand him and, inspired by perestroika, would try to make some changes of their own.'[68] In fact the first to profit from the new possibility 'to make some changes of their own' were the forces of the anti-communist opposition, not so much inspired by *perestroika* as reassured by Gorbachev's clear determination not to resort to violence when dealing with the complex domestic problems of the 'sister countries'.

At the time it was not only a question of Gorbachev and his advisers – practically no authoritative expert, East or West, would have dared imagine the scale of change that would unfold in this apparently tightly controlled region within such a short space of time. Valeri Musatov confirms the fact that neither the department of the Central Committee in charge of socialist countries nor the specialists from the academic institutes that were supposed to act as 'think-tanks' for the top *nomenklatura* ever suggested such a perspective.[69] This confirms the sad conclusion of Georgi Shakhnazarov, who retrospectively admits that there was never any serious attempt to implement the philosophy of 'new thinking' in the particular case of the socialist countries; there was never a strategic plan, a practical analysis or a tactical programme.[70]

Since Gorbachev was convinced that the evolution of the situation in the socialist countries was intimately connected to the success of *perestroika*, he classified the heads of 'sister countries and parties' according to their personal attitude toward his project. This explains why the enthusiastic fans of *perestroika* like Jaruzelski – and to a lesser extent the cautious Kádár, who on one occasion even warned Gorbachev about the danger of repeating the fate of Khrushchev – were listed among his closest political friends and allies, while the sceptics (if not opponents), such as Honecker, Zhivkov and certainly Ceaușescu, were almost overtly despised and ignored.[71]

Yet the main reason for the evident neglect of relations with the East European countries was not Gorbachev's personal lack of interest but ultimately the dramatic aggravation of the situation inside the Soviet Union beginning in the autumn of 1988. Gorbachev was desperately engaged in trying to extinguish the flare-up of nationalism and separatism in various Soviet republics from the Caucasus to the Baltic, which was threatening the preservation of the unitary state. In this context, any idea of maintaining the old-style Soviet empire in Eastern Europe looked increasingly unrealistic.[72]

Throughout most of 1989, starting with the humiliating defeat of the Polish United Workers Party in the free Polish elections in June, when communists failed to win the seats reserved for them according to the terms of the 'round-table agreements' between the government and the opposition, up to the mostly non-violent (with the exception of Romania) dismantling of communist regimes in other countries of Eastern and Central Europe by the end of the year, Gorbachev and his foreign policy team were forced to adjust to the accelerating pace of events, trying to put a brave face on a rather sorry business. The ambiguity of the situation was obvious. On the one hand, having deliberately instigated the wave of profound political change within the Warsaw Pact, rather than denying his own role, Gorbachev had an interest in asserting his paternity in relation to the whole breed of new regimes that emerged from the political turmoil within the alliance; while, on the other, he could hardly claim that the sudden removal of the Soviet Union's friends from power, including the reform-minded supporters of *perestroika*, or the inglorious dissolution of the Warsaw Pact, were in fact the well-calculated and desired consequences of his policy in this part of Europe.[73]

During the US–Soviet summit in Malta in December 1989, where Gorbachev met George Bush, Sr to discuss the outlook for the new world order after the Cold War, the subject of Eastern Europe was hardly mentioned. Conscious of Gorbachev's evident embarrassment over the unpredictable course of political development in this strategically sensitive zone, the American President tactfully gave his Soviet partner to understand that the United States was not at all inclined to create additional problems for the Moscow leader. 'I have conducted myself in ways not to complicate your life,' he told Gorbachev. Yet even the famous phrase of President Bush, who reminded Gorbachev that he had not 'jumped up and down on the Berlin wall',[74] did little to change the general interpretation of the significance of the summit in Eastern and Central Europe. Despite the deliberate reserve of both leaders on this subject, the true meaning of the consensus reached during their discussions was obvious. 'Both Gorbachev's opponents at home as well as representatives of various political currents in Eastern Europe interpreted the US–Soviet Malta "entente" as nothing less than a revision of the Yalta agreements of 1945 between the Big Three, when the Western powers yielded this part of Europe to the Soviet Union.'[75]

Without formally redrawing the famous 'percentage agreement' about the power sharing in Eastern Europe suggested by Churchill at his meeting with Stalin in Moscow on 9 October 1944,[76] Bush and Gorbachev *de facto* proclaimed this divide abolished and announced the emergence of a new map of the continent. Incredulous in the face of such an extraordinary development, Henry Kissinger, the veteran cold warrior, who regarded himself as an expert in forecasting Soviet behaviour in critical situations, proposed to Bush that he offer Gorbachev a 'fair deal' in order to sweeten the pill of unavoidable retreat. He suggested that an official promise be made by the US government not to profit strategically from the eventual withdrawal of Soviet troops from their bases in Eastern Europe. The American President expressed polite interest but preferred to follow James Baker's advice. His Secretary of State, who on the basis of his regular contacts with Gorbachev and Shevardnadze must have understood that they were true believers in the religion of 'new political thinking', according to his terms 'poured cold water' on Kissinger's plan.[77]

The temporizing strategy proposed by Baker proved to be effective, not because of incoherence or naïvety on the part of Gorbachev; rather it was a question of the disintegration taking place within the political framework in which he was operating, the implosion of the Soviet state. By the second half of 1989, Gorbachev and his team were being carried along by the turbulent historic current they themselves had initiated. After more than forty years of imposed subsistence in the shadow of the Soviet big brother, Eastern Europe was waking up and, unexpectedly for Gorbachev, this led to a breach in his frontline facing the West. And yet, as Robert English rightly remarks,

> in 1989 when their commitment to the deeper democratic nexus of foreign policy was challenged in Eastern Europe the leaders of the new thinking chose principle over power. In 1991 this challenge visited the USSR itself. Gorbachev fighting resurgent Soviet reactionaries as well as his own deep allegiance to the Union hesitated but again chose the path of the new thinking.[78]

The last summit meeting of the leaders of Warsaw Pact members took place in Moscow on 4 December 1989, several days after the Malta summit. Its composition reflected the beginning of the historic change that was now under way; among those present were new faces such as Petr Mladenov from Bulgaria, Hans Modrow from the GDR, Miklos Nemeth from Hungary, Tadeusz Mazowiecki from Poland and Ladislav Adamets from Czechoslovakia. Romania was represented by one of the few familiar faces, the eternal Nicolae Ceauşescu, who behaved as if he were immortal, not knowing that there were to be hardly three more weeks of his life remaining.[79] The decision taken 'unanimously' by these men to start transforming the Warsaw Pact from a military into an essentially political alliance was never realized. In the spring of 1991 the military organization of the Warsaw Pact was dissolved. The Pact itself was officially put to death in the summer. Gorbachev preferred not to attend this ambiguous event, which, while marking another of his historic achievements – the dismantling of one of the remaining bastions of the Cold War – also represented an ignominious failure of his diplomatic tactics, depriving him of a valuable trump card in the delicate negotiations with his Western partners/rivals over the political landscape of the post-Cold War world. But nowhere did the boomerang of his 'new political thinking' return with such dramatic effect as in the case of the reunification of Germany.

## Destroying the Berlin Wall

Gorbachev's first personal encounter with the reality of a divided German nation dates from the mid-1970s. In May 1975 the young Party Secretary from Stavropol visited West Germany as a member of an official delegation invited by the West German communists. Viktor Rykin, at that time a functionary in the International Department of the Central Committee, who accompanied him on this trip, recalls that in private conversations Gorbachev several times asked him about the manner in which the division of Germany had been organized by the victorious powers after the Second World War. In public debates, his replies to the questions put by Germans were always quite formal, reiterating the official Soviet position that Germany as the initiator of the Second World War had to pay the price. And although according to Rykin, on the emotional level Gorbachev certainly did not remain indifferent to the feelings expressed by ordinary people who lived the division as a national trauma, there is no reason to attribute to the young provincial Party functionary any conscious willingness to re-evaluate the official Soviet position on the German question. 'At that time Gorbachev was hardly envisaging for himself a future spectacular political career that would raise him to the summit of international policy-making.'[80]

But even when propelled to the summit of the Soviet pyramid of power, at the initial stages of the elaboration of his new foreign policy Gorbachev did not show any particular interest in German problems. At that time the two German states certainly represented for him organic elements of two quite different worlds: West vs East. This is why, in his view, Moscow's relations with the GDR were bound to follow a logic quite distinct from relations with West Germany; one was a 'sister' socialist state, a member of the consolidated 'family' of COMECON and the Warsaw Pact, while the other was a loyal ally of Washington and the stronghold of an 'aggressive' NATO alliance opposing the socialist community. At that time it even appeared that the 'special relations' between the two Germanys were completely subordinate to the general logic of the global confrontation and would never acquire an independent political meaning.

When looking to the West, for evident reasons Gorbachev regarded relations with Washington as the absolute priority. This would explain why Soviet policy with regard to the 'German question' continued to follow the hard-line position set by Gromyko for some time, even after Shevardnadze had arrived on the scene. According to Falin, even Brezhnev considered this stance to be excessively tough, and in order to encourage Willy Brandt's *Ostpolitik*, he preferred to use a specially established direct channel of communication with the Federal Republic's leadership via Yuri Andropov's KGB connections, thus bypassing Gromyko.[81]

In 1985–6, while the GDR was seen as a privileged member of the 'socialist family' for various strategic and economic reasons, the FRG was not a promising political partner for Gorbachev, led as it was by a conservative coalition with a CDU Chancellor, Helmut Kohl. This sceptical appraisal of the Bonn government was aggravated by the fact that unlike other Western European leaders and particularly Mitterrand and Thatcher, the West German Chancellor was not only unimpressed by the new Soviet leader, on the contrary, and in a rather awkward manner, he compared Gorbachev's dynamic style of political offensive toward the West to the propaganda methods used by Goebbels. This unfortunate remark by Kohl resulted in a two-year delay in the development of Soviet relations with West Germany

Gradually, however, Gorbachev's simplified black-and-white image of the two separate German worlds began to evolve.

His growing personal antipathy towards Honecker, who made no effort to conceal his scepticism about *perestroika*, began to affect his relations with the GDR leadership. Also, having begun a re-evaluation of the nature of economic ties with the socialist countries and preparing a reform of COMECON, Gorbachev better realized that the acclaimed economic superiority of the GDR and the relative prosperity of its population in comparison to the other COMECON members and certainly the USSR rested on two pillars: cheap oil and gas supplied by the Soviet Union, often re-exported in huge quantities and for high prices to the West; and the impressive covert economic aid coming from West Germany, to which the GDR was already dramatically indebted.[82]

After a pause caused by Kohl's unfortunate remark, things began to change in relation to the Federal Republic. In summer 1987 the FRG President, Richard von Weizsäcker, paid a visit to Moscow, and with the evident intention of breaking the ice in bilateral relations, he conveyed to Gorbachev an informal apology from Kohl. By that time Gorbachev himself was looking for an occasion to normalize the situation. Internal economic problems had already become a growing concern, while the potential of West Germany to become a privileged Soviet economic partner in Europe was obvious. 'Germany is the main country of Western Europe,' announced Gorbachev in the Politburo session on 16 July, reporting about his meeting with Weizsäcker. 'In our policy of freezing the relations, we have gone to the limit. We have let the West German Chancellor know that we are ready to start movement in relations with each other . . . Kohl should not be treated as a scapegoat in this situation. Otherwise it would be journalism and not politics.'[83]

Despite the announcement of a warming climate in bilateral relations, issues related to the notorious 'German question' remained a taboo. When the West German President ritually mentioned the 'drama of German division', Gorbachev did not go beyond the classical Soviet position: he referred to the 'reality of the two German states', praised the 1970 Moscow Treaty between the Soviet Union and the FRG, but added just one new phrase: 'History will show who is right.' This apparently innocent phrase, which at that point Gorbachev understood to mean nothing more than conceding the possibility of change not earlier than in some hundred years' time, nevertheless allowed the West German President to announce to the press that 'for the Soviet leader the German question is not closed'.

In fact, according to Chernyaev, Weizsäcker had some grounds for interpreting Gorbachev's position in this way: 'Gorbachev was not ruling out German unification.' Nor when Weizsäcker repeatedly stressed the fact that there was only one German people, did Gorbachev protest. Nevertheless in the reports of the Soviet press about the visit, the text of Weizsäcker's speech at the reception given by Gromyko was shortened considerably and among the passages that were excised were those that referred to the theme of German unity as well as hints about 'the Wall'. According to Chernyaev, this was done by the MID on orders from Gromyko; he had to use his authority as an aide of the General Secretary in order obtain the publication of the full text in the *Moscow News*.[84]

Whatever might have been the personal evolution of Gorbachev's approach toward the delicate German issue, until 1989 the question of the eventual German reunification was never formally debated in the Politburo. During internal working sessions, only rare Soviet experts on Germany like Valentin Falin, Nikolai Portugalov or Valentin Dashichev, who were conscious of the extent to which the drama of national division continued to traumatize the consciousness of millions of Germans both East and West, dared to raise the distant possibility of eventual national reunion. At the same time, even timid public statements such as Portugalov's use of the term of 'one German nation' in an interview with a German paper or Falin's suggestion that in the 'common European home' the separate apartments occupied by the two Germanys 'could have interconnecting doors' provoked immediate reprimands from MID officials and even a rebuke by Gorbachev after complaints from Honecker about 'unauthorized improvisations'.

Concerned by the deteriorating economic and political situation, the GDR leadership tried to counterbalance its growing dependence on subventions from West Germany with ostentatious ideological orthodoxy. This inevitably resulted in a demonstrative refusal to countenance any political reforms, with an increasingly overt rejection of Soviet *perestroika*. By decision of Honecker's Politburo, a number of Soviet periodicals considered to be particularly articulate mouthpieces of *glasnost* were banned and could no longer be distributed in the GDR. Falin (at the 28th Party Congress in the summer of 1990 he was elected Secretary of the Central Committee and made head of the International Department) sent warning memos to Gorbachev; he predicted that if there was no change in the prevailing political course of the GDR, the country would experience a dramatic social and political crisis that could push the regime to the use of force in order to neutralize the expressions of discontent. In his notes Falin advised the necessity of proceeding with a measured liberalization of the political system in the GDR, and, voicing the ideas of his long-standing SPD friends Willy Brandt and Egon Bahr, he urged encouragement of a controlled process of *rapprochement* between the two German states in the direction of eventual confederation. But these 'heretical' ideas, according to Falin, appeared to be well ahead of their time and 'were disregarded by Gorbachev'.[85]

While Moscow's relations with Berlin steadily deteriorated, the first half of 1989 marked a real breakthrough in a Soviet *rapprochement* with Bonn. The awakening of Gorbachev's interest toward West Germany can be explained by two considerations. First, there was the Federal Republic's key position in any future 'common European home', which was gradually becoming one of the key elements of Gorbachev's foreign policy strategy in Europe. Secondly, West Germany could play an essential role in assisting the Soviet economy at a time when political *perestroika* started to face serious problems.

Gorbachev's official visit to the Federal Republic in June 1989 made him aware of the impressive economic strength of the country and its potential to become a precious partner for the Soviet Union during its process of economic reform. Personally, Gorbachev and Raisa were deeply moved by the extremely emotional reception they received in West Germany. At first the initiator of *perestroika* was inclined to interpret the enthusiasm of the crowds in the street as an expression of support for his policy of democratic reforms at home. Yet he was soon made aware of the real reason for this unprecedented welcome. During a traditional 'midnight tea party' to which

Gorbachev usually invited representatives of the Soviet intellectual and political elite who accompanied him during his trips abroad, the old German hand Nikolai Portugalov did not hesitate to explain the extraordinary burst of 'Gorbymania' during the visit: Germans expected from Gorbachev 'the solution of their national problem'. Apparently this caused some surprise. Gorbachev reacted by saying: 'But they must know that there can be no imminent unification.'[86] Yet as was frequently the case for the Soviet leader, an unexpectedly new angle on a seemingly familiar problem gave rise to further reflection.

It was certainly more a question of an inner process of reappraisal than the famous 'walk along the banks of the Rhine ' with Kohl (during which the question of eventual German reunification was never even raised, according to Zagladin, who served as interpreter for the two leaders[87]) that led Gorbachev to remark during the final press conference when answering a question about the future of the Berlin Wall: 'Nothing is eternal. I don't exclude anything. History will take care of this problem.' The same ambiguous answer was given by Gorbachev to a direct question put to him two months later in September 1989 by Willy Brandt on a visit to Moscow. Reacting to Brandt's proposal that it was time to 'start reflecting about the future destiny of the Germans. Will they one day be able to live under the same roof?', Gorbachev said: 'We have to wait.' And he once again referred to the slow but steady march of History.[88] At that time apparently neither he nor his interlocutor suspected that History's judgement had already been rendered and was about to be announced.

*   *   *

By midsummer of 1989, relations between Gorbachev and Honecker reached the lowest point, although appearances of fraternal ties between the two 'sister' socialist states continued to be observed. In July during Honecker's visit to Moscow, the conversation between the two leaders took the form of a dialogue of the deaf. Honecker once again gave Gorbachev to understand that the GDR leadership was not seeking any advice from Moscow and remained unimpressed by Soviet encouragement of political reform. Gorbachev in return warned the East

German leader that in case of any domestic complications the leaders of GDR would have to assume all responsibility and rely entirely on their own forces; there would be no support from Moscow and in particular no involvement of the Soviet troops stationed in the Republic.[89]

At that moment, however, the Soviet leadership was not really preoccupied by the future subsistence of the 'first socialist German state', believing that after the eventual replacement of its archaic leadership by a reformist team, the GDR would quickly rebuild its image as a model member of the socialist community. Nevertheless, faithful to his position of total non-interference in the internal affairs of even the closest allies of the Soviet Union, Gorbachev never gave the green light to any of the various scenarios involving an 'assisted' replacement of Honecker by a more modern, younger leader. (Among the names that were discussed by the experts of the International Department and the KGB were Egon Krenz, Hans Modrow and even the head of the GDR Intelligence service, Markus Wolf.[90])

In the meantime, whether sincere or feigned, the confidence of the East Berlin leaders in the stability of their regime and in the perennial separation of the two German states was reconfirmed at every opportunity. In October 1989 the GDR leadership was preparing to celebrate the fortieth anniversary of the foundation of the Republic and was using the occasion to inject an additional dose of official optimism into the minds of its citizens. Obviously all the heads of 'fraternal Parties' and allied states were invited to Berlin for the occasion and Gorbachev, despite all his antipathy toward Honecker and reluctance to participate in the monumental propaganda operation, could not decline the invitation.

In Berlin the arrival of 'the father of *perestroika*' had a tangible effect as a political catalyst. Thousands of the young Germans who gathered to take part in the demonstrations profited from Gorbachev's presence on the official tribune to display their sympathy, ignoring Honecker and shouting: 'Gorbachev stay with us!' The visit to the GDR convinced Gorbachev of the regime's incurable illness. As he observed the striking contrast between the pompous official celebrations and the spontaneous demonstrations of young Germans who were openly challenging the official leadership, probably for the first time he became conscious of the rapidly approaching crisis. 'It looks like a boiling pot with a tightly shut lid,' he remarked to his aides.[91] Standing at his side on the rostrum, Miecislav Rakowski, the reform-minded General Secretary of the Polish United Workers Party, whispered into his ear what Gorbachev must have been thinking himself: 'Mikhail, this is the end.' In fact one did not have to be on the tribune to realize the depth of the political abyss separating the heavy-handed regime from the aspirations of millions of the GDR citizens.

Just several weeks before the celebration of the fortieth anniversary, the GDR had been shaken by emotional images shown on national television of thousands of East Germans storming the gates of the FRG Embassy in Prague and later waving goodbye to their compatriots from the windows of sealed trains that were carrying them across GDR territory to the West. Later in the day Gorbachev addressed the members of the Party Politburo during a special session convened at his demand. At least in this way he wanted to appeal to the younger level of the GDR political leadership over Honecker's head, in order to encourage democratic reforms. It was on this occasion that he pronounced the words that soon became prophetic: 'those who lag behind history end up being punished by it'.[92]

Falin claims that on the day of Gorbachev's departure, disregarding the rules of subordination and without asking for Gorbachev's permission, he decided to encourage the Soviet Ambassador in Berlin, Viacheslav Kochemasov, to let the members of GDR leadership know that Moscow would welcome the long-awaited change.

> On 7 October at the airport, before saying goodbye to Kochemasov, I told him that the events of the last two days showed that the crisis of the regime has reached the stage where any hope of stabilization was directly connected to a change of leadership. This is why it was time to abandon the traditional posture of evading answers to direct questions on this subject. We were too timid, constantly repeating: 'It's your internal affair, please handle it yourselves.' When such questions are asked in the future, it might be reasonable to suggest that we would consider the coming of new people to power as

something natural. Kochemasov asked me if he was formally authorized to act in this way or did he have to wait for additional instructions. My answer was: '. . . sometimes waiting for formal directives means losing time'.[93]

If this conversation really did in fact prompt Kochemasov to act the way Falin proposed, it should be recorded as a first attempt by the former Soviet Ambassador to Bonn to initiate his own personal diplomacy in the face of the 'inexcusable sluggishness' (Falin's characterization) of official Soviet diplomacy when faced with the dramatic acceleration of German history

On 18 October, several days after Gorbachev's departure, the Second Party Secretary, Egon Krenz, pretending that he had previously consulted Gorbachev, took the initiative to convene an extraordinary meeting of the Politburo in order to compel Honecker to resign. The change of GDR leadership occurred according to Gorbachev's wish, 'naturally', without any direct involvement or formal instigation by the Soviets. In the first days that followed Honecker's resignation the prevailing mood in Moscow was one of relief and optimism. It looked as if the most important obstacle to reform in the GDR had been removed and the worst had been avoided in time. Receiving Honecker's successor, Krenz, in the Kremlin on 1 November, Gorbachev encouraged the new GDR leader to undertake 'radical reform and not just a cosmetic repair job'.[94] A week later the inexorable course of history, as so often happens, took the form of a chain of accidental events leading to the fall of the Berlin Wall and opening the road to the reunification of Germany and a total change of the postwar map of Europe.

\* \* \*

The beginning of the landslide can be traced to a telephone call by the Soviet Ambassador in the GDR, Vyacheslav Kochemasov, to Shevardnadze's first deputy, Anatoli Kovalev, informing him that the new GDR leadership was planning to liberalize the conditions of movement for its citizens across the inter-German border, in accordance with the programme of measures mentioned by Krenz to Gorbachev during his visit to Moscow. In its initial form this decision was not intended to affect Berlin or the checkpoints along the Wall. By 'informing' Kochemasov, the GDR authorities apparently wanted to get a formal green light from Moscow for this action.

According to Kovalev, who at that time was replacing the absent Minister and was not aware of the details of Gorbachev's conversation with Krenz, he responded with a rhetorical question: 'Where is the problem?' Kovalev claims that in this way he wanted to convey to the GDR leaders via the Soviet Ambassador that Moscow regarded the rules regulating the border regime between the two Germanys as a matter belonging to the internal affairs of the GDR. Since the cautious Kochemasov was not satisfied with an oral answer and demanded written instructions, Kovalev, 'without asking anybody', signed a cable confirming this position.[95]

Falin blamed Kovalev 'and the persons from whom he might have taken orders' (hinting at Shevardnadze) for 'irresponsible behaviour', since it was not just the Berlin Wall but also the whole inter-German border that served as part of the political frontier and was a line of strategic defence for the Warsaw Pact. Consequently any modification of the border regime could only be regarded as a matter for the collective competence of the political leaders of these countries.[96] These angry remarks by Falin most probably reflect the frustration of a man who felt sidelined in the handling of an event that marked a crucial turning point in the history of Germany and of Europe; he neglects the fact that the first breach of the Warsaw Pact frontline occurred several months before the opening of the Brandenburg Gate in Berlin – on the border between Hungary and Austria.[97]

Although Falin's arguments might have a certain formal validity, in terms of political logic it was Kovalev who was certainly right. Once Gorbachev delivered his speech at the United Nations renouncing the use of force and, by implication, allowing people freely to choose their own social system, the Wall was already doomed. Restating the principle that 'freedom of choice should not know any exceptions' in Strasbourg in July 1989 during his speech before the Council of Europe, Gorbachev not only asserted its universal value, but for the first time applied it to 'friend or ally states'.[98] By the autumn of 1989, Gorbachev's statement had passed convincing tests, first in Poland, with the installation in August of a non-communist government headed by Tadeusz Mazowiecki, in accordance with the results of free elections, and after that in September in Hungary, where the opening of the Austrian border with the silent consent of Moscow, despite the ire of Berlin, allowed thousands of GDR citizens to flee to the West. With the removal of Honecker, the fall of the Wall became just a matter of time.

Yet the course of events on the historic night of 9 November did not simply reflect political disarray in East Berlin and Moscow in the face of pressure from the Berlin 'street'.[99] What determined the behaviour of both the Soviet and the new GDR leaders during those decisive hours was the fear of possible bloodshed and an unwillingness to resort to force. Gorbachev certainly did not choose 'to pull down that wall' on that night, in response to Ronald Reagan's appeal of several years before. He merely dug under its foundation, leaving it vulnerable, so that it would collapse at the first outburst of a political storm. But he, too, was taken unawares by the rapidity with which his declaration of principles set in motion political change on such a colossal scale.

Despite the tremendous symbolic significance of the opening of the Wall, its real political meaning for relations between the two Germanys and the situation in Europe was not immediately understood either in Berlin or Moscow, or in Bonn and other Western capitals. Most politicians on both sides of the now non-existent divide continued to assume that the parallel existence of the two German states would continue for an indefinite period. In fact the plausibility of this prospect was supported by the first polls showing that the public opinion in both German states had not yet 'digested' the sensational change that had taken place and seemed ready to accommodate the new non-antagonistic relations between the two states without raising the question of immediate reunification.[100]

On the other hand, the political and psychological shock of the November events in Berlin, events that threatened a dismantling of the whole postwar order in Europe, led political leaders in both East and West to hold their breath while observing the reaction of the other side, fearing that any imprudent move could provoke a world crisis. In this situation, quite naturally all Western eyes were turned on Gorbachev. An understandable nervousness prevailed in Paris, London and Rome, where political leaders imagined the possibility of completely different but equally worrying scenarios: would there be a furious response by Moscow (coming from Gorbachev himself or imposed on him by the Soviet generals) that could give rise to an extremely grave East–West crisis in the centre of Europe? Or, alternatively, might a dramatic destabilization of Gorbachev's internal position lead to his eventual removal from the Kremlin and the end of *perestroika*? In either case the further evolution of the German question, which remained a highly sensitive issue for a whole generation of European politicians, including Thatcher, Mitterrand and Andreotti, opened up a new uncertainty.

Reporting about Mitterrand's reaction to the collapse of the Wall, Jacques Attali wrote about the feelings of 'grave concern' for the fate of Gorbachev expressed by his boss on 10 November: 'Gorbachev will never agree to go further or else he will be replaced by a hawk. These people [referring, apparently, to the initiators of street demonstrations in Berlin] play with world war without understanding what they are doing.'[101] On the same day Mitterrand received from Margaret Thatcher a copy of her letter to Gorbachev in which the 'Iron Lady' expressed her concern that the evolution of the situation in the GDR and other East European countries could increase the risk of political instability.

In Moscow in those days Gorbachev chose to display assurance and show both his colleagues in the Soviet leadership and his foreign partners that he still maintained total control of events. To do this he had to make everybody believe that nothing extraordinary had happened. His adviser for Western Europe, Vadim Zagladin, was dispatched to carry reassuring messages to the worried European capitals. His task was to calm those who feared repressive unilateral action by Soviet troops in Berlin, while simultaneously producing the impression that Gorbachev was in daily contact with the leaders of both German states and that Moscow was on top of the new situation.[102] In his telephone conversation with Mitterrand on 14 November, Gorbachev told the French President that Kohl had promised that 'he would resist by all means the forces within Germany that were pushing him towards speedy unification'.[103]

In fact Gorbachev's expressions of self-assurance in this period were intended to conceal the evident confusion that reigned in the Kremlin and the fact that there was no existing strategy to deal with events that were no more than the logical consequences of Gorbachev's own policy. Until the fall of the Wall, Gorbachev had reason to believe that his political and moral authority as the initiator of democratic change in the Soviet Union and as the man who had solemnly abolished the 'Brezhnev Doctrine' would allow him to exercise control over the evolution of the situation in Eastern Europe. Yet the completely new predicament that emerged as a result of the unexpected family reunion of the two parts of the German nation continued to escape Gorbachev's notice for at least two months following the 9 November events.

His main foreign policy assistants, Shevardnadze and Chernyaev, were neither sensitive enough nor competent to advise him on the particular complexities of the German problem, while Zagladin did not have enough authority (or strength of character) to draw his boss's attention to the fact that events in Germany were rapidly taking on a force of their own. The only highly placed professional expert who could soberly evaluate the situation and understand that things were getting out of control was Falin. Yet even in his position as a Secretary of the Central Committee he did not have direct daily access to Gorbachev. Observing with growing concern the impotence of the MID along with a growing gap between the Soviet leader's perception of the situation in Germany and the reality of what was occurring on the ground, he finally decided to act on his own.

Referring to the chain of events that followed Honecker's resignation and the fall of the Berlin Wall, Chernyaev suggests that one of the explanations for Moscow's obviously incoherent immediate reaction to the landslide developments within the GDR lay in the power clash and acute 'personal rivalry between the two former Soviet Ambassadors to Bonn: Falin and Kvitsinski'.[104] It is certainly the case that these two top Soviet experts on Germany often disagreed about policy, their views being quite different or even contradictory. Falin believed that Moscow should rely on his long-standing political/personal friends – social democrats of the SPD and in particular the two 'fathers' of Ostpolitik, Brandt and Bahr. He believed, as they did, that Ostpolitik had made a major contribution to the disintegration of the dogmatic communist model in the GDR, which would be followed by a merited victory of social democrats – first in the GDR and afterwards in all-German elections; Kvitsinski, on the contrary, was openly scornful of the social democrats and insisted on a total alignment with the coalition of Kohl and his Free Democrat deputy, Hans-Dietrich Genscher. But the real explanation for Falin's independent moves at this time was not just this debate between professionals.

In fact his dissent from the formal line of the Ministry of Foreign Affairs on the 'German question' went back to much earlier days, to the late 1960s, when, as one of Moscow's principal German hands inside the MID, he did not hesitate to challenge Gromyko's position, insisting on the need to meet Willy Brandt halfway, once a hand had been extended to Moscow. At that time it was only Brezhnev's personal sympathy for Falin as well as his ambition to open a new page of détente in the Soviet Union's relations with the West that saved the maverick official from being ejected from his post by Gromyko. Eventually Falin's view prevailed with the signing of the historic Moscow Treaty by Brezhnev and Brandt in 1970, with Gromyko publicly obliged to compliment Falin for the splendid job he had done in its preparation. Falin soon left for a well-deserved Ambassador's post in Bonn.

Yet despite all his professional disagreements with Gromyko, Falin was not prepared to recognize the authority of Shevardnadze as Gromyko's successor. This was particularly the case when he found himself pushed aside and marginalized in the decision-making process at the very moment when the fate of the German nation was at stake during a period of historic change. Apparently this situation, coupled with the evident embarrassment of the MID and the fact that Gorbachev had been taken unawares by the sudden political collapse of the GDR, pushed him to violate the unwritten laws of state and Party discipline. His rather surprising personal initiatives led to a succession of events that produced unexpected results and accelerated the collapse of the temporary political equilibrium between Bonn and East Berlin. This may explain why in the aftermath of these events, Falin himself had a problem about acknowledging the real role he had played in seeking a resolution of the German puzzle.

Conscious of the fact that German reunification was unavoidable, he came to the conclusion that the only way to adjust this process to suit Soviet interests was to channel it into a predetermined form. His plan was to resort to the formula of a German confederation or a 'contractual community' (*Vertragsgemeinschaft*), which was mentioned as one of the hypothetical options by German politicians already at the time of the preparation of the Moscow treaty of 1970. Legitimizing the *de facto* economic and social reunion of the German nation, this formula had the advantage of securing for an indefinite time the political independence of the GDR. Another motive of Falin's initiative, never publicly acknowledged, amounted to a revival of the dream of most Soviet Germanophiles harking back to the 1920s and the spirit of Rapallo – Soviet–German complicity in the face of an arrogant alliance of Western powers almost equally hostile toward defeated Germany and Bolshevik Russia.[105]

Yet, obviously, this scheme could only work if it were to be discussed between Kohl and Gorbachev. However, for different reasons, neither leader was prepared for such an initiative. Gorbachev, concerned about internal as much as external political considerations, was thinking only of how to slow down or, better still, to freeze the uncontrolled process of German *rapprochement*. Kohl himself was reluctant publicly to raise the question of German reunification even in the intimate circle of his West European colleagues for fear of arousing their anxieties, which in fact happened during the EEC summit in Paris.[106]

This explains why Falin, deprived of direct access to the ear of Gorbachev and moreover not all that hopeful about the possibility of convincing him, chose a roundabout path. He proposed to Chernyaev to activate a dormant channel of direct communication between the Soviet General Secretary and the FRG Chancellor, established during the Brezhnev years to bypass Gromyko. This time, of course, the men to be outflanked were Shevardnadze and Kvitsinski. The idea was to dispatch an unofficial envoy to Bonn, Nikolai Portugalov, who had specialized in this type of mission since the Brandt era. Instead of his usual contact, Egon Bahr, he would now meet Kohl's foreign policy adviser, Horst Teltschik.

Falin presented this delicate mission in a manner that made it seem to coincide with Gorbachev's overriding concern of the moment: to encourage Kohl to show the maximum restraint on the question of *rapprochement* between the two German states in order not to provoke either Soviet conservative forces or Germany's allies in Europe. On the condition that maximum caution was to be observed, suggested Falin, Kohl could be told that 'anything might become possible'. Since for Chernyaev this ambiguous formula did not sound very different from Gorbachev's famous 'nothing is eternal and history will find the proper solutions', without much hesitation he accepted Falin's proposal, 'seeing no harm in it' and also looking for a way to satisfy Falin's pride, apparently wounded by his estrangement from discussions on the handling of the German issue.[107]

What Falin did not tell Chernyaev, however, was that in his conversation with Teltschik, Portugalov would be instructed to develop the idea of a confederative structure uniting the two German states. For Falin, this formula was meant to rationalize the chaos of spontaneous national reunion and also to offer the GDR what might be a last chance to secure and legitimize its state structures in a totally new political context.[108] It was an operation bordering on political adventurism, since Portugalov was going to Bonn with the status of Gorbachev's envoy but was in fact bearing a personal message from Falin to the West German Chancellor.

Falin's real addressee, however, in fact was not Kohl but Gorbachev. Feeling incapable of persuading his boss of the merits of German confederation – for the moment it seemed too radical – he was counting on the Federal Chancellor to do the job for him. Several days later at a meeting in Moscow with the new GDR Prime Minister, Hans Modrow, he repeated the manoeuvre, prompting Modrow to speak in favour of the 'contractual community' during his meeting with Gorbachev. This probably unique exercise in personal diplomacy by a Secretary of the Central Committee without the knowledge of the General Secretary (not to speak of the Minister of Foreign Affairs) was the inspiration behind rather sensational subsequent developments.

Horst Teltschik, after his meeting on 21 November with Portugalov, who told him that 'in the long run the Soviets might be prepared 'to give a green signal to a German confederation, regardless of the shape it may take', immediately seized on the importance of these remarks as a tremendous historic opening for the future of Germany and also as an extraordinary political opportunity for Kohl to emerge on the national political scene as the Chancellor of reunification. 'If Gorbachev's experts on Germany were discussing the possibility of German reunification,' wrote Genscher's chief of staff, Frank Elbe, 'it was high time to take the offensive'.[109]

Already on 23 November Teltschik proposed to the Chancellor that he work out 'a viable concept for German unification'. Kohl's advisers warned him that 'if he let slip the opportunity to publicly present his plan for national unity, Genscher or even the SPD opposition would steal the march on him'. Profiting from the first available occasion – a debate in the Bundestag scheduled for 28 November on the coming year's budget, Kohl presented his dramatic ten-point programme for creating national unity within a framework of confederative structures. 'The real bone of contention was the Chancellor's proposal for a "contractual community" between both German states with the final aim of forming a "federation" from which Germany would emerge reunited.' Kohl treated his ten-point plan as if it was a top secret commando operation. As Teltschik reported later, 'no member of the government [and particularly not Genscher] was to get even the slightest inkling of the coming political coup, in order to ensure a surprise effect.'[110]

Having received what he had taken to be a green light from Moscow, Kohl not only did not bother to inform his allies in the EEC (Mitterrand was particularly furious because in a letter that the German Chancellor had written to him on the day of his Bundestag speech, he did not even mention his intention to address the question of German unity) or even his own Foreign Minister. Genscher learned of the new plan while sitting in Parliament listening to Kohl. The reason for this was obvious:

Kohl's advisers also regarded the whole initiative as 'a significant tactical move as far as the junior coalition partner (FDP) was concerned'.[111]

Meeting the three ambassadors of the allied countries – America, Britain and France – on the same day in order to explain the meaning of the ten-point programme, Teltschik presented the plan as a product of Kohl's own reflection on the subject but enigmatically suggested that there had been consultation with 'friends of Germany', namely with Moscow. Not only did this not reassure German's Western allies, on the contrary it aggravated their concerns. Either Kohl's initiative meant that he had decided to go it alone, or, worse, it could portend a revival of the phantom of Rapallo. For Kohl's West European partners (and above all for Thatcher and Mitterrand), the sudden thrust toward German unity roused instinctive fears; divided after its defeat in war, the German nation had until recently obediently accepted its lot along with the patronage of the victors. What they now heard seemed to border on dangerous rebellion. From their point of view there were also two important omissions in Kohl's ten-point programme: alliance membership (the British concerned about NATO, the French with the EEC) and postwar borders.

For the United States, even if free from the historical European complexes and prejudices with regard to the Germans, the unexpected national upheaval in their safest European bastion provoked a bewildered reaction. For them, too, as for the FRG's other Western allies, in their confrontation with the USSR it was one thing to exploit politically the abnormality of an entire people's division and the monstrosity of the Wall; but it was quite different actually to manage the realization of the German dream of reunification while taking care of their own security concerns, especially in the unwonted situation of the Germans themselves being apparently ready to take care of their own future without seeking advice from their tutors. And all this was taking place in the completely transformed context of the West's relations with a Soviet Union being directed by Gorbachev toward a yet uncertain but exceptionally promising evolution.

Quite naturally with hindsight and interested in stressing the US administration's capacity for foresight, Condoleezza

Rice and Philip Zelikow list among the 'thirteen variables' that played a decisive role in the reunification of Germany George Bush's encouragement of Kohl to revert from the *Ostpolitik* paradigm of 'change through rapprochement' back to the Adenauer paradigm of 'change through strength'.[112] Yet they are wrong, first to undervalue the historic significance of Brandt's *Ostpolitik*, which much more than the Adenauer paradigm was responsible for the determination with which the thousands of Berliners invaded the streets of the GDR capital after they realized that Gorbachev had discarded the 'Brezhnev Doctrine'. It was this popular policy and the impressive manifestation of the retrieved dignity of a nation that changed the tempo of the historical process and forced the politicians to adjust to its new pace. Second, they attribute an extreme coherence and resolution to Washington's position on the question of German reunification as early as November–December 1989, while in reality it took the US administration a much longer time to fine-tune its reaction to the German tornado. As confirmed by some insiders within the White House, Kohl's ten-point plan took the administration in Washington completely by surprise. Bob Blackwill, Senior Director for European and Soviet Affairs in the National Security Council, revealed: 'Above all, we wanted to avoid giving the impression that we were not informed.'[113]

Even more revealing is Brent Scowcroft's comment in George Bush's memoirs, to which he contributed: 'I was concerned by Kohl's unexpected announcement. . . . If he was prepared to go off on his own whenever he worried that we might object, we had very little influence. Suppose, for example, it came to the point that he decided he could get unification only by trading it for neutrality?'[114] As Aleksandr Bessmertnykh has observed, after a certain stage it was neither Kohl nor the Americans who were speeding up the development of events in Germany. 'They all, including Kohl, were just trying to catch up. Events in the GDR, like wild horses, galloped away, escaping any control by politics or diplomacy.'[115]

In Moscow, Kohl's speech produced an indignant reaction from Gorbachev, who was completely ignorant of Falin's personal initiative. His emotional response was not surprising, since he had every reason to interpret the proposal as a unilateral step which flouted all their previous agreements; for Gorbachev this perceived betrayal overshadowed any real merit that might be found in Kohl's plan. The whole Falin exercise thus produced the opposite effect of the one he had intended. Gorbachev toughened his own position, at least for the next two months, while Germany's West European partners were irritated and outraged by the fact that they had not been consulted. The spectre of Rapallo did indeed haunt their deliberations.

Both the East and West German advocates of the idea of a confederative state – Modrow and Genscher – had to listen to Gorbachev's vehement denunciation of the project when meeting him in the days that followed Kohl's speech. Talking to Genscher, for example, Gorbachev (perhaps recalling Kohl's earlier inappropriate Goebbels remark) did not hesitate to say that the German Chancellor was apparently an admirer of military marching tunes. He qualified Kohl's plan as an attempt to annex the GDR. For Gorbachev, there could be 'no doubt' that the GDR must remain an independent state and a member of the Warsaw Pact. These remarks by Gorbachev were immediately amplified by Shevardnadze, who during his conversation with Genscher referred to the 'blitz-unification' and 'diktat', adding: 'Even Hitler did not permit himself this.' Later in a press interview he referred to the 'revanchist forces' raising their head on West German soil.[116]

In this heated environment, Gorbachev's advisers (Chernyaev, Zagladin and certainly Falin), wishing to cool the atmosphere, tried to point to the valuable aspects of Kohl's programme. However, they did not get very far. According to Chernyaev, Gorbachev's reaction to Kohl's speech was mostly emotional and could largely be explained by a feeling of offence. 'He interpreted it as Kohl's attempt to seize the political initiative, a breach of his promise not to push events forward or try to extract one-sided political advantage, and above all it was a violation of their agreement to consult each other on every new move.'[117]

Instead of becoming the basis for an eventual compromise, the abortive plan for a German confederation provoked distrust in Moscow vis-à-vis the real intentions of the Bonn government and stimulated efforts in both Eastern and Western

Europe to 'contain' if not to counter what was interpreted to be the German 'rush for unity'. Gorbachev, who to Kohl's great surprise proved to be allergic to the very term 'confederation', in response to the 'ten-point speech' suggested changes in the established calendar of the Helsinki process, arguing that it was necessary to accelerate the process of building all-European structures so that the unification of Europe did not lag behind the reunification of Germany. On 30 November, during a visit to Rome, Gorbachev proposed that the next Conference on Security and Cooperation in Europe (CSCE) be convened in Paris in the autumn of 1990, two years ahead of schedule.

Mitterrand, who supported Gorbachev's initiative, had additional reasons to be alarmed by Kohl's presentation of German reunification as a practical possibility. As his Minister of Foreign Affairs, Roland Dumas, has testified, Mitterrand was torn by a double uncertainty:

> On the one hand he thought that Kohl was not truly reliable and might be prepared to sacrifice the cause of European integration for the chance of rapid unification on as yet unknown conditions suggested by Gorbachev. On the other, he feared that by being 'overhasty', Kohl could spoil the internal game for Gorbachev provoking the fury of his military commanders.[118]

Mitterrand not only supported Gorbachev's initiative to speed up the process of creating pan-European structures, but also in his own way tried 'to slow Kohl down' by raising the question of a future Germany's Eastern (Polish ) border; solution of this issue would be a precondition for French agreement to reunification. Another of his concerns was to ensure that Europe, as a political player, was not excluded from the elaboration of decisions over the future of Germany. The French President's uneasiness was at the heart of his proposal to Gorbachev to hold a French–Soviet summit immediately after Malta. It took place in Kiev on 6 December. The very fact of this meeting as well as his suggestion to Gorbachev that they go together to Berlin to meet the new GDR leadership made it clear that Mitterrand was trying to bring Europe in as a participant in all deliberations on the German question, which so far seemed only to involve Gorbachev, Kohl and Bush.[119]

Although Gorbachev declined Mitterrand's invitation to join him on his trip to East Berlin, he basically shared the French President's concern that 'improvised' formulas for German reunification which neglected the interests of the former victorious powers could have unpredictable consequences for the European scene. When relating his conversation with Genscher to Mitterrand, Gorbachev said that he had described Kohl's behaviour as an exercise in 'political diktat' and compared the West German Chancellor to the proverbial 'bull in a china shop'.[120]

Yet Gorbachev's real problem at that time was the fact that beyond this 'reactive' position, there was as yet no Soviet strategy for dealing with the new situation. Different, sometimes conflicting views existed side by side within the MID; Shevardnadze largely relied on Kvitsinski's recommendations, while Falin and Chernyaev tended to clash. The new authorities of the GDR evidently were incapable of establishing control over the situation. Having circumscribed his options by flatly refusing to countenance talk of a confederative arrangement, thus depriving himself of the possibility of influencing the inter-German dialogue, Gorbachev was losing precious time. Just several weeks later at the end of January 1990, his rigid position had to give way to its opposite – an acceptance of the by then inevitable collapse of the East German state.

The Central Committee 'seminar' on East Germany convened by Gorbachev on 26 January 1990 with the participation of Prime Minister Ryzhkov, Shevardnadze, Medvedev, Kryuchkov, Yazov, Akhromeev, Yakovlev, Falin and his aides Chernyaev and Shakhnazarov, after the reports from the MID, KGB and Ministry of Defence and several hours of debate, ended with him concluding that, given the process of the rapid dislocation of state structures within the GDR, there was no hope of securing its independent survival. The only way to avoid reunification, according to several participants of the session, would be to use the Soviet army stationed in the GDR to close the inter-German border. Yet from the very beginning Gorbachev had declared his categorical refusal to resort to military force.

In his concluding remarks, Gorbachev did insist that he would resolutely oppose a united Germany's entry into NATO, declaring that in order to avoid this he would be prepared to suspend both the Vienna negotiations on conventional arms and the US–Soviet START talks. Chernyaev claims that during this seminar it was he who suggested the '4 + 2' formula (four victor powers + two German states) as an international negotiating framework to discuss the external aspects of the process of German reunification. In the original MID proposal, the still existing GDR was omitted – it was suggested that the negotiations be limited to five participants, with West Germany representing the future united country. On Chernyaev's insistence, the GDR was included, since 'the country and its leaders were still there'.[121]

In fact within the space of two months Gorbachev's position on the question of German unity shifted almost from one extreme to the other, bordering on the total abandonment of the East German state which just one month before he was promising he would 'never let down'.[122] Two main factors influenced this spectacular change in Gorbachev's position. One, evidently, was the rapid deterioration of the situation in the GDR with the quite real probability that tens if not hundreds of thousands of East German citizens would wish to profit from the new situation and cross the border to the West.

The other element was the awakening of American diplomacy with regard to the German issue. This took place in December after the Malta summit where Bush centred his position on support for *perestroika* and its leader. On that occasion he expressed Washington's determination to avoid complicating life for Gorbachev by attempting to influence developments in Eastern Europe or trying to profit strategically from the sensational changes taking place in this sensitive zone. According to Gorbachev, the two leaders agreed to let events follow their natural course and even to cooperate and act jointly 'in a spirit of consensus'.[123] After Malta the situation began to change.

On the way from Malta to Brussels, where George Bush was planning to inform the US NATO allies about the results of the US–Soviet summit, he formulated his own four-point position that represented the US conditions for support of German reunification. The two most important of them were a guarantee of the US presence in Europe and confirmation of a united

Germany's membership in NATO. During a *tête-à-tête* meeting with Bush in Brussels (Baker suggested that he would not participate in order to avoid Genscher's presence), Kohl thanked Bush for his 'calm' reception of the ten-point plan. He promised not to do anything reckless and said that there was no timetable. Continuing integration with the West was a 'precondition' for the ten points. After free elections in the GDR (scheduled for March), the next step would be confederation, but with two independent states remaining. The third phase, federation, lay in the future. It would take some years, perhaps as many as five, to reach the goal. Bush for his part informed Kohl that at Malta Gorbachev had approached the reunification issue gently. (In fact Gorbachev preferred to elude the subject since at that time he did not yet have an established position on the issue.[124])

When the US President presented his four-point formula to the Brussels NATO summit, Kohl immediately said that there was nothing to discuss: 'The meeting should simply adjourn.' Only Andreotti and Thatcher disagreed. Andreotti spoke up 'after an awkward silence', writes Scowcroft. He warned that self-determination, if taken too far, could get out of hand and cause trouble. 'What if tomorrow the Baltics asserted their sovereignty?' he asked.

Thatcher said she shared Andreotti's concerns, and wanted to study Bush's proposal more carefully.[125] Apparently she hoped that the Four Power framework would allow Britain some leverage, but she quickly understood that 'with the United States – and soon the Soviets too – ceasing to regard this as anything more than a talking shop for discussion of the details of reunification', there was little chance she could influence the process.[126] In her memoirs Thatcher remarks bitterly: '[I knew there] was nothing I could expect from the Americans as regards slowing down German unification. If there was any hope . . . it would only come from an Anglo-French initiative.'[127] A more realistic Mitterrand, instead of trying to slow down the Germans, preferred to speed up the process of European integration. 'German unity should go no faster than the EC,' he told Kohl, making France's support conditional on the establishment of a precise timetable for building economic and monetary union. It was only after he finally obtained Kohl's agreement for the convening in late 1990 of an intergovernmental conference to amend the Treaty of Rome that Paris (and the EEC) endorsed Germany's movement toward reunification.[128]

Unlike the French and the British, the Americans were not at all worried by the possible emergence of a German giant in the centre of Europe. What did, however, give rise to Washington's concern was the danger of a 'neutralized' Germany and its eventual withdrawal from NATO. Fearing that West German leaders might negotiate the conditions for reunification directly with Moscow in exchange for German neutrality or the 'French formula' of non-participation in NATO's military structures, the Bush administration decided to step up its support for Kohl, making it clear that this support was dependent upon the united Germany becoming a member of NATO. During his visit to Moscow on 9 February 1990, James Baker, speaking on behalf of Bush, used two main arguments in order to persuade Gorbachev to agree. First: a neutral Germany unrestrained by its membership in the Western alliance might become less predictable and could one day be tempted to start developing its own nuclear capability. Second: if Germany's entry into the Alliance were to take place, the West would be willing to guarantee that NATO would not extend 'the zone of its jurisdiction or military presence in the East even by an inch'.[129]

Ultimately it was on this basis that the final political and military status of the new Germany was defined. Yet it took Gorbachev more than four months to come to terms with it, during which time he tried by different means to obtain a more flexible formula from the West, one that would look more like a compromise rather than capitulation in the face of a Western ultimatum. He finally gave his formal consent to a reunified Germany joining NATO during the US–Soviet summit in Washington in May 1990 and formally confirmed it to Kohl in July during their meeting in his native Stavropol region at Arkhyz.

The real reason for Gorbachev's hesitation to accept Germany's NATO membership was not a concern that it could compromise the security of the Soviet Union (he came out of the Malta summit convinced that the logic of strategic equilibrium characteristic of the Cold War period could now be abandoned by both East and West), but rather his fear that political prejudice against this unilateral solution could jeopardize support for his foreign policy at home. On every occasion he continued to remind his Western partners that since the last war the 'German question' remained an extremely sensitive issue for the Soviet public. This was largely the reason why both he and Shevardnadze kept proposing rather awkward formulas such as the parallel membership of the two German states in their respective military alliances for a transition period or a simultaneous withdrawal from both entities.

At the same time, Gorbachev maintains that he was never tempted to use the Soviet military presence in East Germany as a political trump card in order to put pressure on the West, contrary to the recommendation of some of his advisers (curiously enough, on this point the positions of such different persons as Dobrynin, Falin and Kvitsinski, all of them coming from the Gromyko school of diplomacy, were rather close). In fact Gorbachev's field for manoeuvre was quite limited. Although Zagladin, too, believed that 'Soviet troops represented the last argument with which Gorbachev could have countered Western pressure',[130] in reality Gorbachev did not possess even this theoretically powerful lever (except, of course, if he had been actually ready to engage in military action rather than use it merely as a means of political pressure). 'After the collapse of the Wall and the likelihood of a single German currency, the Soviet Union did not have the necessary resources to finance the prolonged stationing of its troops [the Soviet contingent amounted to 380,000 men] on East German territory. This is why the presence of the army could not be used as a instrument to postpone unification,' remarks Valentin Kopteltsev, a former Soviet head of mission in Berlin.[131]

Contrary to what has often been said by some of Gorbachev's domestic critics, he could not count on the public support of either Margaret Thatcher or François Mitterrand to stop the steam-roller of German reunification. Certainly in their private conversations with Gorbachev (Thatcher in some cases even asked Chernyaev to stop taking notes), both shared with him their concerns about the 'unpredictable consequences' and the risks of 'international destabilization' that could arise from the speedy German march to unity. Vadim Medvedev, who led a

Soviet Parliamentary delegation to London in March 1990, reports that his face-to-face conversation with the 'Iron Lady' left him with the clear impression that she not only did not welcome the reunification of Germany, but ardently hoped that Gorbachev would block it. Mitterrand's position differed in detail but was basically similar. Possibly because of differences in temperament, he was not as explicit as Thatcher in revealing his preoccupations in public. Yet when speaking to his counsellors, he did not conceal his disappointment with Gorbachev's 'soft' reaction, bordering on 'capitulation'.[132]

However, despite all the prompting he was receiving from Thatcher and Mitterrand, Gorbachev was quite conscious of the fact that neither the British nor the French leader would ever express his or her reservations about the form and timing of German reunification in public. 'They were counting on us to slow it down and if possible to block the process,' according to Zagladin.[133] Chernyaev's interpretation is similar:

> Gorbachev realized that Thatcher and Mitterrand would never conspire with him against the Germans, especially after Bush made his views known. It was also clear to him that they would like to use him as a brake mechanism. Yet since it was obvious that the process of unification had already begun and could not be stopped, he feared that it might go ahead without him and would consequently be directed against him.[134]

Discussing the (still hypothetical) perspective of German reunification with Margaret Thatcher in September 1989, Gorbachev, quite naturally reacting to Thatcher's concerns, said that the Russians did not want German reunification either. 'But,' writes Rodric Braithwaite, 'she had misunderstood Gorbachev: he did not intend to stand uselessly against the tide of history. His problem was a different one: to extract the best bargain he could in exchange for Russia's inevitable retreat.'[135]

All the attempted bargaining about the final formula for German association with NATO was therefore much more a question of form than serious content; Gorbachev was trying to gain needed time in order to let public opinion at home adjust to the new reality, to the new type of relations that were taking shape in the Soviet Union's relations with Germany as well as with the West in general. At the same time he was hoping to get at least partial political compensation from his Western partners for what he believed to be his major contribution to the end of the Cold War.

In May 1990, having realized that all arguments and political tactics (the military option having been excluded a priori) to get a better bargain from the West had been exhausted, Gorbachev took a conscious decision. Chernyaev describes Gorbachev's thinking at this crucial moment as follows:

> When the economic situation inside the country started to deteriorate rapidly and Gorbachev realized that the whole prospect of continuing political reform was at stake, he came to the conclusion that gaining Germany – the state and a great nation, not specifically Kohl or Genscher – as a strategic ally for the future was certainly much more important than to continue small disputes over formulas. This decision became part of his general determination to save *perestroika*.[136]

Naturally this kind of reasoning could hardly gain him unanimous support within the Soviet political elite, deeply divided by the contradictory balance sheet of the years of reform, or even within an already gravely fractured Politburo. Gorbachev would never have been able to obtain a Politburo mandate to agree to Germany's membership in NATO, had he wished it. Actually the official directive which he took with him to Washington for the US–Soviet summit in May 1990 confirmed Soviet opposition to this outcome and obliged Gorbachev to insist on German neutrality or non-aligned status. It was during the discussion of the German issue with Bush on 31 May that Gorbachev took on the responsibility of over-stepping his mandate and accepted a formulation that stipulated a united Germany, free to adhere to the alliance of its choice.

Gorbachev's decision was not in any way an improvisation. Psychologically, he prepared himself for this option before he went to Washington, following his conversation with Mitterrand, whom he had received in the Kremlin on 25 May. During their meeting Mitterrand made it clear to Gorbachev that the Western powers would certainly remain united in rejecting all Soviet alternative formulas. While promising Gorbachev that he would insist on a provision precluding the stationing of NATO troops in the eastern part of Germany 'in order not to disturb the existing balance of forces', Mitterrand at the same time advised Gorbachev to abandon his 'frontal opposition' to Germany's membership in NATO. 'Such a position risks weakening and isolating the Soviet Union without any real chance of success. You can try and harden your position, but this would become a source of destabilization in Europe. And that would be counterproductive in terms of your long-term interests.'

In response to Gorbachev's direct question about his own attitude toward Soviet proposals for German neutrality or the simultaneous membership of the two German states in both military pacts, the French President replied:

> If I say 'no' to the question of German membership in NATO, I'll find myself isolated among my Western partners. Evidently there is no question of us, you and I, uniting against the Germans, even if I tell you that personally I feel more comfortable with you than with them. Yet if I know that at a further stage I'll be obliged to say 'yes', I prefer not to say 'no' in the first place. And besides, what, for example, could I do? Send a division to Germany?' 'I am in a better position', reacted Gorbachev, 'our divisions are already there.'[137]

Gorbachev also knew that he could no more count on the support from the British Prime Minister. 'In June 1990,' writes Rodric Braithwaite, 'Mrs Thatcher came to Moscow for her last visit as Prime Minister. By then her position had changed, and she tried to convince Gorbachev that the presence of a united Germany in NATO would be a positive advantage to the Soviet Union.'[138] From these conversations Gorbachev concluded that on the question of Germany's membership in NATO he was left alone to face the Americans. In the words of Chernyaev:

> Gorbachev took the final decision to accept German membership of NATO after he came to the conclusion that all other compromise possibilities were ruled out; if he wanted to have a friendly Germany at his side, it was crucial to stop objecting. It was a personal decision without any phone calls to Moscow or consultation with the Politburo, since he was absolutely convinced of the correctness of his position and was unwilling

to place a decision of such historic significance in the hands of incompetent people.[139]

Yet it was not only 'incompetent' members of the Politburo or those who diverged from Gorbachev politically but also highly experienced experts on Germany such as Falin and Kvitsinski who were taken aback by a so radical a move on the delicate question of German membership of NATO. Falin, who says that he personally was 'in favour of the unification of Germany but against the *Anschluss*', portrays Gorbachev's position as 'historically right but tactically wrong'. In fact his main reproach was that the Soviet leader, having at first obstinately resisted the very idea of a staged movement toward the reunification of the two German states, ended up surrendering to West German diktat backed up by American pressure. In other words, had Gorbachev followed his (Falin's) suggestion of proposing a confederated state as the framework for channelling the process of reunification, the Soviet Union could have reached a more profitable solution than the 'humiliating' Arkhyz formula.[140] Falin recalls a last-minute effort to dissuade Gorbachev from 'surrendering to NATO diktat', ringing him late at night on the eve of his departure for Arkhyz with Kohl; Gorbachev, having listened to his arguments, reacted wearily and said: 'I am afraid, Valentin, the train has already left the station.'[141]

This critical reaction of a professional diplomat to an agreement that in his view was not well negotiated most probably reflects the bitterness of an old German hand who had devoted his life to building privileged relations between his country and the German nation and whose role, just at the moment when everything suddenly became possible, was reduced to the status of an observer. For Falin the significance of the Soviet–German alliance initiated by the Moscow treaty of 1970 transcended the question of bilateral relations and was intended to serve as the nucleus of a future united Europe. With the collapse of this perspective he saw the major part of his professional career reduced to futility.

> I tend to regret that in the seventies I associated myself with an attempt to devise an appropriate reaction to the *Ostpolitik* of Willy Brandt, one that would have served both our own country and Europe in general. I now see that neither at that time nor at

present were leaders in Moscow ready to understand this project or give it a worthy response.[142]

Naturally Gorbachev's main concerns during the troubled period of 1989–90 went far beyond the question of the final form of Germany's relationship with NATO. For him the fall of the Berlin Wall and even the end of the Cold War, while formidable historic achievements of his foreign policy, were not his primary goals *per se*. Along with many other manifestations of the 'new political thinking' that transformed the foreign policy of the Soviet Union and consequently the international scene, they were above all regarded as the means necessary to achieve his main objective: a successful accomplishment of his main project of internal reforms – *perestroika*.

Political *détente* in relations with the West as well as the possibility of stopping the costly arms race certainly represented necessary preconditions for the launching of this project and opened promising perspectives of international cooperation vital for the recovery and modernization of the Soviet economy. Yet at a certain stage Gorbachev was faced with a paradoxical situation: because of the aggravation of internal tensions within Soviet society, the further application of the principles of 'new thinking', instead of facilitating reforms, began instead to increase their political price.

The reason for this was the growing gap between the spectacular progress in the Soviet Union's relations with its former Western adversaries and the dramatic deterioration of the conditions of daily life of millions of Soviet citizens. After five years, many of those who found that the reforms were not bringing their promised results started to blame Gorbachev for making more of an effort to please the West than to seek solutions for the dramatic and growing problems at home. Gorbachev even complained about this situation to Bush during their meeting in Helsinki on 9 September 1990, just as the Gulf Crisis began to flare up: 'I still have to justify my position in the country, to argue the necessity of the "new thinking". This is not always easy, especially as there are still people in the West pouring oil on the fire with their views based on the past, something that only further complicates my predicament.'[143] Behind this sad remark one can perceive not only an emotional reaction – the initiator of an unprecedented change in Soviet foreign policy believed that he was not receiving the treatment he deserved; but one can detect also a cry for help addressed to the West, at a moment when the chances of survival for the policy of 'new political thinking' were becoming increasingly less certain.

# 4

# UP TO THE PEAK AND DOWN THE SLOPE

## Gorbachev's 'Anti-Fulton' Speech at the UN

Gorbachev's speech at the UN General Assembly on 7 December 1988 received a standing ovation and truly can be described as a manifesto of 'new thinking', proclaimed *urbi et orbi*. It was not only a question of its content and style, which represented a clear departure from traditional communist ideology as well as typical Soviet phraseology. According to Hans-Dietrich Genscher, 'the speech was in the spirit of Hans Jonas, a great German/American philosopher, who was compelled to leave Germany in the 1930s because he was a Jew. His book *The Imperative of Responsibility* taught us to understand that our responsibility extends beyond everyday routine, that we are responsible for the future.'[1]

In an address so different from the propaganda rhetoric of his predecessors, Khrushchev and Brezhnev, the Soviet leader hardly bothered to confirm the 'peace-loving goals' of Soviet foreign policy. Outlining the new principles that would govern his country's relations with the outside world, he talked in terms of concrete action, announcing deep unilateral troop cuts (half a million soldiers) and arms reductions along with the withdrawal of six tank divisions from Eastern Europe. In this way he publicly made it crystal clear that the 'Brezhnev Doctrine' was dead.[2]

Gorbachev solemnly declared the Soviet leadership's intention to respect 'freedom of choice' for all peoples to determine their own political and economic systems, and he appealed to all members of the international community to renounce the use of force in the settlement of international disputes. 'Force and the threat of force cannot be and should not be an instrument of foreign policy. . . . Freedom of choice is . . . a universal principle, and it should know no exceptions.'[3]

Throughout the world, the speech was headline news. Its key elements, however, had already been formulated by Gorbachev in 1987 and were formally endorsed in the summer of 1988 at the 19th Party Conference in June/July. Convened at a critical stage in the development of *perestroika*, the Conference was intended to clarify the course of reforms, apparently stalled, and to clear up the ambiguity that continued to cloud the long-term orientation of the project. Addressing Party activists (as well as the general public, since the proceedings of the Conference were broadcast live by the main Soviet TV channels), Gorbachev outlined his proposals for the radicalization of reform, expecting to obtain from the Conference a mandate to embark on the democratic transformation of the Soviet political system. However, the political direction he was proposing to the Party *nomenklatura* almost inevitably led to a fragmentation of the heterogeneous coalition of the first supporters of *perestroika* that initially had assured widespread support for Gorbachev within the Soviet political elite.

If for Gorbachev, Yakovlev, Shevardnadze, Chernyaev and other liberal elements within the academy or the world of the Moscow intelligentsia it meant a real democratization of political life and above all a definitive rejection of the Bolshevik model of socialism, the majority of top Party, army and KGB *apparatchiki* interpreted modernization of the system merely as a necessary condition for its preservation. Sooner or later the clash between these different political approaches would inevitably rise to the surface.

At the initial stage of *perestroika*, seemingly abstract questions of foreign policy did not seem to endanger the power, status or privileges of the Party *nomenklatura*. 'For a certain time the foreign policy of the Soviet Union remained an island of national consensus in the stormy sea of internal *perestroika*.'[4] Yet, sensing the subversive potential of the philosophy of 'new thinking', the conservatives launched an attack against one of its core propositions, an affirmation of the priority of 'universal human values' over 'class interests'. The debate was first provoked by the text of the 'Theses' for the Conference when Yegor Ligachev, the number two in the Party hierarchy, proposed balancing the mention of 'universal human values' with a statement reaffirming the necessity of basing Soviet foreign policy on the defence of 'class interests'. In the end, both terms were dropped from the final text, which nevertheless kept a reference to 'the primacy of law and common human morality'.[5]

Presided over by Gorbachev, the Conference ratified the positions of the reformers on all important political issues. Despite the fact that foreign policy questions occupied a rather modest place in the debate, the basic principles of the 'new thinking', including the 'freedom of choice', were formally endorsed by its participants, providing Gorbachev with a formal endorsement for his future speech at the United Nations. Former US Ambassador to the Soviet Union Jack Matlock recalls that having studied the text of the 'Thesis', received by fax late at night, he immediately called the White House and informed Reagan, who was preparing for a visit to Moscow, that apparently the text of the 'Thesis' signalled serious change: 'This is a Party text, yet the language it uses is closer to the American Constitution than to Marx or Lenin.'[6]

Speaking at a meeting at the MID several days after the Conference, Shevardnadze expanded the political offensive against the conservative camp: 'The "new thinking" places the principle of peaceful coexistence squarely in the context of the realities of the nuclear age. We refuse to regard it as a specific form of class struggle.'[7] The leading conservative, Ligachev, reacted immediately. Twice in the course of August 1988, speaking in Gorky on 5 August and in Tula on 31 August, he challenged the resolutions of the Party Conference and declared: 'We proceed from the class character of international relations. Any other presentation of the issues sows confusion among the Soviet people and among our friends abroad.'[8] Despite the fact that Ligachev ostensibly was reacting to

Shevardnadze's statement, his real target was in fact the General Secretary.

No one had any illusions – a seemingly abstract debate over the postulates of 'new thinking' barely concealed the deepening political conflict within the Soviet leadership with regard to the general orientation of the future reforms. Seeking to underline the real significance of what was taking place, Chernyaev wrote in a note to Gorbachev, who at the time of Ligachev's speeches was on holiday in the Crimea: '[Ligachev] is clearly implying that your Report at the 19th Party Conference which spoke of the "priority of humanitarian values" has brought confusion'.[9]

It was in this atmosphere of growing political tension within the Politburo that Gorbachev worked on his speech for the United Nations. Later Ligachev would claim that the text of the speech 'announcing the de-ideologization of Soviet foreign policy, contrary to the existing rules, had never been submitted for approval or discussion in the Politburo'.[10] Yet his memory must have failed him since both the basic conception and the main lines of the speech were presented by Gorbachev to the Politburo on 24 November before his departure for New York, and it did receive formal approval.[11]

The first draft was written by Chernyaev, who collected contributions from Yakovlev, Shevardnadze, Dobrynin, Falin and Akhromeev. After that, according to Chernyaev, Gorbachev himself rewrote the whole text. His ambition was far-reaching: Gorbachev thought of it as an 'anti-Fulton speech', an allusion to the occasion when Churchill first announced the existence of an 'iron curtain' that for so many years was destined to divide Europe and, indeed, the entire world. Apart from declaring important unilateral reductions of conventional forces in Eastern Europe (one of the reasons for this was the Soviet leadership's intention to eliminate its never before admitted conventional arms and troops superiority over NATO on the European continent before the beginning of the scheduled CFE – Conventional Forces in Europe – talks), Gorbachev wished to formulate a 'new doctrine' for the United Nations in what he believed to be a 'new period of world history'. He later wrote: 'I wanted to show the international community that we are entering an entirely new period of history where the former traditional principles of relations between states based on competition and the balance of power should yield place to cooperation and solidarity.'[12]

It was certainly not a coincidence that Gorbachev's formal proposal to Gromyko that he resign from the post of Chairman of the Supreme Soviet (and member of the Politburo) was made in November 1988. Addressing the UN General Assembly several weeks later, Gorbachev clearly did not want to feel the disapproving glance of the former 'Mr *Nyet*' at his back. As a loyal *apparatchik*, Gromyko obediently complied and only in conversation with his son commented bitterly on his forced retirement. He believed that Gorbachev fired him before going to New York with the obvious intention of impressing the West, and his judgement was harsh: 'When economic problems start to cause trouble at home, all Soviet leaders launch themselves in the foreign policy arena. Gorbachev is no exception.' According to Gromyko, his last conversation in the Kremlin with the man whom in March 1985 he helped to propel to the position of supreme power turned sour: 'I warned him: you are heading towards the reefs.'[13]

Gorbachev himself described his address to the United Nations as a 'watershed' for Soviet foreign policy. But certainly no less important boundaries and points-of-no-return were crossed by him domestically in his relations with the conservative section of the Party bureaucracy at home. In Chernyaev's estimation:

> It would be going too far to say that in his speech in New York Gorbachev completed his break with the psychology and manner of a Party official. But a conscious ideological retreat from orthodox class theory and methodology in the analysis of international affairs as well as in the formulation of our foreign policy (although not in every instance) did occur at precisely that time.[14]

Yet in the aftermath of his speech, Gorbachev had to come to terms with the fact that his emotional and perhaps visionary appeal to world leaders that they unite their efforts to construct a more rational, interdependent world did not produce many more enthusiastic supporters than his programme for the total elimination of nuclear weapons proposed almost two years before. 'Gorbachev's address did not get a broad response at that time; most of the "ruling circles" in the West also missed its meaning,' says Genscher.[15]

The initial reaction to Gorbachev's UN speech within the Party apparatus and even in senior military circles was mostly positive. Despite the first public clashes during the 19th Party Conference, the real internal contradictions of *perestroika* had not yet touched the public consciousness, mainly because the economic stability of the country was still largely unaffected. The breathing space offered to Gorbachev and other reformers because of the hopes awakened by the promises of *perestroika* had not yet been totally squandered, while the conflicts involving rising nationalist forces in the Soviet republics were still largely under control. Foreign policy priorities such as the withdrawal from Afghanistan and ending the arms race were still part of the consensus that continued to unify the post-Brezhnev political elite. And the consequences of the far-reaching diplomatic initiatives undertaken by the Gorbachev–Shevardnadze team did not yet touch the immediate interests of the Party apparatus or the military establishment.

The same harmony initially prevailed in Shevardnadze's relations with the Soviet military, since during the first years of *perestroika*, top Soviet military commanders shared the rest of the political elite's belief in the necessity of profound reforms and readily accepted Gorbachev as their symbol. Despite a degree of normal professional friction between the MID and the General Staff over the practical aspects of implementing decisions on the withdrawal from Afghanistan or the tactics to be used in the course of arms negotiations, both partners always managed to find compromise solutions and their representatives cooperated efficiently within the Zaikov Commission.

Yet at the beginning of 1989, within a relatively short period of time, this rather idyllic picture of national unity behind the innovative diplomacy of 'new political thinking' rather unexpectedly broke into pieces. Gorbachev's speech at the UN did in fact become a 'watershed', although not exactly in the sense that he intended.

## 1989 – The Year of 'the Great Turn'

Certainly the determining factor was the political trajectory of *perestroika* within the Soviet Union. The 'revolution of hopes', as Gorbachev himself once labelled *perestroika*, in the absence of concrete improvement in the daily lives of millions of people, began to arouse feelings of weariness and impatience and encouraged the radicalization of the 'democratic wing' of reformers united around Andrei Sakharov, Gavriil Popov and Boris Yeltsin.

On the other side of the political spectrum, the Party *nomenklatura* began to realize that the political reform for which it had voted in obedience to Gorbachev was turning into a trap. The first elections to the new Soviet Parliament in the spring of 1989 – the Congress of People's Deputies and the Supreme Soviet – turned into a political humiliation for leading Party cadres and sounded an alarm even for those who managed to pass the first test of plural candidacies. Gorbachev ceased to be the uniting figure for heterogeneous political currents and certainly was no longer taken to be a magician by a population that had invested its hopes in his project much as it would invest in a financial pyramid scheme.

Dangerous cracks appeared in the monolithic wall of the Soviet people's 'internationalist' unity. From the Karabakh enclave in the Caucusus[16] to the national elites of the Baltic republics, increasing numbers were defiantly challenging the central power. While some most radical and impatient representatives of ethnic minorities like the Crimean Tatars had already begun to protest outside the walls of the Kremlin as early as July 1987, demanding a recognition of their national rights, the republican national elites waited until the aftermath of the Party conference and the beginning of the real political changes inside Russia. On the night of 8–9 April 1989, Georgian nationalists clashed with soldiers sent to disband the popular demonstrations in Tbilisi. This confrontation turned into a tragedy with casualties among the civil population. The opening of the 1st Congress of People's Deputies on 25 May 1989, designed to mark the political triumph of Gorbachev's democratic reform, was thus overshadowed by the call to mourn the victims of Tbilisi.

In these circumstances Gorbachev was more than ever in need of a show of success, and this could be produced by foreign policy. With hopes rapidly fading for any quick, spectacular achievements on the home front, it was the mission of diplomacy to play the role of *perestroika*'s political safety belt. From the beginning of 1989, public debates on questions of foreign policy ceased to be merely formal or ceremonial and began to acquire an importance of their own, since the new approach in foreign policy began to affect the real interests of the Soviet *nomenklatura* and the military establishment.

The first signs of new embarrassing problems were related to the unforeseen development of the situation in Eastern Europe, and more precisely in Poland. In the Parliamentary elections of June 1989, the first pluralist elections in Eastern Europe after those of the Soviet Union, the Polish Communist Party headed by the new reformist General Secretary, Miecislav Rakowski, suffered a humiliating defeat. This sounded an alarm bell. During his visit to Moscow in April 1989, General Jaruzelski had discussed in advance with Gorbachev the possibility of sharing of power with the opposition in accordance with the provisions of the Roundtable Agreement of early 1989 reached between the Communist Party and the opposition.[17] Now, as the Polish Politburo discussed the catastrophic outcome of the elections, Jaruzelski firmly declared that he would respect the results of the popular vote. Most probably it was this stance which one and a half months later in July 1989 led to the General's impressive victory in the Presidential election. Curiously enough, despite his personal hesitation about running, he was eventually convinced to stand as a candidate by persons as different as Lech Wałęsa and George Bush, the latter visiting Poland at the beginning of July.[18]

Despite the fact that Gorbachev himself, in accordance with the declared principles of 'new thinking', gave the green light for power sharing in Poland between the Communist Party and the opposition ('Gorbachev believed that Soviet acceptance of Solidarity as a legitimate political player in Poland could have a moderating effect on its behavior'[19]), in the Soviet Union this first political retreat by a communist regime in Eastern Europe had a quite discernable negative effect. The fact that Solidarity won an absolute majority in the upper chamber in a political landslide and occupied its entire (pre-agreed maximum) quota of 35 per cent in the lower chamber not only meant the advent of the first anti-communist government in a member country of the Warsaw Pact, but also could potentially lead to the withdrawal of Poland (the place where it was born!) from the Pact.

Psychologically, the significance of an eventual Polish defection from the socialist camp was even more important than any hole it might leave in the strategic wall of Eastern bloc defences. The failure of the Polish communists represented a spectacular political setback for the East European 'Gorbachevists' – Jaruzelski and Rakowski were probably the closest political allies of Gorbachev in the whole 'socialist community'. Since the popular vote in Poland was a literal exercise in the use of the 'right of choice', it was a very tough first test for the principles of the 'new political thinking' that had been proclaimed by Gorbachev several months earlier at the United Nations.

Polish voters were also the first to mark the important difference in attitude toward Gorbachev's *perestroika* between public opinion in the West and in the countries of the Soviet zone. Evidently given a really free choice and relieved from the fear of an application of the 'Brezhnev Doctrine', people who had lived for several decades under the iron heel of the Soviet 'Big Brother' were much less euphoric, if not sceptical, about the momentous promises of *perestroika* and the capability of its leader to fulfil them.

For Gorbachev and his political advisers, who sincerely believed that the 'wind of democratic change' from Moscow would be met in Eastern Europe with gratitude similar to that which greeted the Red Army at the liberation from the Nazi occupation (it should not be forgotten that Gorbachev's two closest aides, Chernyaev and Shakhnazarov, had fought in the war), the shock of coming up against the disturbing reality of Eastern Europe was an astonishing and painful experience.[20] Apparently the Soviet presence in its 'zone of influence' rested exclusively on military force; in a spectacular manner the Polish case proved that having been victorious in battle, the Soviet Union failed to win the postwar peace in Eastern Europe and was on the way to an eventual defeat in the Cold War.

At the beginning, the events in Poland were interpreted by Gorbachev and his advisers as a special case with a number of specific explanations. First and foremost came the traditional Polish mistrust of the Russians and the anti-Russian complexes of the Polish intellectual elite, exacerbated during the years of Soviet postwar domination. Since the open expression of these feelings had been harshly suppressed by the pro-Soviet regime, it was only natural that with the liberalization of the political climate, even if as a direct consequence of democratization within the USSR, they logically would rise to the surface.

Another feature of Polish singularity was the fact that already prior to *perestroika* and without waiting for the arrival of Gorbachev, for some years Poland had lived the experience of a massive anti-communist opposition movement that united *Solidarność* with the cream of the Polish intellectual elite and also, certainly, the Catholic Church; the Church's spiritual (and political) influence in the country was considerably strengthened by the election in 1978 of Cardinal Karol Wojtyła, Archbishop of Kraków, as Pope John Paul II.

Yet if this reasoning helped Gorbachev and his aides to think of Poland as a kind of 'weak link' in the Warsaw Pact, it certainly did not mean that they could count on the obedient behaviour of the other members of the socialist family. After all, each Warsaw Pact member in its own way represented a 'special case' with its own unsettled accounts with the Soviet patron. After the electoral shipwreck of the Polish communists, it was the turn of relatively stable Hungary. In June 1989 the ceremony of the reburial of remains of the late Prime Minister, Imre Nagy, who had been executed by order of the Soviet government after the brutal suppression of the massive popular revolt in Budapest in November 1956, turned into a massive political demonstration with the participation of about three hundred thousand people.

This 'quiet uprising', reminiscent of the popular response to the Soviet intervention of 1956, forced another team of East European Gorbachev supporters, headed by the Party leader, Károly Grósz, who had succeeded János Kádár in 1988, to look for more spectacular ways to mark their independence from their Soviet patron. On 10 September 1989 the Hungarian government, 'without asking for Moscow's permission in order not to embarrass Gorbachev', took a decision to allow free passage to the West for several tens of thousands of East German tourists eager to flee from the GDR across the Hungarian–Austrian border that had been open for Hungarian citizens since May. 'As long as Gorbachev was in the Kremlin,' according to Gyula Horn, former Hungarian Prime Minister, 'we were assured that we should not fear any kind of sanction and certainly not a military action'.[21]

The meeting of the Political Consultative Council of the Warsaw Pact leaders in Bucharest in July 1989 had all the characteristics of a burial service, its participants in a state of dissonant confusion. East Germany's Defence Minister, Heinz Kessler, compared the meeting to an 'assembly of ghosts'.[22] While Honecker deplored the failure to resist the West's 'human rights demagogy', the Hungarians insisted on applying Western standards. Behind the scenes Ceauşescu and Honecker tried to raise the 'Polish question', hoping to persuade their colleagues of the imperative need to render 'fraternal aid' to Poland (as in the case of the 1968 Warsaw Pact intervention in Czechoslovakia).

Gorbachev's optimistic concluding statement at the end of the session rejected the notion of socialism in full retreat and was designed to save appearances: 'We should not produce the impression that socialism is living in hard times.'[23] This certainly was not enough to assure the survival of the alliance.

Even if Gorbachev was desperately trying to present the situation as one in which there was still a chance of keeping the socialist regimes of Eastern Europe afloat (and perhaps he actually believed it), the conservative opposition at his back could observe that the leader of the USSR was no longer in control of the events and processes that he himself had unleashed. Gorbachev's political opponents logically interpreted the eruption of anti-communist opposition as the direct consequence of the replacement of the 'Brezhnev Doctrine' by the principles of 'new thinking'. Quite naturally, most were concerned that the uncontrolled developments in Eastern Europe could be a forerunner of change that would threaten their own status; it was this that troubled them even more than any potential threat to the geo-strategic position of the world's second superpower.

For the Soviet generals, already unhappy about Gorbachev's intention radically to reduce the numbers of troops stationed in Eastern Europe as announced in his UN speech, the spectre of Warsaw Pact disintegration was equivalent to a revision of the results of the last world war. As for the Party *nomenklatura*, given the events in Poland, the possibility of estrangement from power by popular vote suddenly became a genuine probability which meant the end of the world as they knew it. By the spring of 1989, the most outspoken representatives of these two sections of the Soviet power structure that continued to occupy dominant positions in the Party's Central Committee were shifting to the offensive against the 'capitulationist' foreign policy of Shevardnadze, although in reality their displeasure was directed against Gorbachev. By the end of the year it was already the General Secretary himself who for the first time in Soviet political history was exposed to public accusations during the session of the Central Committee of 'pursuing pro-American foreign policy and receiving instructions from the Vatican'.[24]

Even inside the foreign policy elite it was no longer a question of understandable grumbling coming from the former 'dinosaurs' of Soviet diplomacy – Gromyko and Kornienko – sent into retirement. (Andrei Gromyko at his dacha, expressing his opinion about Shevardnadze to his son, once said: 'Gorbachev and his team are Martians who have landed on Earth by chance. Shevardnadze is hopeless. He is not a Soviet diplomat, this is a nonsense. One can't even say whose interests the "Georgian" is representing.'[25]) Kornienko, for his part, denounced the escalation of 'unilateral concessions based on the belief that the West was ripe to follow us on the road of "new political thinking"'.[26] But now it was not just the former bosses of the MID but also those who only several years before had been Gorbachev's enthusiastic followers who began to express their doubts (although in the case of most of them, retrospectively).

Anatoli Dobrynin, for long Gromyko's rival, remarked in a lecture he gave in Moscow in 1999: 'There certainly was a chance to end the Cold War without losing the achievements accumulated by Soviet foreign policy under the direction of Andrei Andreevich Gromyko – I mean by this, on equal terms

with the West.'[27] Another active member of the Gorbachev–
Shevardnadze team, the Deputy Foreign Minister, Anatoli
Adamishin, again with hindsight, blamed Gorbachev and his
former boss, Shevardnadze, for 'amateurism and naïvety'.[28] As
we have already noted, Valentin Falin was another once
devoted 'Gorbachevist' and one of the ghost writers of the
'manifesto' of 'new thinking', Gorbachev's Report to the 27th
Party Congress; but after the reunification of Germany he
became a bitter critic of Gorbachev's 'incompetence' in foreign
policy matters.

In order to gain public support for his political initiatives,
Gorbachev did not hesitate to introduce *glasnost* into the closed
world of diplomacy and tended to use every occasion, whether
during trips abroad or at his multiple public appearances at
home, to explain his actions on the international scene. This
was particularly the case in a most spectacular way after
Reykjavik and on the occasion of the signing of the INF Treaty
in Washington in December 1987.

Defending his boss against the accusations of naïvety,
Chernyaev seeks to present Gorbachev's nonconformist performance in foreign affairs as the conscious, well-calculated
tactics of a politician with his eyes wide open. 'Gorbachev
believed that a renovated Soviet Union would one day
become a real competitor of the West. Yet such reasoning
pushed him to conclude that in order to obtain a substantial
change in the West's attitude towards the Soviet Union and
destroy persisting suspicion, "we have to be the first to start
changing".'[29]

In a conversation with the UN Secretary General, Javier
Pérez de Cuéllar, whom he received in Moscow on 29 June
1987, Gorbachev in fact confirmed this ambition of his policies: 'Our tactic is to tow our partners behind us. Somebody
has to take the initiative of taking the first step – if our partners are not ready to do it, we must do it ourselves.'[30] Despite
the fact that he was referring to a concrete case – the Soviet
decision to stop listing French and British nuclear weapons in
the calculation of East–West strategic parity – Gorbachev's
explanation reflected not only his diplomatic tactics applied to
a specific case but also his general philosophy and personal
style.

Analysing this style, Chernyaev underlines Gorbachev's candour and 'artlessness'.

> He could readily accept acting on the basis of the word of honour given by his partner, assuming the apparent community of everyone's interest to stop the arms race and assure Russia's divorce from the old political system. But not all of his partners were playing according to the same rules. Noticing this, he once did not hesitate to say to Jim Baker: 'You are playing with me, it's indecent.'[31]

## Malta – a Belated Triumph

Gorbachev was particularly disappointed by the extremely restrained reaction to his breathtaking panorama of a new world coming from the new United States administration of George Bush. Having spent more than three years on attempts to build a climate of confidence in relations between Moscow and Washington and believing that he had paid a sufficient political price, Gorbachev was hoping that Soviet–American relations had acquired a solid new base for future development. Having heard Reagan publicly declare in Red Square during his visit to Moscow in May 1988 that he no longer regarded the Soviet Union as the 'evil empire',[32] he felt reassured that confrontation and mistrust in US–Soviet relations were finally gone. This explains his frustration when a 'meditation pause' in foreign policy was announced by the Bush administration, imposing something of a moratorium on political contacts with Moscow.

This disquiet on the part of Gorbachev reflected his lack of understanding of the functioning of institutions of American democracy and of the complex process involved in the elaboration of national strategy undertaken by every new US administration. But it also showed the profound asymmetry of priorities prevailing in Moscow and Washington and consequently of the working timetables of each of the two leaders. Pushed from behind by the aggravation of the internal crisis of *perestroika*, Gorbachev was impatient to be able to present a positive account of his foreign policy to the Soviet public.

George Bush, however, was taking his time. Flanked by James Baker and Brent Scowcroft, he wanted to make sure that the whole Gorbachev phenomenon and his transformation of the Soviet system had crossed the point of no return.

However, it was not yet easy to make this judgement. Not everyone in Washington, including the inner circle of Bush's team (starting with the Vice President, Dan Quayle, who characterized Gorbachev's proposals as 'marginal' and the whole *perestroika* project as 'a form of Leninism' ), was convinced of the sincerity of Gorbachev's conversion to democracy or of his chances of overcoming the growing resistance of the Party apparatus and the powerful military lobby. Analysis produced by the CIA shortly after Gorbachev's speech at the United Nations maintained that Gorbachev's 'foreign policy strategy remains in the Leninist tradition. It calls for weakening the main enemy – the United States – by exploiting "contradictions" between it and other centers of capitalist power.' The paper argued that Gorbachev was interested in weakening American global political influence, 'decoupling' Western Europe from the United States, and preserving in some form Soviet hegemony in Eastern Europe while generally trying to 'promote the interests of the USSR at the expense of the United States and other "enemies" '.[33]

At the beginning of 1989, Gorbachev certainly was not aware of all the various pressures on Bush that complicated the working out of his approach to the Soviet Union and its leader. There was also the question of Bush's natural wish to emerge from the 'shadow of Reagan' with a distinct international strategy of his own. The search for an effective counter-ploy against Gorbachev in Europe in a situation where the Soviet leader seemed to be effectively downgrading American influence was a natural part of the process of 'meditation'. Ignoring or neglecting these factors, Gorbachev felt offended by the fact that his newly discovered 'friend George' was not ready to render him the support he so badly needed.

Apparently the 'prudent' Bush, even if ready to believe in the sincerity of the Soviet leader's personal convictions and intentions, was reluctant to assume that the changes introduced by Gorbachev's domestic policies in the USSR had a real chance of transforming the existing system and surviving their initiator. The hesitations of the American President were shared and indeed inflated by his closest aides on the White House staff. Bush's National Security Adviser, Brent Scowcroft, was categorical in a public statement of January 1989: '. . . the Cold War is not over'. Several months later, in May, the White House spokesman Marlin Fitzwater accused Gorbachev of 'playing a PR game', and compared his initiatives on arms control to the behaviour of a 'drugstore-cowboy', a barb for which he received immediate and enthusiastic support from Dan Quayle.[34]

The prevailing slogans in the White House at the beginning of 1989 were 'test the Soviets' and 'let Moscow stew in its own juices'. Bush himself, explaining why he chose the 'no hurry' tactics in relations with Gorbachev, often repeated that if the opportunities Gorbachev offered were real, they would not vanish.[35] This mood contrasted sharply with that of Gorbachev, under increasing pressure to present at least some practical results of *perestroika* to his national public in order to temper the growing impatience of the Soviet population; he also was extremely conscious of the fact that the fragile achievements of the reforms he was struggling to introduce could easily vanish as a result of a counterattack by conservative forces.

Yuli Vorontsov, the former First Deputy to Shevardnadze and at one time the Soviet Ambassador in Washington, thinks that the leaders of the two countries missed a 'rendez-vous' with each other, and explains this by the 'difference in political cultures' of Bush and Gorbachev: 'One [Gorbachev] believed too much in the importance of a policy based on good personal relations, the other [Bush] was coolly concentrated on national interests.'[36] Though quite accurate in presenting the difference in psychological profile of the two leaders, this explanation underestimates the tremendous asymmetry of political conditions in which Bush and Gorbachev were operating, and consequently of their priorities. Yet the width of the gap that separated them, especially at the beginning of Bush's mandate, only heightens the value of their common effort and of the results they achieved, building personal trust and *de facto* accomplishing a synchronization of their foreign policy activity.

It was not before a public speech in May 1989, addressing the question of US policy towards the Soviet Union, that George

Bush for the first time pledged to move 'beyond containment'. It was not only Gorbachev's own statements and performance at home and on the international scene that eventually allowed him to pass the test in the eyes of the White House. During the 'pause' in American contacts with Moscow, most European allies of the United States in different ways tried to influence Bush's position, encouraging him to support Gorbachev and his efforts more energetically.

Already in the first years of *perestroika*, European leaders were more enthusiastic about Gorbachev and less suspicious about his intentions than the Americans. Yet if the Thatcher and Mitterrand initial 1984 and 1985 recommendations to Reagan to treat Gorbachev with all seriousness were based largely on instinct and the surprise discovery of an atypical leader in the Kremlin, two years later in February 1987, Hans-Dietrich Genscher, speaking in Davos, appealed to Western colleagues to 'to take Gorbachev at his word and not to miss a chance offered by history'.[37] By then his views were based on the first results of Gorbachev's reforms.

By the spring of 1989, most European political leaders were convinced that *perestroika* in the Soviet Union deserved active encouragement and support from the West. Some, like Mitterrand, were worried by the possibility that with the change of President in Washington, the process of democratization of the Soviet system could be deprived of the West's backing and consequently interrupted. During the first NATO summit attended by Bush in Brussels (May 1989), Mitterrand chose enthusiastically to express his support for the new US President's proposals to innovate NATO, just to ensure that Bush would not ignore his appeal to pay attention to the 'colossal changes in the East initiated by Mikhail Gorbachev'.[38]

Sensing this concern on the part of his European partners, Gorbachev willingly shared with them his embarrassment at Bush's enigmatic 'pause'. On a number of occasions throughout 1989, he tried to use his contacts with European leaders to exercise pressure on Washington, or at least to convey to the American President his impatience. Gorbachev's nervousness inflamed by his southerner's temper and the gravity of domestic problems that could no longer be solved without outside help regularly gave rise to the suspicion that the US administration was seeking to 'discredit' him and to counter his 'new thinking' diplomacy with an American offensive in Eastern Europe.

After his speech at the UN, Gorbachev believed that the question of the Soviet Union's relations with the West had finally been clarified. He was convinced that his display of goodwill and his statement of intentions as well as his show of resolve to reform Soviet socialism were sufficient for his Western colleagues to accept him as a trustworthy partner. But as he failed to observe any reciprocity from Washington, he began to suspect that Bush 'had in mind . . . to undermine the Soviet Union's international initiatives'.[39]

Remembering the crucial role that Margaret Thatcher had played in establishing his fruitful personal relations with Ronald Reagan, Gorbachev appealed to the 'Iron Lady' once again: 'Apparently our reforms frightened the administration and the US has begun to look for ways to check Gorbachev's international influence,' he complained to Thatcher, referring to himself in the third person. He even shared with her 'information he had acquired through his own channels [meaning the KGB] that the CIA and State Department had created a special commission whose goals included discrediting perestroika and its initiator'.[40]

Kohl, meeting Gorbachev in Bonn in June 1989, tried to reassure him, saying: 'I can tell you that Bush is able and willing to do business with you.'[41] The French President did the same. Meeting Gorbachev in Moscow, Mitterrand told him that Bush was quite positive about *perestroika* and about Gorbachev personally, and that there was no need to fear a double-dealing US policy in Eastern Europe.[42]

Mitterrand was right. Although in his memoirs Bush retrospectively writes that upon embarking on his official duties, he decided to balance the existing privileged US–Soviet relations with a stronger accent on Eastern Europe, nevertheless during his visits to Poland and Hungary in the summer months of 1989, he explicitly stressed the crucial importance of Gorbachev's success in the Soviet Union for the advance of their own democratic reforms.[43] In fact it was after these visits that Bush, having observed the formidable change taking place in Eastern Europe under the direct influence of reforms in the

Soviet Union and weary of his aides' repeated reservations, declared to his inner circle: 'This guy IS perestroika', and that he wanted him to succeed.[44]

Just as Bush had to resist the pressure of his 'Gorby-skeptics' in Washington, Gorbachev in turn was constantly up against the 'America-phobes' in his own entourage. The KGB chief, Kryuchkov, regularly submitted reports about the 'anti-Gorbachev' scenarios elaborated by the CIA, while Falin curiously inherited the credo of his despised former boss, Andrei Gromyko: 'never make any concessions to the Americans since they don't understand any language other than that of force and don't respect weak partners'.[45] This may explain why even on his way to Malta in November 1989, Gorbachev continued to complain about Bush's 'duplicity' during his meeting in Italy with Giulio Andreotti.[46]

It was only after he met George Bush during the 'seasick summit', as it was dubbed by NBC news anchor Tom Brokaw, which took place aboard the Soviet cruise liner *Maxim Gorky* in the rough waters of the bay of Malta on 2–3 December 1989, that he finally abandoned his remaining complexes and suspicions; he could not fail to be impressed by the degree of confidence shown to him by his American colleague and by his apparent willingness to move 'beyond containment' toward the integration of the Soviet Union into the international system. Chernyaev has acknowledged that it was only at Malta that Gorbachev and his team discovered the extent of the 'genuine and laborious "homework"' in which the Bush administration had been engaged during the 'pause' between January and May 1989, as well as the degree of resistance they had to overcome in order to arrive at a turning point in the attitude towards Gorbachev's policies. 'At Malta, Gorbachev was truly impressed by the fact that Bush and Baker came with concrete proposals that confirmed their resolve to begin a new stage in US–Soviet relations.'[47]

Despite the troubled sea (or perhaps also because of it) at Malta, the two Presidents quickly established good personal relations. There was not much controversy between them during the discussions. When the US President raised the question of Soviet support for Castro's Cuba, Gorbachev evaded a direct answer and said, 'You are exaggerating our possibilities of influencing him.' About military aid to the Sandinistas in Nicaragua, however, he reassured the Americans that the Soviet Union had already stopped the shipment of weapons since April 1989.[48]

Bush paid back Gorbachev in his own coin when the two Presidents moved to the German question and Gorbachev suggested that both states refrain from interfering in the complicated situation, i.e. allowing its natural evolution without 'pushing from outside'. Bush mildly remarked: 'We cannot be asked to disapprove of German unification.' At the same time he reminded Gorbachev the he had conducted himself in ways not to complicate his life. 'That is why I have not jumped up and down on the Berlin Wall,' repeated the American President.[49] On the whole both discovered many more subjects on which they could agree. Their new *'entente'* was confirmed by the exchange of two solemn statements made during the summit. Bush and Baker told Gorbachev that they were convinced that he wanted real democratic change in his country and that the US government was ready to discuss different ways to assist him. Bush went as far as to promise to Gorbachev to waive the Jackson–Vanick amendment, which since the Brezhnev years had prohibited the 'Most Favored Nation' status to the Soviet Union. 'For the first time the Americans made a commitment to give economic support to perestroika, to our reforms,' writes Chernyaev, adding: 'We know now that it was a long way from promises to real actions, and we never received what was pledged.'[50] Gorbachev for his part declared to Bush that the Soviet leadership no longer regarded the United States as the enemy and that Moscow considered the American military presence in Europe as a factor for stability.[51]

Curiously the most lively debate was provoked by a philosophical rather than a political subject. Bush praised the recent events that had occurred in the East European countries as proof of the 'efficiency of Western values'. Gorbachev objected, joined by Yakovlev, since in his view such a reading of events downgraded the significance of democratic reforms in the Soviet Union. The compromise formula that found its place in the final communiqué referred to universal 'democratic values'.[52]

At the conclusion of the summit, Gorbachev had good reason to be satisfied. He told Bush before their joint on-board press conference: 'What we had expected from the US President was not just a statement of facts but concrete steps in line with those statements. Now we've seen those steps.'[53] At the press conference Gorbachev announced to the journalists that the USSR no longer regarded the US as its adversary.

Observed from the outside by other political leaders, the Malta summit appeared to be an indisputable triumph for Gorbachev. According to Jacques Attali, the reaction of Mitterrand was unequivocal: 'George Bush confirmed his support for Gorbachev's policies and expressed his intention to integrate the USSR into the international community.' As for the position of Gorbachev himself, according to the French President, 'he has never looked so strong. He's managed to dominate the Party leadership and progressively eliminate his political enemies.'[54]

Yet Gorbachev's psychological triumph at Malta unfortunately came too late. If he felt finally rewarded for his efforts (and patience), his satisfaction had a bitter taste; in order to reach this place he had invested an enormous amount of effort and taken numerous unilateral steps. As a result he had wasted an important part of what probably was his most valuable asset, his window of time to prove to the people of his country that his project was worth following and would bring rewards.

Finally recognized as the 'intimate partner' of the West, he was no longer in a position adequately to fulfil this role, due to the progressive weakening of his internal position. While less and less in control of events at home because of the accelerating deterioration of the economic situation, he was increasingly dependent on Western help. In this new political environment, the initial function of foreign policy was transformed: once Gorbachev's political trump card and the most effective way to promote the 'new political thinking', it increasingly had become *perestroika*'s last resort. Consequently the diplomatic sphere, which until then had largely been exempt from internal political battles, unexpectedly turned into a front line. 'In the summer of 1989 the Supreme Soviet without a single opposing vote ratified my nomination to the position of Minister of Foreign Affairs,' Shevardnadze writes bitterly, 'but in October 1990 a number of People's Deputies accused me of causing damage to the national interest.'[55]

During the last two years of Gorbachev's stay in power, the foreign policy of *perestroika*, no longer reflecting a consensus within the political class, largely turned into his own personal fiefdom. Without any doubt this situation was the necessary condition that allowed to him to accomplish a number of historic breakthroughs on the world political scene, yet for the same reason it additionally threatened his position, making him more vulnerable and politically isolated at home.

The end of 1989 thus marked for Gorbachev the crossing of a psychological Rubicon in his relations with the West. The important shift initiated by his speech at the UN was complete by January 1990. Starting the year resolved to 'conquer the West' and win the confidence of its leaders in the hope of persuading them to join him in the implementation of his messianic project to construct a non-violent and interdependent world, he ended it having gained the full trust of his partners while abandoning many of his own stereotypes and prejudices. He thus took an important step forward, parting with his initial, rather ideological, although certainly no longer communist project, and accepting the much more realistic perspective of building a partnership in order to reach commonly established goals.

## On the Other Bank of the Rubicon

Soon after the Malta summit, a further aggravation of the political and economic situation within the Soviet Union and the obvious deep cracks in the walls of the Warsaw Pact dramatically weakened Gorbachev's position, putting the agreements he had reached with the US President to a serious test.

Foreign policy issues suddenly intruded during debates in the plenary sessions of the Central Committee. Not only Shevardnadze but also the General Secretary himself was subjected to increasingly aggressive criticism by other the members of the Party leadership, a scene hardly conceivable a year earlier. The accelerated meltdown of Soviet superpower status and the shrinking of its sphere of influence throughout the world but above all in Eastern Europe added oil to the fire. Shevardnadze was the one most exposed to censure and became the principal target. But it was clearly understood that he was not being denounced by the conservatives for engaging in 'Shevardnadze diplomacy' but for implementing Gorbachev's foreign policy. Shevardnadze later would compare the attacks against him in these months to 'McCarthyism'.

'The resistance to the new diplomacy was much more aggressive than our own political offensive, since, after all, we tried to advance using only political methods and, I would say, wearing white gloves,' said the former Deputy Foreign Minister, Anatoli Adamishin. He was specifically referring to the practice introduced by Yegor Ligachev – the number two in the Party hierarchy – who 'at times would not hesitate to rewrite the protocols of the Secretariat, editing them in the way he preferred and often completely changing the conclusions reached during the debate'.[56]

In the spring of 1990, Ligachev, by this time certainly Gorbachev's leading political opponent, sent him a letter in which he wrote: 'The Party expects from the Central Committee an analysis of the situation in Eastern Europe. The socialist community is falling apart and NATO is gaining force. The German question has come to the fore. I am convinced that historically this means only a temporary retreat for socialism and that eventually the communist idea will triumph.'[57]

Not only the conservative Party *apparatchiki* but also the traditionally obedient generals (in accordance with Soviet political tradition, they occupied a number of prestige slots on the Central Committee) dared openly to challenge the General Secretary, who was in fact their Commander in Chief. In June 1990, a month after Gorbachev's return from the US–Soviet summit in Washington, General Makashov launched the offensive: 'The Soviet army is leaving the countries that our fathers liberated from fascism without a fight,' he said during the Plenum of the Central Committee.[58] Several other speakers did not hesitate to define Gorbachev's political triumph at Malta as a 'Munich'. Speaking in the Supreme Soviet, Shevardnadze dismissed this challenge, arguing that the use of force in Germany to block reunification would have provoked the danger of a 'third world war'.[59]

As for Gorbachev, he never bothered to answer Ligachev's letter. At the time the General Secretary was busy building an alternative political base which would derive its legitimacy from the new Soviet Parliament rather than the Politburo. With the evident breakdown of the initial consensus on foreign policy, Gorbachev and his foreign policy team were determined not to swerve from their avowed political course or fail to fulfil the obligations they had undertaken with regard to their Western partners; they therefore had to seek ways to bypass the barrier of obtaining obligatory approval from the Politburo. After his election by the Congress of People's Deputies on 15 March 1990 as President of the USSR, although Gorbachev remained General Secretary of the Party and was still obliged to consult the Politburo on major political issues, he no longer had to fear the possibility of dismissal by his Party colleagues, as in the case of Khrushchev.[60]

Since the first plural Parliamentary elections in 1989, the new Parliament and the Party functioned as separate political actors, with the former no longer taking orders from the latter. Moreover, with the revision of Article 6 of the Soviet Constitution initiated by Gorbachev, the Communist Party lost its formal designation as the 'nucleus of the Soviet political system'; in other words, its legal status as the 'ruling party'.

This consequently transformed the previously unquestionable authority of the highest Party bodies, the Politburo and the Secretariat of the Central Committee. The Secretariat, chaired for several years by Ligachev, was abolished soon after the 28th Party Congress in the summer of 1990. As for the Politburo, from its role as the supreme authority, the directing organ, it became a 'consultative body'. The President was thus able to profit from the freedom assured by his new status; he began to reduce his consultations with the Party hierarchy to a pure formality, sometimes ignoring it altogether.

With regard to domestic political problems, even in the new circumstances, Gorbachev was obliged to function within the framework of the existing system of checks and balances; almost daily he had to manoeuvre between the Parliament, Politburo and leaders of republics, constantly improvising new political compromises. Gorbachev naturally kept the Minister of Defence, Yazov, informed about his most important foreign policy moves, especially in the sphere of disarmament, but even that was not systematic, since nothing obliged him to do it.[61] 'Having become President, the General Secretary *de facto* turned into a Tsar,' remarked General Starodubov. 'There remained nobody to challenge him.'[62]

The Politburo sessions, except for rare occasions, gradually transformed into information meetings where no serious problems involving state responsibility were genuinely debated. With good reason it might be suspected that this was a conscious tactic adopted by Gorbachev and largely supported by his most radical aides, such as Chernyaev and Shakhnazarov as well as Yakovlev, who regarded the Politburo and more generally the whole Party structure as an annoying impediment to the great reform.

However, no other political structure was created to replace the Politburo as an embodiment of the traditional principle of 'collective leadership'. A new Security Council created in November 1990 to replace the Presidential Council practically never met. Previously established procedures for the circulation of documents among the members of the Politburo and Secretariat were increasingly neglected; records of Gorbachev's meetings with foreign political leaders were only occasionally distributed among a haphazardly chosen group of recipients, whereas several sensitive political subjects, including German reunification, were, even at the most crucial stage (from the autumn of 1989), 'totally withdrawn from collective debate in the Politburo'.[63] Consequently the whole process of decision-making gradually evolved into sporadic meetings convened in the President's office with the participation of one or several of his assistants and an indeterminate number of advisers and heads of relevant agencies designated personally by him.

The only exception was the Zaikov Commission, which continued to function. Yet its status had changed considerably. In previous years the authority of *piaterka* recommendations was assured, not only because it was the meeting place for the most competent experts from the MID, the Ministry of Defence, the KGB, the VPK and the International Department, but above all by the fact that the heads of these bodies were almost all members of the Politburo. With the spectacular downgrading of the Politburo within the Soviet system, the weight of the *piaterka* also declined. Its competence was now limited to the 'technical' discussion of purely military subjects; political directives for most important negotiations with the West were now drafted by the assistants of Gorbachev and Shevardnadze and formally circulated among a limited number of members of the Politburo and the Security Council. 'We were no longer receiving written directives from the Politburo,' recalls Shevardnadze's aide Sergei Tarasenko, 'and formulated them ourselves in accordance with the logic of negotiations.'[64] More often than not, the Minister of Foreign Affairs discussed policy directives directly with the President, with Zaikov summoned afterwards and instructed to obtain formal ratification by the Commission.

This situation created new problems not only for Gorbachev's relations with the conservative wing of the political establishment, but also with his close political allies, who sometimes learned of important diplomatic moves or shifts in the official Soviet position only after the fact from Shevardnzde's reports or during his press conferences. Further difficulties were caused by the progressive estrangement from the decision-making process of all alternative positions or those holding different opinions, including experts of the International Department or the academic institutes.

The case of Valentin Falin, certainly one of the most competent German specialists in the Soviet foreign policy establishment, was particularly striking. Simply because he was head of the International Department of the Central Committee, he was excluded from the consultations on the question of German reunification at the most crucial point in time, largely at the behest of Shevardnadze. His memoirs sum up his disappointment with Gorbachev's practice of diplomacy: 'The price for Gorbachev's "universal human values" turned out to be the decay and finally the demise of the Soviet Union.'[65]

Chernyaev has on many occasions provided justification for Gorbachev's assumption of almost total responsibility for all major strategic decisions. In his view, retrospectively confirmed by Gorbachev, the progressive distancing of the Politburo from decision-making on crucial foreign policy issues was necessary because 'if we had followed all the formal procedures, bringing such hot topics before the conservative majority in the Politburo, we never would have achieved real results'. In addition to this classical reformer's argument, Chernyaev adds: 'After all, most of them [the Politburo members] were in no way competent to discuss these complex subjects and perhaps were even unable to understand them.'[66]

These self-justifying arguments produced by Gorbachev and his most loyal aides of those days have considerable validity. Similar explanations for the new, 'simplified' procedures have been given by Shevardnadze's former assistants Teimuraz Stepanov and Sergei Tarasenko, athough both stressed the point that their boss was still handling official directives from the Politburo with extreme caution. On a number of occasions (the most prominent example, his speech at the Berlin meeting of Foreign Ministers of the '2 + 4' countries in June 1990), Shevardnadze was capable of expressing an overtly hard-line position, sounding rather like his predecessor Gromyko. It is difficult to know for sure whether this reflected some of his own frustration and hesitations about the out-of-control advancing process toward German reunification or whether it was a tactical ruse, as claimed by Tarasenko, intended to demonstrate the limits and ineffectiveness of direct confrontation with the West to his colleagues in the Politburo several weeks before the 28th Party Congress.[67]

In July on the eve of the Congress, in order to be able to defend his position (and protect the delicate process of German reunification), Shevardnadze even 'conspired' with James Baker, convincing him to issue a statement during the London session of the NATO Council confirming the West's readiness to engage in a serious reform of NATO in response to Soviet concerns. The document adopted by the Council was in fact the first time in NATO's history in which the Soviet Union was referred to as a 'partner' rather than as a potential enemy; it announced a revision of NATO's strategy of 'gradual containment', replacing it with a new doctrine according to which nuclear arms could only be used as an ultimate 'last resort'. Shevardnadze's Secretariat was the first body to receive this text in the USSR, before it reached all the news agencies, including, of course, TASS. This tactic gave Shevardnadze the chance to produce his own positive public assessment of the new NATO strategy before its significance could be analysed by the Soviet General Staff – Marshal Akhromeev was in fact about to dismiss it as a 'propaganda trick'.[68]

Yet despite the fact that after heated debates, the 28th Congress formally approved Gorbachev's positions on both domestic and foreign policy, to some extent it was a pyrrhic victory. In the months that followed, there was a deepening antagonism between representatives of the Party and military establishments and the Gorbachev–Shevardnadze duo. 'The generals hated Gorbachev and Shevardnadze for the decision to evacuate the GDR and Eastern Europe,'[69] and by the autumn of 1990 they no longer felt any obligation to conceal their fury. In November 1990, at the signing of the CFE Treaty in Paris, the Soviet Defence Minister, Dimitri Yazov, who was present at the ceremony, was angry enough to lose all reserve and say to the other members of the Soviet delegation: 'This Treaty means we have lost World War III without a shot being fired.'[70]

By the beginning of 1991, given the development of a grave political crisis in the country with the mobilizing potential of *perestroika* largely exhausted, the monopolization of decision-making power in the hands of Gorbachev gradually turned into a trap. Feeling more and more politically isolated, he felt obliged even further to reduce the circle of persons involved in the elaboration of his most important decisions, but at the implementation stage he had to depend on the apparatus and on collaborators in whom he did not have full confidence. In addition, Gorbachev's sources of information (controlled by conservative lieutenants such as Kryuchkov and Boldin[71]) and his range of choice were becoming increasingly hazardous and circumscribed.

More and more often the President was forced to take solitary decisions, which increased the risk of miscalculation or error. In this situation, as the processes of internal destabilization rapidly accelerated while dramatic developments on the international scene continued apace, he was compelled to take a great number of crucial political decisions based largely on instinct, intuition and of course his convictions and moral principles. It was perhaps the world's historic good fortune and without any doubt a proof of the outstanding qualities of the man that he basically managed to avoid the wrong choices.

One of the gravest international crises to surface at that moment put the new Soviet diplomacy to an extremely difficult test – the invasion of Kuwait in August 1990 by Saddam Hussein.

## The War in the Gulf and Shevardnadze's Resignation

Had George Bush wanted to check the sincerity of his new 'partner's' declarations, he could hardly have staged a better test than the invasion of Kuwait by Saddam Hussein. At that moment Gorbachev was on summer holiday at his Crimean dacha at Foros. The adviser on international affairs who accompanied him, Anatoli Chernyaev, received the news in a phone call from Shevardnadze on the night of 2 August 1990.

It was already morning in Eastern Siberia where the Minister was having talks in Irkutsk with the US Secretary of State, James Baker, from whom he learned the news before it was later confirmed by Soviet military intelligence. Baker was supposed to go to Ulan Bator on that very day, but after brief hesitation and consultation with George Bush, he decided to shorten his visit to Mongolia and to return to Washington, making a stopover in Moscow. Speaking to Chernyaev, Shevardnadze suggested that it was a profitable opportunity to synchronize American and Soviet positions and issue a joint statement condemning Saddam's aggression. Naturally he wanted Gorbachev's approval.

Chernyaev records that he supported the idea of a common statement but decided not to wake up Gorbachev in the middle of the night, telling Shevardnadze that he did not expect Gorbachev to oppose the idea. Yet by morning, having collected all the night's information and entering Gorbachev's study for his daily report, he confesses that he was no longer totally sure about his boss's reaction. After all, just as most other Arab countries throughout the decades of the Cold War, Iraq was a traditional strategic partner and client of the Soviet Union in the Middle East. Additionally, by 'giving up' Saddam, Moscow would sustain heavy risk and material loss (oil and weapons contracts worth $1.2 billion plus the presence in the country of large numbers of Soviet military and civilian experts).[72]

To his great satisfaction, Gorbachev's immediate reaction was the one he had hoped for. 'He described Saddam's action as aggression, saying that it could not be tolerated. Naturally he approved the idea of a strong common US–Soviet condemnation as proposed by Shevardnadze.' Later in the day, when Bush called him in Foros, Gorbachev stated unequivocally that this aggression could not be justified. By reacting in this way, writes Chernyaev, 'Gorbachev showed that ideological considerations had absolutely given way to principles of morality and law. Gorbachev proved by this action that he truly considered these principles to be the core of world politics from the point of view of Soviet–American relations.'[73]

Of course, along with moral considerations, there were other, political factors that were pushing Gorbachev to react in this way. As noted by Sergei Tarasenko, 'at that time the international status of the Soviet Union, weakened by the development of the country's internal crisis, depended on proximity to the United States'.[74] This analysis is confirmed by the message Gorbachev asked Arbatov to transmit to his friends in the Arab countries in the autumn of 1990: 'Tell them that we will not sacrifice our alliance with the US for this.'[75]

Commenting on the US–Soviet common front *vis-à-vis* the invasion of Kuwait and referring specifically to the joint statement he signed with James Baker at Vnukovo (the airport just outside Moscow) on 3 August 1990, Shevardnadze writes in his memoirs: 'Had the international community not condemned the aggression against Kuwait, it would have meant that the world gained nothing from the end of the Cold War and the abandonment of confrontation.'[76] Yet while Shevardnadze (and Tarasenko) retrospectively tend to identify Gorbachev's position totally with that of his Foreign Minister, Chernyaev introduces a certain nuance. In his view the difference of approach that subsequently developed into a sizable distinction explains the 'Primakov case', which several months later provoked an irritated reaction from the 'touchy Georgian' (see below).

In fact while Shevardnadze, in total agreement with Baker, was ready to escalate the pressure on Saddam, threatening him with punitive military action, throughout the evolution of the

Gulf crisis practically until the beginning of the war Gorbachev was looking for the possibility of finding a solution without the use of force. He 'never wavered on the issue of having to push back the aggressor or that the principles of the reborn UN had to triumph. . . . However he was repelled by the mass use of modern weapons and deeply concerned to keep casualties to a minimum.'[77]

Another key element of Gorbachev's reaction to the invasion of Kuwait was his immediate suggestion to involve the United Nations. This important 'detail' suggests an additional reason why Gorbachev chose to stay close to Bush from the very beginning of the Gulf crisis: it was 'his wish to use all means to keep the search for a solution of this international crisis within the framework of the UN and the Security Council in order to assure its legality from the point of view of international law'.[78]

'We knew perfectly well that the US was capable of punishing Saddam on its own,' remarks Tarasenko.

> Yet the fact that they accepted the need to seek a UN mandate was extremely important and had to be supported. Having stuck by the United States, we could continue to play a certain role in these events. We did manage to postpone the beginning of the war providing additional space for diplomacy. Whereas if we had taken an anti-American position, we would have obtained nothing.[79]

Shevardnadze gives a more political, perhaps philosophical evaluation of the significance of the unprecedented cooperation established by the two superpowers, both concerned by the Iraqi dictator's challenge to world stability:

> For the first time in political history an act of aggression by one state against another was punished strictly on the basis of international law, following a mandate from the Security Council. This could only have happened thanks to the fact that the 'new political thinking' was applied to international relations, creating a unique chance to build effective mechanisms for defending law and justice.[80]

With this interpretation, Shevardnadze follows Gorbachev's presentation of 'new thinking' as a form of universal ideology for a global world, capable of revitalizing the United Nations, whose role since its creation in 1945 was considerably limited by the confrontation between the two superpowers. Like Shevardnadze, Gorbachev saw the new relations between the Soviet Union and the United States, confirmed by the Gulf crisis, as a historic opportunity for the UN to start functioning for the first time in its history in accordance with its Charter as the international arbiter and protector of international peace and stability.

The date 29 November 1990 can justly be considered to be a crucial moment in the history of the United Nations. On this day the Soviet and US representatives on the Security Council, supported by the majority of its members, voted for resolution 678 authorizing the use of 'all necessary means', including force, to compel Saddam Hussein to evacuate Kuwait.[81] There was now reason to believe that in the future, the functioning of the UN supreme body would no longer be restricted by ideological confrontation between the two superpowers or their strategic rivalry.

In this context, James Baker's remark associating the real end of the Cold War with this vote in November 1990 becomes understandable. His Soviet colleague Shevardnadze, as Aleksandr Bessmertnykh recalls, not only actively supported the draft proposed by the Americans, but, unexpectedly for many, was the one who energetically advocated the eventual use of force against Baghdad. Shevardnadze's critics at home (Falin among them) interpreted this zeal as a sign that the Soviet Minister had by this time virtually identified his position with that of his American 'friends'.[82] (Perhaps unknowingly, Falin was echoing the views of his despised former boss; as noted earlier in this chapter, Gromyko once told his son that he did not know 'whose interests the "Georgian" is representing'.)

Such strong language can naturally be explained by political divergence, but certainly also by the personal rivalry that separated these veteran Soviet diplomats from the outsider who had intruded into their closed corporate world. Needless to say, the interpretation of a certain emotional fervour on Shevardnadze's part provided by his aides (e.g. Tarasenko) is different: they report how repugnant he found the cynicism and perfidy of Saddam's action and refer to the Soviet Minister's 'Caucasian temperament'. However, it would be reasonable to seek additional reasons for his energetic behaviour.

One explanation has been suggested by Bessmertnykh, who at the time was the Soviet Ambassador to Washington. In his view, Shevardnadze went to New York with the evident intention of presenting the Soviet position in an uncompromising manner, seeking to 'kill' the mission of Evgeny Primakov, who had been dispatched by Gorbachev to Baghdad in order to try to persuade Saddam to evacuate Kuwait voluntarily and accept the demands of the Security Council. Shevardnadze in fact went much further than intended at that time by Gorbachev. While on a number of occasions during the autumn of 1990 Gorbachev maintained that 'he would stand by Bush in any situation', during his numerous telephone conversations with the US President (one of them, on 18 January, a week before the beginning of the US land operation, lasted for an hour and a half), he kept emphasizing the need to use all possible means to search for a political solution which in his view would be infinitely preferable to the use of force.[83]

The idea for Primakov's mission, according to Chernyaev, came out of the one-day US–Soviet summit in Helsinki on 9 September 1990. As he says, it was Bush himself who, with the apparent intention of proving to Gorbachev that Saddam was 'hopeless', suggested that the Soviets 'use their contacts in the region' to make an attempt to obtain the evacuation of Kuwait peacefully. Primakov, a member of the Presidential Council and long-time Soviet expert on Middle East affairs, went to Baghdad several times to meet Saddam and try not only to get him to agree to the liberation of Soviet experts and other foreign citizens who had been taken hostage (he succeeded), but also to convince him to accept the conditions of the Security Council's resolution.

Primakov's activity profoundly irritated Shevardnadze, not only because the two men approached the possible ways of finding a solution differently. While Shevardnadze was an almost unconditional supporter of US tactics, having apparently promised Baker that he would have Moscow's total support, Primakov, with many personal friends among the Arab leaders, was more reserved about the American position. According to Primakov, the purpose of the first Gulf War for the United States was to a large extent 'the wish to demonstrate American military supremacy, much like using the A-bomb in Hiroshima in 1945'. This in his opinion explains why the Americans 'were not interested in a political solution'.[84]

Yet the basic reason for what became an almost open conflict between Gorbachev's two close associates was largely personal, since the perhaps over-sensitive Shevardnadze viewed Primakov's mission as a sign of Gorbachev's mistrust, a feeling that only got stronger after he learned that Gorbachev intended to send Primakov to London and Washington to report to Thatcher and Bush about the results of his trip to Iraq. At a most crucial moment, it looked as though another Soviet political figure had appeared on the international stage, while Shevardnadze was pushed into the shadows. 'This situation certainly damaged the relations between Gorbachev and Shevardnadze,' remarks Bessmertnykh.[85]

The rivalry between the two men (Shevardnadze and Primakov) led to an unprecedented episode in the history of Soviet diplomacy: on behalf of Shevardnadze, the Soviet Ambassador to Washington advised the American President not to take seriously any information brought to him by Primakov, despite the fact that the latter was coming as Gorbachev's personal envoy. After Falin's exercise in personal diplomacy on the German question, Shevardnadze's escapade illustrates the growing degree of indiscipline, if not chaos, that reigned in Moscow in the daily administration of foreign affairs.

Primakov also cites a 'very unhappy' phone conversation during which Shevardnadze alluded to rumours according to which Primakov was seeking to become his successor.[86] Later, Gorbachev assumed that one of the main reasons that might explain Shevardnadze's surprise announcement in the Supreme Soviet of his resignation on 20 December 1990 was his feeling that he did not have the complete trust of the President during the delicate period of the Persian Gulf crisis. 'He must have interpreted the involvement of Primakov as a sign of personal mistrust. Also, he was very upset by the possibility that this situation could undermine his status in the eyes of his Western colleagues,' assumes Gorbachev.[87]

In fact by the late autumn of 1990, Shevardnadze had a number of reasons for feeling alienated. Not only had he partly been discharged from the handling of the Kuwait crisis, he was also exposed to growing political pressure from conservative forces. The Minister's relations with the military, irremediably damaged ever since the army's involvement in the bloody suppression of popular demonstrations in Tbilisi in April 1989, were progressively deteriorating. According to Tarasenko, Shevardnadze's personal relations with the Chief of General Staff, Marshal Akhromeev, were 'horrible'; they certainly were not improved by the fact that the Minister did not hesitate to challenge the position of the military on such sensitive issues as the 'nonconformity' of the Krasnoyarsk radar station to the provisions of the ABM treaty or to denounce their 'cheating' when calculating the number of the Soviet tanks to be eliminated in the framework of the CFE.

By December 1990, Shevardnadze's reserves of patience were apparently exhausted. Later he would say that he was still ready to stand firm against the attacks of his political opponents in the Parliament and in the Party but could not endure the lack of political support from Gorbachev. The man who only a year before had personified what united the broad political coalition of initial supporters of *perestroika* (including Gorbachev) ended up marginalized and fiercely attacked by the military, the old Party bureaucracy and even an important part of the new-born Parliament. After his resignation he stayed on in office at the behest of Gorbachev until his successor could be appointed in January 1991 – the former USSR Ambassador to the US, Aleksandr Bessmertnykh.

The resignation of Shevardnadze marked a symbolic end to a whole chapter in the trajectory of *perestroika*. (The personal alliance between Gorbachev and Shevardnadze was never restored, although after the August coup Shevardnadze acceded to Gorbachev's request and returned to the post of Minister of Foreign Affairs; he lasted for less than two months, only to be chased out of office in a humiliating way by Yeltsin's Foreign Minister, Andrei Kozyrev.) Shevardnadze's gesture can in fact be seen as an honest recognition of the fact that he could no longer claim to speak on behalf of his country or its deeply divided leadership on the international stage. Ultimately it would be fair to say that Shevardnadze was pushed off the Soviet proscenium not as the Foreign Minister but as one of the key figures of the liberal camp.

He was not the only one. Various other members of the initial intimate circle of Gorbachev's devoted supporters, such as Yakovlev, Medvedev, Petrakov and also Primakov – all representing the reformist wing of the political leadership – were obliged to retreat at the time of Gorbachev's 're-centring' of his position in the winter of 1990–1. This political divorce was a signal that an important component of the programme of democratic reform had succumbed to the resistance of conservative forces.

The sad irony of the situation was confirmed by the fact that when on 10 December 1990 the Nobel Committee announced its decision to award the Peace Prize to Gorbachev, he felt obliged (as in the case of the two other outstanding Nobel laureates from the Soviet Union, Solzhenitsyn and Sakharov, although obviously for very different reasons) to decline the invitation to go to Oslo. He was represented at the ceremony by the Deputy Foreign Minister, Anatoli Kovalev, and the text of his speech was even not published by the Soviet media. Commenting on the event, *Time* magazine entitled an article: 'Praised Abroad and Cursed at Home'.

Gorbachev apparently sincerely believed that he would be able to limit his unavoidable 'shift to the right' to domestic questions while keeping faith with democratic principles in foreign affairs. In a letter to Bush written on 25 December 1990, five days after the departure of Shevardnadze and precisely one year before his own resignation from the post of the Soviet President, Gorbachev wrote: 'I can't tell you who'll be the next foreign minister. I haven't decided myself. But let me assure you that our new policies, the policies of "new thinking", the strengthening of trust and collaboration between our countries will continue.'[88]

Yet by the end of 1990, and for the first time in the brief history of *perestroika*, the two tracks of Gorbachev's democratization project, domestic and foreign, visibly began to split. Gorbachev attempted to persuade his Western partners (and probably himself as well) that by making some sacrifices to the conservative forces at home he would be securing the possibility of forging ahead with his great endeavour, the transformation of

world politics. To him the 'new political thinking' acquired a different role: once an auxiliary instrument assigned to service the
project of internal reform, it had evolved into an independent
asset, valuable in its own right and worthy of being secured and
protected.

In the middle of the Baltic crisis of the winter of 1991,[89]
during which Gorbachev strangely appeared to be either a
genuine supporter of the conservatives or perhaps their impo-
tent hostage, he received the US Ambassador Jack Matlock in
the Kremlin. It was 24 January 1991. Gorbachev asked him to
transmit to Washington the following message: 'Tell my friend
George Bush: whatever pressure is put on me regarding the
Persian Gulf War, the German question or the ratification of the
conventional arms treaty, I'll keep to our agreements. I'll do
everything . . . My deepest desire is to keep our radical
changes from drowning in blood.'[90]

However, his attempt to buy time in order to reanimate the
domestic reform agenda at the cost of temporary concessions
to his political foes proved to be futile, even counterproductive. Hoping that a temporary split between the foreign and
internal aspects of what was initially an organic project would
secure, as for separated Siamese twins, an independent life for
each, he soon discovered that it was in fact endangering the
viability of both. After the grim ordeal of bloody clashes in
Vilnius and Riga and the precarious confrontation between the
radical supporters of Yeltsin and conservative revanchists in
Moscow,[91] forced to make a choice, Gorbachev confirmed his
determination to continue with democratic reforms. From this
moment, having openly defied the Party and military establishment, he staked the fate of *perestroika* (and his own political
future) on the promised hypothetical dividends it would one
day bring to the everyday lives of the millions of Soviet citizens
in some uncertain future.

Yet since by this time most of the internal resources of the
national economy as well as the patience of the population
were exhausted, Gorbachev had no alternative other than to
address an appeal for help to the outside world, which had
profited so much more from his reforms than had Soviet
society. He certainly remained convinced that the changes he
had initiated in the political reality of his country would in the

end finally bear fruit. Yet at this critical stage, increasingly isolated at home, he was obliged to seek support from his Western partners.

## The G7 in London: The Summit of a Last (Lost) Chance

Already following his return from the Malta summit in December 1989 Gorbachev was obliged to confront an acute deterioration of the political situation within the USSR. In fact he had to deal with the parallel development of at least three grave crises threatening the further advance or even the ultimate survival of *perestroika*: an upsurge of nationalist movements in various Soviet republics (after the Baltic region, the Caucusus and Central Asia, a congress of the Ukrainian popular front, Rukh, gathered in Kiev in December 1989); the beginning of the deterioration of the economic situation, which started to have a very damaging effect on the living conditions of the population; and, last but not least, the sharpening of the political attacks against him from both the conservative and radical democratic camps.

Events that were taking place on the foreign policy scene throughout the previous year – the withdrawal of Soviet troops from Afghanistan, the fall of the Berlin Wall and the succession of 'velvet revolutions' in Eastern Europe – while obviously strengthening Gorbachev's popularity abroad, were at the same time making his position at home increasingly fragile. Meeting Mitterrand in Kiev in December several days after the Malta summit, the Soviet President appealed to his French colleague to help him 'contain the march of the two Germanys towards unification, since otherwise', he said, 'you will see a general in my place in the Kremlin'.[92] Yet it was much more the example of a transformed Eastern Europe than the prospect of German unity that was threatening his position; as the unexpected testing ground for the policies of 'new thinking', it became a stimulus for the national elites of the Soviet republics.

The first to draw lessons from the successes of the 'velvet revolutions' within the Warsaw Pact were the Baltic countries.

In January 1990 Gorbachev was obliged to go to Vilnius, charged by the Central Committee to try to put down the revolt of the local communist party, which had proclaimed its independence from Moscow. His mission turned into a fiasco which encouraged the Lithuanians, followed by the other Baltic nations, radically to speed up their advance towards full sovereignty.

Next came the turn of the Caucasus. Here, in contrast to the process of gradual but inexorable progress pursued by the prudent Balts, the explosion of suppressed nationalism took the form of violent clashes that provoked bloody inter-ethnic conflict. In January 1990, facing a wave of anti-Armenian and anti-Russian pogroms in the Azerbaijani capital, Gorbachev reluctantly decided to declare martial law in Baku and ordered the army to intervene. The operation resulted in more than one hundred dead and almost one thousand wounded.[93] 'New thinking' discovered its limits when applied to the rude reality of Soviet home territory. Unlike Moscow's heavy-handed behaviour in the Baltic republics one year later, this show of force by Gorbachev was met with 'understanding' by the Bush administration, despite the bloodshed that accompanied it.[94]

Still, as long as the phenomenon of rising nationalism was limited to the periphery of the Soviet empire and did not yet challenge the survival of the state, Gorbachev could believe that the political dynamics of democratic change emanating from Moscow would be strong enough to keep the USSR together, on condition that he found solutions to intensifying economic problems. It is at this point, in the spring of 1990, realizing that he could no longer afford to postpone long-awaited economic reforms, that Gorbachev turned to the West as the source of desperately needed economic aid.

Just as in the first years of *perestroika*, when he believed that in order to launch the process of disarmament it would be enough to persuade Western leaders of the futility of continuing the arms race, he now hoped that his new strategic partners would realize that assisting the survival of *perestroika* by sharing at least some part of the 'peace dividends' he had helped them to obtain would correspond not only with his but also with their own political interests.

When preparing for the summer 1990 summit in Washington, Gorbachev showed a particular interest in the prospect of the signing of the US–Soviet Trade Agreement believing, as recalls Aleksandr Bessmertnykh, the then Soviet Ambassador to Washington, that it would 'solve most of his internal problems'.[95] Initially, in the winter of 1990, when the preparation for the summit had just begun, Bush, worried by the prospect of the eventual 'neutralization' of a united Germany if Moscow were to proclaim this to be a condition for reunification, was ready to promise anything to Gorbachev as compensation: not only a commercial agreement but 'Christmas in June'.[96]

However, by the time Gorbachev arrived in Washington in late May, the situation had substantially changed. The dynamics of German reunification had taken on an irresistible force, leaving Gorbachev apparently no lever to slow down the process or to resist the combined pressure of the Bonn government and its Western allies for the entry of a united Germany into NATO. In addition Gorbachev's position was seriously weakened by the sharpening conflict between Moscow and the dissident Baltic republics, whose Parliaments by this time had formally proclaimed independence. Gravely concerned by the prospect of the first dominos falling and pushed by the conservatives, Gorbachev was engaged in a balancing act between threats of the use of force against the separatists and measures of political and economic pressure.

His American host was certainly not interested either in the weakening of Gorbachev's position at home or in the collapse of the Soviet state. According to Bessmertnykh, 'the Bush administration was against the break-up of the Soviet Union in general and initially even against the separation of the Baltic republics from the USSR, ready to accept their being given a special status'.[97] But strong pressure was coming from the US Congress, demanding the liberalization of Soviet emigration laws and more energetic administration support for nationalist aspirations in the Baltics as conditions for its agreement to the Trade Agreement.

All this led Washington to inform Gorbachev during Baker's visit to Moscow in May 1990 that it might be impossible to sign the trade agreement during the summit. The news was very badly received by Baker's counterpart, Shevardnadze, who tried to explain to the US Secretary of State that the Soviet Union was entering the stage of painful economic reforms, that the rescue of *perestroika* would require at least twenty billion dollars in aid from its friends, and that the moment when friendship counts had come. Baker, avoiding a direct answer, suggested that there were two serious obstacles in the way of any decision in favour of aid to the Soviet government – the threat of repression against the Baltics and Soviet economic/military assistance to the Castro regime in Cuba.

Upon his arrival in Washington, when, during the first day of talks with the US President, Gorbachev was told that the prospect of signing a trade agreement remained rather dim, he was aggrieved, understanding it as the unwillingness of Bush to come to his rescue in a situation when his help was very much needed. Bush's arguments about the opposition in Congress did not seem convincing. As a true Soviet leader, Gorbachev could hardly imagine that a man as powerful as the President of the number one world superpower would need to seek approval for a political move that he genuinely wanted to make. At the end of the second day of talks, he admitted that there was a stalemate, saying: 'I have to accept the fact that today, support for the Baltic nationalists is more important for the President of the United States than all other considerations.'[98]

That was certainly an unfair appraisal of Bush's position. Obviously if faced with a choice between support for the President of the Lithuanian Parliament, Vitautas Landsbergis, or for Gorbachev, Bush without any hesitation would have chosen the latter, a preference made clear in April 1990 when he encouraged Kohl and Mitterrand to send a joint letter to the flamboyant Lithuanian leader, inviting him to moderate his ardour and suspend the independence declaration in order to avoid creating additional political difficulties for Gorbachev. One of the reasons for Gorbachev's misinterpretation of Bush's position, his underestimation of the real problems the latter was facing, was the fact that, as the former US Ambassador to the Soviet Union, Jack Matlock, has observed, 'despite his for-midable record in relations with the West, the Soviet President had a poor understanding of the nature of relations between the administration and the Congress'.[99]

Yet on the last day of the US–Soviet summit, Bush, obviously hurt by Gorbachev's remarks, finally announced that the US government was prepared to sign the Trade Agreement (subject to Congressional approval), news that exerted an important psychological effect on Gorbachev, since he believed that economic aid from the West would save *perestroika*. But this was unrealistic: on the one hand, since real money only began to flow some two years after these appeals and conversations – and by then not to the USSR but to Russia; on the other, because there was no coherent strategy or mechanism for their use. Even those credits that were provided to Gorbachev following his pressing demands (mostly by West European governments, but also by Saudi Arabia and Kuwait on American advice) were quickly squandered, evaporating like a drop of water in a red-hot pan.

*   *   *

The London meeting of the G7 in July 1991 was a final chance for Gorbachev to strike a new strategic deal with the West. It was also the last opportunity for a common economic strategy, a new 'Marshall Plan' for the Soviet Union, devastated by decades of totalitarian rule and isolated by the Cold War, that could merge Gorbachev's project of democratic transformation with Western economic tutelage. Gorbachev's interest in being invited to these closed sessions of the unofficial 'world government' dates from early 1989 and represented for him a logical development of the position expressed in his UN speech of December 1988. At that time his motives for joining the G7 were largely political. He believed that the very fact of being invited to attend these sessions would have officially confirmed the achievement of his grand project – integration of the Soviet Union as an equal partner of the Western powers in the world's political family.

In a letter addressed to President Mitterrand, who was hosting the annual meeting of the G7 in the summer of 1989, Gorbachev wrote: '*Perestroika* is inseparable from a policy aimed at our full participation in world economy.'[100] At the time of this statement the Soviet leader was at the height of his international authority and, far from positioning himself as a petitioner, he was declaring his wish to join the club of the world's top political leaders on his own terms. At that time Gorbachev's letter disrupted the agreed agenda of the meeting and aroused obvious irritation on the part of the American delegation, since the meeting in Paris was intended to mark the solemn entry of the new American President onto the world stage. James Baker exclaimed, addressing the circle of Bush's aides: 'Gorbachev is trying to hijack the summit.'[101]

One year later, with growing political tensions and especially the deteriorating economic situation within the USSR, Gorbachev's priorities had changed, as had the tone of his address to the G7. Having not without difficulty obtained Bush's signature on the Trade Agreement, he appealed to the G7 session in Houston, seeking financial help for *perestroika*, unofficially. When asked by Dennis Ross at Camp David during the Bush–Gorbachev summit about the approximate amount of the aid that was needed, Evgeny Primakov replied: 'About sixty billion during the three-year period.'[102]

George Bush, however, expressed his reservations to the participants of the session; he feared that offering credits and loans without a concrete plan for their use would be equivalent to 'pouring water on sand'.[103] He was supported by Margaret Thatcher and the Japanese Prime Minister, Toshiki Kaifu, while other Western leaders – Kohl, Mitterrand and the Canadian Prime Minister, Brian Mulroney, advocated a more receptive approach to Gorbachev's appeal as a token of the West's political support for his reform policies.

In the absence of a consensus, on Bush's suggestion the participants at the Houston summit replied to Gorbachev with a letter of encouragement for *perestroika* and a proposal to send economic experts to study the situation of the Soviet economy before deciding upon the form and volume of eventual aid. In plain, non-diplomatic language this meant a 'thinly disguised rejection'.[104] One of the explanations of the US government's position, aside from the economic arguments cited by Bush, was probably the fact that from the summer of 1990 the Bush administration had started to reach out beyond Gorbachev to other political leaders in the USSR.

By the spring of 1991, following six years of reforms, the political and economic situation of the Soviet Union reached the critical stage. Having resisted the attempts of the central power forcefully to suppress their aspirations for effective sovereignty, the Baltic republics were heading toward a formal separation from the Union. The dangerous trial of strength between the radical supporters of Boris Yeltsin and the conservatives in Moscow in March momentarily put the country on the verge of civil conflict. Gorbachev's political rivals and adversaries from both the radical democratic and the conservative camps were demanding his resignation – the former accusing him of attempts to install dictatorship, the latter blaming him for accepting the 'partition' of the Soviet Union and 'selling out' the country to its deadly enemies.

Yet by the end of April 1991, Gorbachev had succeeded in extinguishing one hotbed of potential conflagration after another. Despite the sovereignty declarations by the Baltic republic parliaments, by staging and winning the 17 March Referendum on the preservation of the Union, he managed to reverse the process of its progressive disintegration.[105] In April he obtained the agreement of the leaders of the nine republics to launch the 'Novo-Ogarevo process' with the purpose of drafting a new Union treaty and at the same time restored his relations with the democratic supporters of *perestroika*.

But what remained an unsolved and rapidly worsening problem, threatening a potential explosion, was the rapid deterioration of the economic situation. Under the double pressure coming from the government (Ryzhkov) and from Parliament (the future putschist Lukyanov), Gorbachev had balked at the chance to launch a first real economic reform in the summer of 1990 on the basis of the Shatalin/Yavlinsky '500-Day Programme'. Instead, in the winter of 1990–1, he tested unsuccessfully the set of 'anti-crisis measures' proposed by the newly appointed conservative Prime Minister, Valentin Pavlov. The result was a further decline of the economic situation, a rise of social tension with massive miner and rail worker strikes, and a catastrophic depletion of the state's food and currency reserves.[106]

In late April 1991, assuming the likelihood of the eventual ratification by Congress of the Trade Agreement, Gorbachev sent a letter to Bush asking for an immediate loan of $1.5 billion to finance the purchase of US grain on the world market. Gorbachev's plea arrived on Bush's desk shortly after the

American President had been able to announce a victory in the Gulf War, which meant that he was no longer concerned to get Soviet support in the United Nations. Perhaps for this reason the letter aroused only irritation: 'This guy seems to think we owe him economic help because we support him politically,' he complained in the Oval office to Baker, Secretary of the Treasury Nicholas Brady and Scowcroft. 'Loans have to be made for sound financial and commercial reasons.'[107]

When he learned of this reaction, Gorbachev reflected bitterly to his aides: 'When they started the war in the Gulf they had no problem finding 100 billion. Now when it's not a matter of going to war but assisting a new strategic partner it becomes problematic.'[108] Certainly at that time Gorbachev would not have known that Yeltsin's emissary, Andrei Kozyrev, who paid a visit to the White House in May on behalf of his boss, had pressed the American administration not to give any subsidies to the central government in Moscow, arguing that the credits would not be used efficiently.

Yet despite the feelings of betrayal Gorbachev certainly experienced when he received this flat refusal from Bush, his general assessment of the level of cooperation and mutual confidence prevailing in US–Soviet relations remained positive – he had no reason to doubt the fidelity of the American administration to the principal political undertakings agreed at Malta. In this general context Washington's reluctance to respond to Gorbachev's demands could be interpreted as an episode. In any case, Gorbachev was then engaged in a much larger strategic proposal to the West as a whole, an appeal to invest in *perestroika* not just politically but also economically and on a long-term basis; he was expecting an answer from the G7 members, due to gather in the British capital in mid-July 1991.

Gorbachev was conscious of the fact that this meeting could turn out to be his last chance to obtain a life insurance policy for what remained of his reform project. The first and probably the easiest element of the task he had set for himself was to obtain an official invitation to attend the gathering. This was quickly resolved since none of the members, starting with the host of the meeting, the British Prime Minister, John Major, could imagine refusing to invite (in the status of a guest) a man with Gorbachev's political record who had recently become a Nobel Prize laureate. President Bush was an exception; knowing in advance that the leaders of the most developed Western countries most probably would not respond favourably to his request, he tried to dissuade Gorbachev from coming.

In fact Bush had definitely made up his mind well ahead of the London summit. His sceptical attitude toward the deal proposed by Gorbachev remained unshaken. He was not impressed by the three-year plan for the financial backing of Soviet economic reforms, jointly elaborated by Grigori Yavlinsky and the Harvard economist Graham Allison, called 'The Grand Bargain', and still less by the visit to Washington of a Soviet preparatory team headed by Primakov at the end of May. Nor was he moved by an emotional appeal from Margaret Thatcher, transmitted to him via the US ambassador in Moscow, Jack Matlock, 'to stop looking for excuses and find a way to help Gorbachev'.[109]

Bush's reluctance to accept Gorbachev's proposal was based on a number of considerations. The American President and his team were receiving multiplying signals indicating the progressive weakening of Gorbachev's internal position and pointing to the 'rising star' of Boris Yeltsin. One such judgement came from the former US President, Richard Nixon, who, having visited Moscow in the spring of 1991, conveyed to Bush his conclusion that 'Soviet society was tired of Gorbachev'. The fact that on 12 June, one month before the London summit, Yeltsin had impressively won an election victory to become President of the Russian Republic, certainly strengthened this impression.

Yet it was not only a classical 'wait and see' attitude on the part of the prudent Bush, yielding to the advice of his aides urging him to start 'looking beyond Gorbachev'; the obvious incoherence of the programme that had been proposed also affected Bush's attitude. In response to Primakov's presentation of the 'Grand Bargain' project as a chance to demonstrate the new interdependence of the world, George Bush evasively repeated the same promises he had already given to Gorbachev during their meeting in Malta.

In fact Gorbachev lost his London wager before he flew to Britain. His last attempt to persuade his future hosts of the merits of his plan did not bring about the desired result. What he was in fact proposing to his Western partners looked like a new version of the 'Marshall Plan', which in his view was justified by the end of the Cold War; it had been earned by the Moscow reformers' proven fidelity to the democratic course of internal reforms and the principles of 'new thinking' in foreign policy. The obvious difference from the Marshall Plan era was the fact that Gorbachev would not have accepted a comparison of the Soviet Union with a devastated Europe and certainly did not consider himself to be the leader of a defeated power (and for obvious internal political reasons could not allow himself to be treated in this way), which is why he thought he could be considered an equal partner when negotiating the conditions of his economic surrender to the West. His principal political argument may have been valid and found considerable resonance among the G7 members; however, the concrete solutions that Gorbachev was proposing remained unconvincing.

Certainly Gorbachev was received with due honours on the last day of the G7 meeting on 17 July and received high praise from its members for the advances achieved by his political reforms. Yet in response to his request to set up a hard currency fund to stabilize the rouble with loans to purchase consumer goods when prices were freed, he merely received good wishes for success and promises of technical assistance. Gorbachev's final warning of the danger of a communist revival if the economic situation of the country was not stabilized was interpreted by the American delegation as an attempt to impress the audience. 'We let him down', considers Roland Dumas, who says that Mitterrand, supported by Kohl, tried to persuade the other G5 to support Gorbachev. 'But the Americans would not hear of it.'[110]

The true explanation for the failure of accord between Gorbachev and his Western strategic partners cannot be reduced simply to the contradictions and technical weaknesses of the proposed rescue package. Certainly most if not all of the G7 members had a political interest in helping him to overcome his new difficulties and prolong his stay in power. The problem was that their reasons for this were specific in each case and often divergent. The US administration was concerned to profit as much as possible from the 'window of opportunity' offered by Gorbachev to finalize the agreements on strategic arms limitation. The Bonn government wished to assure a smooth transition to German reunification and a continuing troop withdrawal from the former GDR. All the West Europeans were interested in was the implementation of what was agreed in the CFE Treaty, signed in the autumn of 1990, and the evacuation of the Soviet army from the territory of the former Warsaw Pact members.

Sensing that Gorbachev's days in the Kremlin were numbered, they were trying as hard as they could to push forward all these agendas and 'lock in' the change offered by the 'Gorbachev chance'. During the G7 Gorbachev had a mini-summit meeting with Bush entirely devoted to the finalization of the START Treaty. The American side was pressing for the last details to be cleared up so that the Treaty could be signed at the next official US–Soviet summit, scheduled to take place in Moscow during the last days of July. Once again taking on the sole burden of a political decision, Gorbachev persuaded the Soviet General Staff to give the green light for the signing of the Treaty. In London the two Presidents could declare that the road to the next summit had been cleared.

Paradoxically this last-minute agreement, which apparently satisfied Bush, instead of strengthening Gorbachev's position at the session in fact had the opposite result. Most of what the West was hoping to get from Gorbachev, things that could not have been dreamed of just several years before, had been obtained: thanks to Soviet support on the UN Security Council, the American war against Saddam Hussein had been transformed into a successful international police operation, now over; basic strategic agreements between the United States and the Soviet Union on nuclear disarmament had either been signed or were on the way to conclusion; and the CFE Treaty put an end to the long-standing supremacy of Soviet conventional forces in Europe, inaugurating the superiority of the American contingent for the first time since the Second World War.

The Warsaw Pact members adopted a decision on self-dissolution without demanding any reciprocity on the part of NATO, while at Malta, Gorbachev could reassure Bush, worried about eventual European pressure for American withdrawal, that he would not demand the evacuation of US troops from the continent. The unity of Germany was achieved on Western terms with the absorption of the GDR by West Germany and with the reunited German giant becoming part of NATO.

Yielding on a number of occasions to Western positions in order to achieve these results, Gorbachev did not regard these simply as unilateral concessions, since in his view this new reality represented a new world order that no longer would be based on the balance of reciprocal fear or strategic nuclear parity but rather on interdependence and a common concern for indivisible security. All he wanted to obtain in return was a recognition of the reformed Soviet Union as the equal partner of the West and an integral part of this new world balance. Yet it turned out that in the eyes of his Western partners, having wasted his trump cards and overtaken by political crises at home, Gorbachev no longer possessed his previous value.

By July 1991 it would seem that most of what he could deliver both on the home front and in foreign policy had been produced and consumed, with the danger of a return to the Soviet past most improbable; however, Gorbachev's capacity to implement further reforms looked increasingly problematic. Out of all the Western leaders, possibly only Mitterrand was alarmed by what could occur if the second nuclear superpower were suddenly to implode: 'envisaging the worst, he feared a planetary version of the breakup of Yugoslavia with unpredictable consequences,' recalls Roland Dumas.[111] Yet his appeals to his colleagues to come to Gorbachev's rescue, not out of sympathy or gratitude for what he had done but in order to secure the West's own interests, remained unheeded. 'The West had to experience the August *putsch* to understand how serious the danger was,' says Chernyaev.[112]

Gorbachev's *perestroika* appeared to be an exhausted project that no longer promised attractive returns and therefore was no longer worth additional investment. After a successful summit in Moscow, George Bush remained loyal during his visit to Kiev to the political rapport he had established with Gorbachev at Malta; once again he offered public support, exhorting the Ukrainians to give preference to freedom (meaning *perestroika*) rather than to independence.[113] But in the conditions of acute confrontation between Gorbachev and his increasingly aggressive opponents, no words could replace the concrete emergency aid that might have saved the vessel of *perestroika* from political shipwreck.

In one of his conversations with Roland Dumas, commenting on Gorbachev's extraordinary political adventure, Mitterrand remarked: 'Certainly Gorbachev's survival depended ninety per cent on his capacity to maintain control over events at home. With all its sympathy, the West could not provide more than ten per cent of the assistance he needed. Yet it is quite possible that at a critical moment precisely that missing ten per cent might have led to his undoing.'[114]

\* \* \*

On 18 August 1991 a group of top Soviet Party and government officials, including Vice President Yanaev, Prime Minister Pavlov and the heads of the KGB, Defence and Interior Ministries, having declared Gorbachev 'incapable' of fulfilling his constitutional duties due to 'serious illness', interned him at his vacation residence in the Crimea and announced the creation of the GKTchP – the State Committee for the Emergency Situation. They were tacitly supported by the Speaker of the Supreme Soviet, Anatoli Lukyanov.

With Gorbachev categorically refusing to endorse their action and up against resolute opposition by the Russian President, Boris Yeltsin, supported by thousands of Muscovites, three days later this bizarre Soviet '*pronunciamento*' turned into a fiasco and collapsed. Gorbachev returned to Moscow, but his political position had been fatally damaged, and the Soviet state, dramatically shaken by political crisis in Moscow, began its accelerated slide toward disintegration.

With the programmed disappearance of the Soviet state announced at the meeting of the three republican leaders (the Presidents of Russia, Ukraine and Belorussia) on 8 December 1991 in the forest of Belovezhskaya Pushcha (near Minsk, the capital of Belorussia), Gorbachev was not only about to lose his job as the first and the last President of the USSR, but what was even more dramatic for the initiator of *perestroika*, he would lose his political leverage and would no longer be in a position to promote democratic change or influence the complex reality of his country. Having served him as an effective tool for the implementation of 'new thinking' in the international arena, in the end the Soviet Union became its victim.

It was only three years since the optimistic initiator of *perestroika* proclaimed before the General Assembly of the United Nations his inspiring vision of a new world order based on rationality, cooperation and the supremacy of international law. Yet after his policy of 'new thinking' led to the fall of the Berlin Wall and the destruction of the 'iron curtain', the boomerang of *perestroika* launched by Gorbachev returned to the Soviet capital to crush the walls of the Kremlin, putting in motion the collapse of the ideological state that had been created in 1922. Gorbachev proved to be right: the 'new political thinking' was indeed a formidable instrument for the transformation of world politics – East and West. But he had to pay for this triumph with his resignation.[115]

# 5

# THE WINDS OF CHANGE

The sudden ending of the Cold War, surely the dominant feature of the second half of the twentieth century, continues to be one of the most unexpected and perplexing phenomena of our time. Explanations provided by the winners and losers differ considerably, often contradict each other, and even taken together they produce no answer to the key question: *'Why* did it happen?'

The Cold War came to an end peaceably; but because its happy conclusion was not formalized by any act of capitulation or postwar congress such as the Potsdam Conference of the summer of 1945, there remains a significant diversity of views even with regard to timing. When did it actually happen? There is no agreement even about that. In fact since the very term 'Cold War', as Archie Brown justly observes, is a metaphor, there can be no definitive – still less a 'scientific' – answer to the question.[1] Anyone can chose his or her own version, selecting a date or event to mark the moment in accordance with his or her understanding of what the metaphor actually meant.

According to prevailing opinion, the Cold War came to an end in 1989, although among the many extraordinary events that took place during that year, different analysts choose different symbols. For some it is quite naturally 9 November, the fall of the Berlin Wall. Others refer to the US–Soviet December summit at Malta, where in their joint press conference on board the Soviet liner *Maxim Gorky*, Bush and Gorbachev announced to the world that the leaders of the two superpowers no longer considered their countries to be adversaries.

Archie Brown, while reminding us that the Cold War was an ideologized struggle – and not only on the Soviet side – also places its formal end in 1989. He writes: 'The Cold War began with the Soviet takeover of Eastern Europe in the form of acquisition of power by Moscow-dominated Communist Parties. It ended when the countries of Central and Eastern Europe became non-Communist and independent.' Yet he recognizes that from the ideological standpoint, the Cold War was over a year before it ended on the ground, citing two important speeches by Mikhail Gorbachev in 1988: one at the 19th Party Conference in the summer of that year and another in December, his 'anti-Fulton' address to the United Nations.[2]

Gorbachev's UN speech is also chosen by Matthew Evangelista, who sees it as a trumpet-call proclaiming the end of some fifty years of East–West strategic confrontation; Anatoli Chernyaev focuses on this moment as well, although for different reasons. For Evangelista this speech, in which Gorbachev announced a substantial unilateral reduction of Soviet troops and conventional arms, 'marked the end of the Cold War in Europe as it rendered Soviet forces incapable of either a standing-start invasion of the West or a major intervention to maintain control of the "fraternal" allies of Eastern Europe'.[3]

Chernyaev chooses a different argument.[4] For him the most important thing was Gorbachev's new philosophical approach to the handling of foreign policy, his renunciation of the use of force as a way to solve international problems along with the recognition of people's sovereign right to choose their own political systems. With this statement the last General Secretary of the Soviet Communist Party formally severed his filial ties to his predecessors; it was not just a question of Stalin, the 'godfather' of the Yalta accords, or Brezhnev and his ill-fated 'Doctrine', but Lenin as well, since for the first time a Soviet leader was ready publicly to admit that he did not necessarily consider communism to be the world's final destination, in accordance with a scientifically programmed 'end of history'.

And yet apart from these 'romantic' analysts of Gorbachev's statement of intentions, there were of course also the 'realists', like the US Secretary of State, James Baker, who preferred to wait for the promises to be carried into effect. It would not take long before this happened. Already in 1990 the Soviet–American political *entente* declared at Malta was put to the test by two major challenges: first, the need to handle the delicate issue of a reunited Germany's future membership of NATO; and, secondly, the question of Saddam Hussein's invasion of Kuwait in August 1990 – what would be the Soviet reaction? In both cases Gorbachev did not deviate from his stated principles.

During the US–Soviet summit meeting in Washington in May 1990, he confirmed to George Bush his acceptance of the future German state's 'right to chose' its future alliance, fully aware of the fact that it was going to be NATO. Following the Iraqi aggression against Kuwait, Gorbachev did not hesitate to describe it as a brutal violation of international law that could not be justified. According to Baker, the crucial moment came on the day in August 1990 when he and Shevardnadze read their joint communiqué to the press, condemning the Iraqi incursion and demanding the evacuation of Kuwait: 'a half-century after it began in mutual suspicion and ideological fervor, the Cold War breathed its last at an airport terminal on the outskirts of Moscow'.[5]

The common position taken by Moscow and Washington in the face of an act of aggression against a sovereign state represented for Baker 'a historic demonstration of superpower solidarity'; it signalled the encouraging picture of a stable and secure post-Cold War international order. Two days after his mini-summit with Gorbachev in Helsinki, it was this prospect that inspired the US President George Bush in his speech to Congress on 11 September (with hindsight, an ironic date) to promise to Americans and to the whole world a ' "new world order" based on the rule of law and not on the law of the jungle'.[6]

Bush had reasons to be optimistic at that time, and not only because Gorbachev had just assured him of Soviet support for the American position. There were also other areas of the world where 'superpower solidarity' seemed to be extremely productive, facilitating the resolution of chronic conflicts of the Cold War decades. Europe was heading towards the historic Paris summit of the CSCE, which in November would adopt the Charter of Europe that declared an end to the era of division and confrontation. The CFE Treaty signed on 19 November, after years of futile bargaining, announced significant cuts in the manpower and weapons of the Warsaw Pact armies that for so many years had aroused fears in the West of a Soviet blitzkrieg.[7] The Warsaw Pact and NATO, following disarmament, would be non-antagonistic, serving as an infrastructure for a new pan-European security system built on a strengthened and institutionalized CSCE, soon to be transformed from a 'Conference' into an 'Organization', the OSCE (the Organization for Security and Cooperation in Europe).[8]

In Africa, the continent that for many years had served as a battleground for East and West acting through their local clients, new opportunities emerged for the resolution of several long-term regional conflicts, and finally the shameful apartheid system of South Africa came to an end. Following the December 1988 Agreement jointly brokered by Soviet Deputy Foreign Minister Anatoli Adamishin and his American counterpart, Chester Croker, Cuba agreed to withdraw its troops from Angola. And a year later, in November 1989, South Africa withdrew its troops from Namibia, ending the occupation of seventy-five years and opening the road to Namibian independence. In South Africa itself the newly elected President de Klerk, likened, as already noted, to Gorbachev by his Minister of Foreign Affairs, R.F. Botha,[9] decided to meet the imprisoned Nelson Mandela, who was subsequently released after twenty-seven years of incarceration on 11 February 1990.

Even the most long-standing and seemingly hopeless of the regional conflicts, that of the Middle East, began to show signs of possible positive evolution. True, there had to be a delay until the war in the Gulf was over, but the new level of US–Soviet cooperation achieved during their collective management of the Gulf crisis encouraged the extension of this experience to the search for a solution of the Israeli–Palestinian conflict. Formally, the Soviets and particularly the Americans preferred to deny any direct relationship between international action to force Saddam to evacuate Kuwait and the proposal to convene a Middle East peace conference, yet the connection between the two was obvious. Gorbachev started to push Bush in this direction ever since their meeting in Helsinki in September. At first the Americans were reluctant to agree out of fear that the linkage between the two could be interpreted as a reward to the aggressor. Yet at the end of January 1991, when the preparations for the ground offensive against Iraq were in their final stage, James Baker accepted the mention of the project for a Middle East peace after his meeting with the newly appointed Soviet Foreign Minister, Aleksandr Bessmertnykh, to whom he said: 'it is a reward for Gorbachev, not Saddam'.[10] (The Conference under the joint chairmanship of Bush and Gorbachev eventually convened in Madrid at the end of October 1991.)

In Latin America, not only did the Soviet Union stop its military aid to the Sandinista government from the spring of 1989, as Gorbachev informed Bush at Malta; now, according to James Baker, the USSR would 'join the United States with strong support for negotiations, searching for a political settlement of civil conflicts' in Nicaragua and El Salvador.[11]

During these crucial months it was not only the many regional conflicts across the globe, nourished by Cold War confrontation, that suddenly seemed to acquire the possibility of resolution; the general structure of global politics was considerably strengthened, with major institutions regaining the chance to function effectively. Speaking at the opening of a meeting of the UN Security Council on 29 November 1990, convened to discuss sanctions against Saddam Hussein, James Baker had every reason to say: 'With the Cold War behind us, we now have the chance to build the world envisioned by the founders of the United Nations. We have the chance to make the Security Council and this United Nations true instruments for peace and justice across the globe.'[12] In fact after Malta the American vision of the emerging 'new world order' was not very distant from Gorbachev's 'new political thinking'; it was Gorbachev's belief as well that a new international order should move on from a 'balance of forces' to a 'balance of interests', and that this would be achieved through the strengthening of international organizations and gradual transfers of national sovereignty to the United Nations.[13]

It is striking to discover in the memoirs of both leaders, Soviet and American, amazing similarities of tone when referring to this period; with a certain nostalgia they tell the story of the extraordinary political romance between the two superpowers that brought about an end to decades of mutual fear and mistrust. Describing the atmosphere that reigned at Camp David on the day following the Washington summit of May 1990, Baker writes:

> The President, Scowcroft, and I spent the . . . day at Camp David, discussing regional issues with Gorbachev, Shevardnadze and Akhromeyev in a very relaxed way and in casual attire. . . . We covered conflicts from Kashmir to Cuba and Ethiopia, to North Korea . . . the discussion reminded me of some of the talks the President had held with Kohl and Thatcher – thinking out loud, comparing notes and creating stronger personal relationships.[14]

And now compare to this Anatoli Chernyaev's notes about the Bush–Gorbachev summit that took place one year later in Novo-Ogarevo (a kind of Soviet Camp David):

> Gorbachev and Bush had agreed to spend at least one day outside Moscow in a relaxed atmosphere, outdoors, 'with their ties off' discussing anything and everything in an intimate circle. . . . They talked about the Middle East, disarmament, including the chemical and biological aspects, Angola and South Africa, Yugoslavia and Eastern Europe. . . . Gorbachev suggested discussing a new concept of strategic stability on a global scale, because the former foundation – nuclear parity between the two superpowers – was losing its significance. . . . I had the impression that I was present at the culmination of a great effort very much along the lines of 'new thinking'.[15]

Gorbachev confirmed Chernyaev's impression in a conversation with the author: 'I remember sitting with Bush and Baker discussing the prospects for the solution of other [post-Gulf War] regional conflicts. . . . As we would have done between ourselves.'[16]

In these converging stories one can sense much more than mere 'superpower solidarity', and certainly no inclination to strike a geo-strategic deal in a form of a future condominium across the globe. The new US–Soviet relationship emerging from the spirit of confidence enjoyed between the two leaders reflected their concern and feelings of common responsibility for the as yet unknown world that they were about to set free from the weight of their confrontation, a confrontation that had lasted for almost half a century.

Yet less than half a year later, the would-be reliable partner of the US President for the building a 'new world order', Mikhail Gorbachev, was compelled to abandon his post; one of the presumed bastions of the future construct – a democratized Soviet Union – fell into ruins. To many in the West it was this break-up of the historic rival of the Western world that signalled the real end of the Cold War. History seemed to have reached a happy ending, this time not in its communist incarnation but as a liberal, democratic triumph. It was assumed that nothing could now inconvenience the sole remaining superpower or disturb its imposition of its own version of law and order on the rest of the globe.

We all now know what happened next. The political universe that emerged after the end of Cold War unfortunately is now referred to as the world 'post-9/11'. Instead of living in the comfort of Fukayama's 'end of history' we face unprecedented challenges, most, such as international terrorism, on a new and global scale. Certain former problems have returned as well. US–Russia relations, at least in terms of the rhetoric employed by political elites or the tone of the press, can seem reminiscent of the days of the Cold War. A number of strategic issues thought to have been successfully resolved at the time of Reagan–Bush/Gorbachev political collaboration are back on the political agenda, including: conventional and nuclear disarmament, weapons modernization, systems of mutual confidence building, NATO's expansion to the East, anti-ballistic missile defences, the presence of intermediate-range missiles in Europe, etc. History gives the impression of going round in circles.

It is now obvious that during the years when the Soviet Union was headed by Gorbachev, US–Soviet relations enjoyed much greater predictability and seemed to be heading toward a more promising future, in contrast to the present relations between the Kremlin and the White House. As some Western analysts argue, since 'the Cold War ended more than two years before the Soviet Union itself ceased to exist', it was not the formal preservation or the disappearance of the USSR but rather the *nature of the Russian state* and the chances of its political evolution in the direction of community of values and interests compatible with those of the West that should be regarded as the factor determining the effective end of the Cold War.[17] Hence the indissoluble relationship between the unprecedented opening up of Soviet foreign policy in the direction of the West and the internal reform initiated by Gorbachev; while the failure of *perestroika*, the deviation of Russia's development from its original objectives during the Yeltsin/Putin years, had an undermining effect. Gorbachev himself believes that the break-up of the Soviet Union deprived the world of an important factor for stability, rendering more hazardous the positive transformation of the international political scene dreamed of by the two superpower leaders at Malta.[18]

And yet an obvious question arises: how realistic was Gorbachev's strategy? Could a reformed Soviet Union have been transformed into a solid bastion of a new international order? Was there no contradiction between his project for profound democratic political reform and the wish to preserve the Soviet state that carried the stigmas of the Bolshevik project? Replying to these questions, Gorbachev reminds us of his intention to reform the Union state, turning it into a loose confederative structure. He also cites the convincing figures of the vote of approval for the preservation of the Union in the referendum held in March 1991. He then presents his final argument: the draft of the new Union Treaty, approved by the leaders of nine Soviet republics and supported by the autonomous republics as well, was scheduled to be signed on 20 August 1991. The plotters of the August *putsch* chose 18 August for their action in order to disrupt the ceremony.

However, these formal arguments do not stand up against the political logic flowing from Gorbachev's own *perestroika* policies: the liquidation of monopoly rule by the Communist Party, a key result of his reforms, gave rise to the progressive erosion of the regime and prepared the ground for the collapse of the state, based as it was on ideological dogma and coercion. It was through his practical policies, however, that Gorbachev provided a better and more convincing answer to the above embarrassing question: by renouncing the use of force to preserve the Union state, he made it clear that he would not sacrifice the democratic core of his project in order to maintain a rigid shell.

Undoubtedly the ultimate fate of the Soviet Union was directly related to Gorbachev's biography and political career; it must be remembered that this first elected President of the USSR was in that office for only twenty months. And yet in addition to his personal destiny, the verdict of history on him will be determined by the concrete record of his rule and influenced by the judgement of his compatriots as well as by world public opinion. Mixed, if not negative, assessment of the Gorbachev years by many Russians is understandably affected by the contradictions, ambiguities and inconsistencies of Russia's post-communist reforms and development. Yet the appraisals of Gorbachev's role by some Western historians and analysts present his actions as of almost marginal importance.

Some seem to share John Lewis Gaddis's claim (in his book on the Cold War) that 'Gorbachev was never a leader in the manner of Václav Havel, John Paul II, Deng Xiaoping, Margaret Thatcher, Ronald Reagan, Lech Wałęsa – even Boris Yeltsin. They all had *destinations* in mind and maps for reaching them. Gorbachev dithered in contradictions without resolving them.'[19] Others argue that the major real incentive for Gorbachev's revolutionary transformation of the Soviet relations with the West was the USSR's 'material decline', which in fact did not really leave any freedom of choice for the Soviet leader.[20] These authors basically reproduce the evaluation of Gorbachev's policy given by Robert Gates at the time he was the Director of the CIA, when he declared that the 'new thinking' had grown 'out of need for breathing space'.[21]

Curiously, while some contemporary Russian historians (Utkin, Narochnitskaya, Myalo, Sheviakin) do not hesitate to present the foreign policy of the Gorbachev–Shevardnadze team as the realization of a long-time Western dream of destroying Russia or even of a CIA conspiracy,[22] there are also quite a number of Western analysts who, while recognizing the historic dimension of the change inaugurated by Gorbachev, present the transformation of the international scene as an unexpected byproduct of his utopian reform plans, unforeseen and unwanted by Gorbachev himself, who simply lost control of the forces he had unleashed and behaved like a politician who was both naïve and unprofessional.

It seems to me that the testimony collected in this book produces an adequate counter-weight to most of these assertions and helps better to define the true significance of the 'Gorbachev factor'.[23] And yet the question of Gorbachev's 'naïvety' perhaps requires some additional comment. It was the 'naïve' Stavropolian who for more than six years successfully presided over the extraordinary process of peacefully dismantling the world's most powerful and feared totalitarian regime of the second half of the twentieth century, leading the first successful 'velvet revolution' of the East. 'It was Mikhail Gorbachev not Ronald Reagan or George Bush who ended communist rule in the Soviet Union,' testifies Jack Matlock, one of the most effective US Ambassadors in Moscow and a shrewd observer of Soviet society at a time of unprecedented change.[24] To achieve this, unlike the promoters of democratic transformation in Germany or Japan, the reformist General Secretary could not lean on a military defeat of the ruling caste or major assistance from victorious powers; when he launched the introduction of democratic procedures and institutions and attempted to protect them, he had to mobilize and lead thinly scattered, disorganized democratic forces within Soviet society itself, including within the ruling party.

Despite tremendous political pressure at home that on a number of occasions risked sinking the boat of political reform, it was he who remained uncompromising on the principle of 'freedom of choice' – the sovereign right of people to determine their own political systems and to choose their leaders and strategic alliances; he accepted the dissolution of the Warsaw Pact and the break-up of, first, the Soviet 'external empire' and later of the Soviet Union itself, sparing the world the nightmare of a continental-size 'Yugoslavia with nukes'. 'The nations of Eastern Europe, in the course of a free expression of the will of the people, chose their own path of development based on their national needs. The system that existed in Eastern and Central Europe was condemned by history, as was the system in our own country,' writes Gorbachev.[25]

It was Gorbachev, whose father had fought the Germans, and who himself survived Nazi occupation in 1942–3, who, on behalf of a whole nation that had suffered so grievously during the last war brought the German Chancellor to his native village to offer historic reconciliation to the German people (as well as the long-awaited reunification), an achievement comparable to the other crucial example of postwar reconciliation between the leaders of France and Germany. The admission of Germany, finally sovereign and reunited, as an equal member of the family of its former victorious adversaries not only marked the end of the Cold War but also brought closure to any remainder of the unhappy legacy of the Second World War.

The 'naïve' Gorbachev succeeded where several generations of postwar leaders, both East and West, had failed: he managed to recast the formal ritual of disarmament talks, which up until then with a few exceptions had brought no results. From serving merely as alibi for both sides to continue the arms race, negotiations were transformed into a genuine common endeavour, a search for effective schemes to reduce the most dangerous weapons arsenals along with reliable procedures for mutual inspection. Having chased secrecy from the sensitive sphere of the strategic balance of power, *glasnost* fatally undermined the possibilities of the military-industrial complexes of both sides to dominate over politics and the politicians.

To break this circle of futile bargaining and reciprocal suspicion, Gorbachev did not hesitate to resort to a risky gamble, making to his partners offers they could not refuse and proposing sensational unilateral concessions and asymmetric arms cuts in order to involve the other side in practical negotiations. Amazingly for the professionals in the trade, eventually the gamble worked far better than containment; within a period of two to five years a number of disarmament treaties were concluded that radically reduced (or even totally eliminated, in the case of intermediate nuclear missiles) not only the nuclear arsenals of both sides but also conventional forces and weapons to an extent unimaginable during the preceding decades of the Cold War. Even certain totally unilateral gestures by Gorbachev paid off in the end, such as sacrificing the shorter range 'Oka' tactical missile, despite the fury of his generals since there was no American equivalent; it was this action that persuaded the US to renounce the modernization of the 'Lance-II' missiles, earmarked to be deployed in West Germany to match the Soviet analogue.

Could these impressive results lead to the conclusion that in order to achieve ephemeral political success, Gorbachev did not hesitate to squander the hard-built military might and authority of the Soviet superpower? This line of argument could be and has been taken only by those who ignore his primary goal: to liberate Soviet society from the devastating burden of the arms race and from the quest for strategic parity, matching not only US capabilities but also those of its allies in NATO, with China included as well. It was a price that the country could no longer afford to pay.

Yet if carefully calculated political gambling was part of Gorbachev's negotiating tactic, it was in the end not tactics that helped him to achieve the desired results but rather a profound shift in the logic that determined relations between all the parties engaged in the Cold War. It is amazing to see the similarity of the arguments that were used by decision-makers in Moscow and Washington when discussing strategy *vis-à-vis* the adversary. In January 1982, presenting his view about the way to face the challenge posed by the Soviet Union, Reagan cited Winston Churchill, who 'observed that they [the Soviets] respect only strength and resolve in their dealings with other nations'.[26] In Moscow in those years it was common at Politburo meetings to hear similar reasoning coming from Andropov, Ustinov or Gromyko : 'The Americans understand only strength.' The same argument was repeated by the conservatives (KGB Chairman Viktor Chebrikov) in 1986, after the failure of Gorbachev's attempt to reach an agreement with Reagan at the Reykjavik summit; they wanted to demonstrate the naïvety of any alternative foreign policy based on the vague postulates of the 'new thinking'.[27]

And yet, convinced that it was precisely this logic of mutual mistrust and demonization that had pushed East–West relations into their present impasse, at times bringing the entire world to the verge of catastrophe, Gorbachev continued to insist on the need to replace the logic of confrontation with a strategy of partnership. After initial attempts to persuade the

West of the seriousness of his intentions, he realized that the only way to introduce real change was to set an example. Whereas in the traditional logic of superpower relations, reducing Soviet nuclear forces in the face of the SDI challenge would have been virtually unthinkable, Gorbachev managed to negotiate a strategic arms reduction treaty while essentially evading the Star Wars issue. 'His accomplishment marks a key turning point in the Cold War endgame because it removed SDI as a stumbling block to internal and external demilitarization and achieved the first significant reductions in the arsenals of strategic nuclear weapons of Russia and the US,' writes Matthew Evangelista.[28]

Naïve, idealist or visionary? The distinction between these assessments is often quite thin and any final judgement, almost always elusive for contemporaries, can only be given by history. The opinions of analysts continue to diverge, even with the privilege of hindsight. For Jacques Lévesque, 'seldom in history has the policy of a great power continued to be guided, despite difficulties and reversals, by such an idealistic view of the world, one based on universal reconciliation, one in which the image of the enemy gradually blurs until it virtually disappears as an enemy'.[29] Gorbachev 'allowed circumstances – and often the firmer views of more far-sighted contemporaries – to determine his own priorities,' writes Gaddis.[30] Vladislav Zubok reproaches the Soviet leader for an excessively 'rosy' view of the brutal reality of the world, leading him to a 'psychological dependence on former enemies and geopolitical rivals'. For that author, the fact that Gorbachev was too 'soft' on his Western partners and too conciliatory, that he neglected to draw certain 'red lines' before making concessions, makes him (at least partly) responsible for the excesses of triumphalism that characterized Western (American) behaviour after the end of the Cold War.[31]

Even unconditional supporter and loyal aide Anatoli Chernyaev remarks: 'Gorbachev made a few faulty decisions and mistakes in assessing his foreign counterparts, often expressed unwarranted optimism, he exaggerated the effects of personal charm and relied on ungrounded predictions.' He also testifies to the personal style of Gorbachev diplomacy: 'the man hated confrontation, fist banging, he preferred compromise and consensus'.[32] Gorbachev himself would not hesitate to acknowledge: 'I prefer to trust people.'[33] These characterizations illustrate the nature of Gorbachev as a politician as well as a human being.

But it may be precisely his determination to embrace the quest for personal integrity, rather rare for a professional man of power, that made him different from the crowd of 'political animals' that too often surrounded him; it was this quality that made him unexpectedly similar to another powerful state leader, the man whom he was fated to encounter and collaborate with – Ronald Reagan. Meeting Gorbachev before Reykjavik, as noted in Chapter 2, Mitterrand described Reagan in the following manner: 'Reagan is among those leaders who intuitively want to put an end to the existing status quo. In contrast to other American politicians, Reagan is not an automaton. He is a human being.'[34]

Another testimony to Reagan's character comes from George Shultz, someone who certainly observed him from much closer range than Mitterrand: 'I think that [Reagan's] characteristics were important . . . when Reagan said, "Yeah, I think this man is different," . . . that was an expression of this internal confidence, as I see it, and willingness to stand against people all around him if he felt this was the right course.'[35] Perhaps because the words 'confidence' and 'trust' meant so much to both men, these two very different individuals developed a certain chemistry in their relations and managed to achieve a historic breakthrough in the annals of the postwar world.

Reagan, reflecting on his first meeting with Gorbachev in Geneva on 19 November 1985, wrote in his memoirs: 'Looking back now, it's clear that there was a chemistry between Gorbachev and me that produced something very close to a friendship.'[36] It would seem, after all, that Gorbachev's reliance on personal diplomacy, his inclination to trust others, was not as naïve as some may have thought and could even be said to have paid off.

And so where, then, does the truth actually lie? Was this 'new political thinking' romantic a man cut off from the brutal reality of the world, a compliant follower of partners with a stronger hand? Or was he a visionary who refused to accept the absurdity of the world that he had inherited? Was he blinded by the original decision to choose partnership with the West and personally in thrall to his Western partners to the point where he could no longer distinguish between the national interests of his own country and those of the major Western powers? Was he absolutely unable to admit the existence of strategic rivals and adversaries? Was it simplistic to believe that by proposing new rules of the game and putting the accent on common interests in the face of common challenges, he would be able to transform enemies into partners?

It may be useful as a way of rescuing Gorbachev's reputation as an effective politician to cite the reaction to his initiatives and performance by his more experienced Western partners. Reagan certainly did not view him as a dilettante. The American President did find Gorbachev's obsessive attachment to the idea of a de-nuclearized world seductive (despite warnings from Defense Secretary Caspar Weinberger and a vigilant Robert Gates against 'naïve'(!) support of Gorbachev), to the point that in Reykjavik he almost accepted Gorbachev's proposal for the progressive elimination of superpower nuclear potential; this gave rise to panic on the part of the French and the British.[37]

Gorbachev's dream of a 'common European home' was initially received sceptically by Mitterrand; but the French President was soon persuaded to share the logic of this project and even suggested a practical way in which it might be realized in the form of a European Confederation.[38] The 'prudent' George Bush obviously borrowed some of the ideas for his 'new world order' from Gorbachev's 'new political thinking'; announcing his intention to go 'beyond containment', he gave the green light to his Secretary of State publicly to discuss (in a Berlin speech of 8 December 1989) ideas for a 'new Atlanticism for a new era' along with the possibility of a new common security system including the Soviet Union and extending from Vancouver to Vladivostok.[39] Impressed by Gorbachev's position in the aftermath of Saddam Hussein's aggression against Kuwait, Bush would not hesitate in his address to the joint session of Congress on 11 September 1990 to speak not only about the building of a new relationship with the Soviet Union but of the 'new partnership'.[40]

It is true that most of these ideas were born in the climate of euphoria that accompanied unprecedented changes on the international scene at the end of the 1980s; what was taken for granted was the continued existence of the USSR as a key player in world politics, even if in a transformed state. Another explanation is suggested by Jacques Lévesque: 'messianic and ambitious though it may have been, the project [of Gorbachev] was not wholly devoid of realism, and it did embody political aspirations that had currency in both East and West'.[41] But previously unimaginable events suddenly took on a momentum of their own. With the progressive and rapid disintegration of their presumed partner in the East and the crumbling of Gorbachev's authority under the multiple blows coming from insurgent Warsaw Pact members along with the rising popularity of Boris Yeltsin, optimism in the West about constructing a new, more rational architecture for the world as a joint venture with Gorbachev quickly evaporated.

'The stock market is heading south,' announced Baker in January 1991 to his colleagues in the State Department. 'We need to sell.'[42] 'Selling' meant 'locking in' the change during the uncertain but already limited time that was left to Gorbachev to stay in power. The Americans were concerned, above all, to get a rapid end to the war in the Gulf and a finalization of the START Treaty, as well as some initial progress in the Middle East. Observing the accelerated weakening of Gorbachev's position at home, his Western partners abandoned the projects of 'castles in the air' promised by his 'new thinking' and soberly returned to 'realpolitik' reflexes in their relations with Moscow. In a certain sense the West was faster and better than the initiator of perestroika at adapting to the winds of change that it had set swirling across the world political scene. Yet it did it mostly by retreating into the habitual past rather than agreeing to answer the challenges of the future, and in this way by its reaction contributed to the reintroduction in international relations of the age-long ploys of the 'win-lose' games between the great powers.

Forgotten were the 'no winners, no losers' slogans that held sway during the Malta summit. Nor was there any more needless bargaining with Gorbachev over the reunited Germany's affiliation with NATO. ('We prevailed and they did not,' remarked Bush. 'We can't let the Soviets snatch victory from the jaws of defeat.'[43]) Gorbachev's desperate appeals for economic aid to 'save *perestroika*' were met with nothing more than polite if sympathetic words, first at the G7 summit in London and finally at the last official meeting between the US and Soviet Presidents in Madrid in October 1991, after the August *putsch*. The US administration abandoned its promise to convince Congress to drop the Jackson–Vanick amendment, a remnant of the Brezhnev era that limited US–Soviet trade relations in response to Soviet restrictions on Jewish emigration. (At a later stage, under the pretext that the Soviet Union had ceased to exist, Bill Clinton repudiated the commitment given by Baker to Gorbachev that NATO would not extend eastward.[44])

At the time of discussions with Baker in May 1990 dealing with the question of a reunited Germany's entry into NATO, Gorbachev opposed the idea using an argument from his domestic political context: 'It is going to mean the end of *perestroika*.' 'People will say that we are losers,' added Shevardnadze.[45] In reality it was not the West's imposition of Germany's NATO affiliation that sank *perestroika* but the opposite: the misfortunes of Gorbachev's ambitious reform plan and the resultant break-up of the world's last remaining empire doomed the 'new political thinking' to failure.

And yet even after the passage of time and the publication of piles of books on *perestroika* and its author, the final question remains unanswered: how will Mikhail Gorbachev finally go down in history, as a winner or a loser? To say that his balance sheet is mixed would be a too easy answer, in fact an evasion and profoundly unfair.

After his less than seven years in power Gorbachev left behind him a peacefully dismantled totalitarian system in the biggest country of the planet and a different Russia reconciled with the rest of the world. He raised the 'iron curtain' that came down after the Second World War and allowed and encouraged the reunification of Germany and Europe after more than forty years of division. He succeeded in initiating, together with his Western partners, a disarmament process which for the first time in postwar history slowed down, even turned back, the arms race. Without any doubt Gorbachev's policies gave a powerful impetus to globalization. What more impressive appraisal could there be for a statesman who always was obliged to remember that politics is the art of the possible?

On the other hand, Russian public opinion today rates this man (at least for the time being) as one of the least popular national leaders of the twentieth century. Post-Gorbachev Russia is smaller and much less powerful than the Soviet Union before *perestroika*, and under Gorbachev's successors the country seems to be heading away from the democratic goals proclaimed by *perestroika* and *glasnost*; many observers have represented the current uncertain trend as 'back to the USSR'.

As for the world today in general, it is light years away from the inspiring vision of 'new political thinking'. The Cold War has been replaced by a multitude of 'hot' conflicts across the globe, and although the threat of annihilation in a nuclear catastrophe has been lifted, the number of victims of terrorist violence, inter-ethnic and religious conflicts and local wars (including those that are waged with the proclaimed objective of countering terrorism, promoting democracy and securing human rights) surpasses the annual rates of the darkest Cold War years.

The promised stability of international relations has yet to arrive and force remains the accepted way of handling conflicts, new and old. The 'peace dividends' have never been shifted from the military budgets of the developed countries to development aid or ecological programmes, while the volume of defence spending and international arms trafficking has considerably surpassed Cold War levels. The system of international disarmament treaties that covered the whole spectrum of weaponry is being reconsidered, and some key East–West agreements achieved after years of effort on the basis of hard-reached compromises have been suspended or even annulled.

Contrary to the assurances given to Gorbachev by Western leaders, NATO has expanded to Eastern Europe and has entered the territory of the former Soviet Union, provoking frustration in Russia and giving rise to nationalist, anti-Western currents in Russian public opinion. As for Gorbachev's project of a 'common European home', it is indeed being realized, but without the participation of Russia, while Moscow's relations with the West are once again, as during the Cold War years, marked by mutual accusations, propagandistic campaigns and spy scandals.

The new generation of politicians in both East and West, who never lived through the worst experience of the Cold War years, apparently has no hesitation about resorting to the spirit of confrontation and using enemy imagery as an instrument of domestic policy in order to consolidate public opinion behind national leaders. Such a regressive slide towards the atmosphere and reflexes of the past may result in, if not a new version of the Cold War, then at least a very cool peace, quite different from the rosy perspective suggested by 'new thinking'. This perhaps confirms the fragility of the historic changes which at the end of the last century seemed irreversible.

With such a contradictory balance sheet, should not Gorbachev's historical record in fact be portrayed as a global failure? Would he not himself appear to be a commander who, though he won numerous battles, ultimately lost the main war? And yet the controversy around this figure persists, both in Russia and across the globe, despite the passage of years. Why?

I am convinced that had Gorbachev been an average politician he would have been allowed to live quietly in retirement – after all, how many statesmen have really kept the promises given to their nations or their foreign partners? But Gorbachev's case is different. Because his project aroused so much hope and expectation, because his actions set in motion such important social forces and processes in his own country and the world over, many cannot forgive him for his failure. At times one almost has the impression that he is being judged not as a politician or a normal man but as a new Moses who failed to lead his people to the Promised Land. What adds a degree of complexity is the fact that quite often it is difficult to be clear whether we (Russians and non-Russians alike) are blaming Gorbachev (again with the wisdom of hindsight) for his errors and inconsistencies, or ourselves for not having effectively used the chance that was offered.

But is it really a failure after all? Gorbachev had the courage to push the old world aside and, with it, the old thinking; they were consigned to the past, where they belonged. He possessed the wisdom to welcome and assist the birth of a new reality, however controversial, with all its as yet unknown dilemmas and contradictions. And whenever it came to a conflict between interests (including his own) and principles, he invariably chose principles.

Mikhail Gorbachev was himself very conscious of the enormity of the challenge he had chosen to face. When his aide, Georgi Shakhnazarov, informed him that *Time* magazine had designated him the 'man of the decade', he did not seem to be particularly touched or flattered. 'The scale should be different, Georgi,' he said.

> It's not about me, the scale of our design is global. Look, we've turned our country upside down. Europe will never be the way it was. And the world will not return to the past. . . . Once again it's turned out that our new revolution is not only national, Russian, but global. At least we've managed to launch the beginning of world *perestroika*.[46]

Is this messianic ambition? Megalomania? Hardly, under the circumstances. Perhaps it is just one more 'gamble' on history by a politician who believes to the end that he correctly guessed the sense of history's movement and was on its side.

# NOTES

## Introduction

1. This way of presenting and interpreting the reasons that provoked the radical change of Soviet foreign policy during the Gorbachev years as well as its astounding evolution is particularly present in the works of: Michael R. Beschloss and Strobe Talbott, *At the Highest Levels: The Inside Story of the End of the Cold War* (Boston: Little, Brown, 1993); John Lewis Gaddis, *The Cold War: A New History* (New York: Penguin Press, 2005); Robert M. Gates, *From the Shadows* (New York: Simon and Schuster, 1996); Richard Pipes, 'Misinterpreting the Cold War: The Hard-liners Had It Right', *Foreign Affairs*, 74/1 (Jan.–Feb.1995), pp. 154–60; Georges-Henri Soutou, *La guerre de cinquante ans: Les relations Est–Ouest 1943–1990* (Paris: Fayard, 2001); and Philip Zelikow and Condoleezza Rice, *Germany Unified and Europe Transformed: A Study in Statecraft* (Cambridge, MA: Harvard University Press, 1995).
2. The organic interrelation of the internal and external aspects of Gorbachev's reforms explaining the origin and the initial motivation behind the 'new political thinking' is, however, extensively developed in: Archie Brown, *The Gorbachev Factor* (Oxford: Oxford University Press, 1996); Robert D. English, *Russia and the Idea of the West: Gorbachev, Intellectuals, and the End of the Cold War* (New York: Columbia University Press, 2000); Jack F. Matlock, Jr, *Autopsy on an Empire: The American Ambassador's Account of the Collapse of the Soviet Union* (New York: Random House, 1995); Jacques Lévesque, *The Enigma of 1989: The USSR and the Liberation of Eastern Europe* (Berkeley: University of California Press, 1997); and Lilly Marcou, *Le defi de Gorbatchev* (Paris: Plon, 1988).
3. Author's interview with Mikhail Gorbachev, 28 April 1999.

4. Author's interview with Aleksandr Yakovlev, 16 August 1999.
5. Beschloss and Talbott, *At the Highest Levels*, pp. 32–3.
6. James A. Baker, III, with Thomas M. DeFrank, *The Politics of Diplomacy: Revolution, War and Peace, 1989–1992* (New York: G.P. Putnam's Sons, 1995), p. 563.
7. On this see, for example: Pipes, 'Misinterpreting the Cold War'; and James W. Davis and William C. Wohlforth, 'German Unification', in Richard K. Herrmann and Richard Ned Lebow (eds), *Ending the Cold War: Interpretations, Causation, and the Study of International Relations* (New York: Palgrave Macmillan, 2004), pp. 131–53.
8. Eduard Shevardnadze, *Moi vybor: V zaschitu demokratii i svobody* (Moscow: Novosti, 1991); Aleksandr Yakovlev, *'Gor'kaia chasha': Bol'shevizm i reformatsia v Rossii* (Yaroslavl: Verhne-Volzhskoe izdatel'stvo, 1994); Anatoli Chernyaev, *My Six Years with Gorbachev* (University Park: Pennsylvania State University Press, 2000); Georgi Shakhnazarov, *Tsena svobody: Reformatsiya Gorbacheva glazami ego pomoshchnika* (Moscow: Rossika Zevs, 1993); V.A. Medvedev, *V komande Gorbacheva: Vzgliad iznutri* (Moscow: Bylina, 1994); Georgi Arbatov, *Zatyanuvsheesya vyazdorovlenie (1953–1985): Svidetel'stvo sovremennika* (Moscow: Mezhdunarodnye otnosheniya, 1991); and Pavel Palazchenko, *My Years with Gorbachev and Shevardnadze: The Memoir of a Soviet Interpreter* (University Park: Pennsylvania State University Press, 1997).
9. Georgi Kornienko, *Kholodnaia voina: Svidetel'stvo ee uchastnika* (Moscow: Mezhdunaronye otnosheniya, 1995) (at the beginning of the 1980s, Kornienko was the first Deputy Minister of Foreign Affairs of the USSR); Anatoli Dobrynin, *In Confidence: Moscow's Ambassador to America's Six Cold War Presidents (1962–1986)* (New York: Random House, 1995) (Dobrynin was Soviet Ambassador to the USA and later Secretary of the CPSU Central Committee); Yegor Ligachev, *Inside Gorbachev's Kremlin* (New York: Pantheon, 1993) (Ligachev was a member of the Politburo in the Gorbachev years, *de facto* number 2 in the Party apparatus, and reputed to be head of the conservative wing); Vladimir Kryuchkov, *Lichnost i vlast'* (Moscow: Prosveshchenie, 2004) (Kryuchkov was former aide and deputy to Yuri Andropov in the KGB, later Chairman of the KGB, as promoted by Gorbachev); Yuli Kvitsinski, *Vremia i sluchai: Zametki professionala* (Moscow: Olma Press, 1999) (former Soviet Ambassador to the USA, later Deputy Foreign Minister); Nikolai Ryzhkov, *Perestroika: Istorya predatel'stv* (Moscow: Novosti, 1992) (Ryzhkov was Secretary of the CPSU Central Committee, later Prime Minister under Gorbachev, 1985–91); and Valentin Falin, *Bez skidok na obstoyatel'stva: Politicheskiye vospominaniya* (Moscow: Respublika, Sovremennik, 1999) and *Konflikty v Kremle* (Moscow: Tsentrpoligraf, 1999) (Falin was a former Soviet Ambassador to the FRG, later Secretary to the CPSU Central Committee).
10. Author's interview with Mikhail Gorbachev, 22 June 2000.

## Chapter I   Preparing the change

1. Aleksandr Yakovlev, *'Gor'kaia chasha': Bol'shevizm i reformatsia v Rossii* (Yaroslavl: Verhne-Volzhskoe izdatel'stvo, 1994), p. 392.
2. Khrushchev's speech at the 20th Congress in February 1956 broke significantly with Stalinist dogma: a new world war was not 'fatalistically inevitable'. Different countries could take *different* roads to socialism; even a peaceful, *non-revolutionary* path to socialism was possible. See William Taubman, *Khrushchev: The Man and His Era* (New York and London: W.W. Norton & Company, 2004).
3. The deaths of Soviet Prime Minister Alexei Kosygin in 1980 and of chief ideologue of the CPSU Mikhail Suslov in January 1982 were followed by that of the CPSU's General Secretary, Leonid Brezhnev, in November of the same year. Next came the turn of the last member of the *'troika'* that had ousted Nikita Khrushchev in 1964: Nikolai Podgorny – former Chairman of the Presidium of the Supreme Soviet (1983). The year 1984 was marked by the deaths of Brezhnev's successor in the post of General Secretary, former Chairman of the KGB Yuri Andropov (February), and the powerful Minister of Defence Dimitri Ustinov (December). This chain reaction of mortality within the supreme leadership culminated in March 1985 with the death of Konstantin Chernenko, who briefly replaced Andropov in the position of the Party's General Secretary.
4. *Understanding the End of the Cold War, 1980–1987*, transcript of an oral history conference, Brown University, 7–10 May 1998, ed. by Nina Tannenwald, Watson Institute for International Studies, pp. 29, 32.
5. Author's interview with Viktor Starodubov, 26 April 1999.
6. Transcript of interview with N.S. Leonov, conducted by O.I. Skvortsov, Moscow, 21 April 1999, in Matthew Evangelista, 'Turning Points in Arms Control', in Richard K. Herrmann and Richard Ned Lebow (eds), *Ending the Cold War: Interpretations, Causation, and the Study of International Relations* (New York: Palgrave Macmillan, 2004), p. 89.
7. L.I. Brezhnev, 'Report of the CPSU Central Committee and the Immediate Tasks of the Party in Home and Foreign Policy', 24 February 1976 (Moscow: Novosti Press Agency Publishing House, 1976), pp. 10–12.
8. Author's interview with Viktor Starodubov, 26 April 1999.
9. Author's interview with Anatoli Chernyaev, 10 September 1998.
10. Anatoli Gromyko, *Andrei Gromyko v Labirintakh Kremlia* (Moscow: IPO 'Avtor', 1997), p. 56.
11. Yuri Andropov, especially during the short period when he succeeded Brezhnev in the post of General Secretary, was reputed in the West to be almost a liberal. This perception is amazing considering his previous record as the ruthless head of the KGB. That it was at odds with reality is borne out by Ambassador Oleg

Grinevsky, former chief Soviet negotiator at the CFE (Conventional Forces in Europe) talks, who often heard Andropov's remarks on questions of foreign policy, and recalls this typical observation: 'The international situation is very tense. The Americans can't be trusted. The only language they understand is the language of force' (interview with Oleg Grinevsky, 13 October 1999).

Andrei Gromyko, as reported by his son, spoke the same language. For example, when arguing in favour of maintaining the Soviet military presence in Central Europe, he said: 'Central Europe is our advance defensive line. It should be strengthened by all available means rather than weakened. That is why we could agree only to the symbolic reduction of Soviet troops in this region. That was our common line – mine and Andropov's – and within the Politburo it was regarded as an axiom' (Gromyko, *Andrei Gromyko v Labirintakh Kremlia*, p. 183).

12. During his best years, as his advisers have confirmed, the General Secretary could impose his personal style of diplomacy on Gromyko, as he did during the delicate moments of finalizing the 1970 Moscow Treaty with the Federal Republic of Germany; he could prevail over Prime Minister Kosygin and invite Richard Nixon to Moscow despite the US bombing of Haiphong Harbour. But by the end of the 1970s, these days were over.

13. *V Politburo Ts K KPSS . . .* [Records of Politburo sessions according to notes of Anatoli Chernyaev, Vadim Medvedev, Georgi Shakhnazarov (1985–1991)] (Moscow: Alpina Business Books, 2006), p. 377.

14. Author's interview with General Nikolai Detinov, former deputy Director of the Defence Department in the Central Committee, 8 February 2000.

15. Ibid.

16. Author's interview with Anatoli Chernyaev, 26 March 1998.

17. McFarlane was addressing his Soviet counterparts during an oral history conference at Brown University on 7–10 May 1998 (see n. 4). *Understanding the End of the Cold War, 1980–1987*, p. 48.

18. Ibid. p. 54.

19. Author's interview with academician Nikolai Petrakov, aide to President Gorbachev on economic affairs in 1990–1, 15 September 1999. Nikolai Kosolapov, assistant to Aleksandr Yakovlev and before that a close collaborator of the Director of the Institute of World Economy and International Relations (IMEMO), academician Nikolai Inozemtzev, does not hesitate to contest these official statistics, arguing that the real figures of military spending in the USSR at the end of the Brezhnev years were much higher. According to him they should not be less than 36 per cent of GNP (author's interview with Kosolapov, 27 May 2007).

Gromyko tried to explain his support for the position of Ustinov and Andropov in an unsent letter to Gorbachev cited by his son:

'The American government aspired to destabilize the situation on the southern flank of the Soviet borders. . . . Brezhnev believed that [Afghan President Hafizullah] Amin's group might gang up with the USA' (Gromyko, *Andrei Gromyko v Labirintakh Kremlia*, pp. 187–8).

20. The former head of East German Intelligence, Markus Wolf, says that in a meeting with the GDR Minister of Security, Erich Mielke, Yuri Andropov warned that nuclear war was 'a real danger'. 'The USA is seeking nuclear supremacy. A preemptive nuclear strike against the Soviet Union or its allies cannot be excluded' (Markus Wolf, *Igra na chuzhom Pole: Tridtsatj let vo glave razvedki*, Moscow: Mezhdunarodnye otnosheniya, 1998, p. 251). It is certainly difficult to establish whether this remark of Andropov reflected his true convictions or was just a rhetorical formula meant to impress his East German colleagues and call them to order at a time when the GDR leadership was starting to develop an independent strategy of relations with the FRG. Chernyaev, himself citing his friend Aleksandr Bovin, a member of Andropov's immediate entourage, confirms the view that at the time he became the CPSU General Secretary, Andropov considered Ronald Reagan capable of launching a first nuclear strike against the Soviet Union (interview with Chernyaev, 10 September 1998).

   In his turn, Professor Georgi Mirsky – one of the leading Soviet specialists on the developing countries, who was often invited to the brain-storming sessions organized by the International Department – quotes Boris Ponomarev, head of the ID, saying in a closed circle in 1973: 'Under no circumstances can we afford to let the Americans achieve even a small degree of military superiority, to rise one notch above our level, because in this case the next US President (after Carter) may be tempted to strike at our country.' (Georgi I. Mirski, 'Soviet–American Relations in the Third World', in Kiron K. Skinner (ed.), *Turning Points in Ending the Cold War*, forewords by Pavel Palazhchenko and George P. Shultz, Stanford: Hoover Institution Press, 2007, p. 151).

21. Author's interview with Oleg Grinevsky, 13 October 1999.
22. Gromyko, *Andrei Gromyko v Labirintakh Kremlia*, p. 57.
23. *Understanding the End of the Cold War, 1980–1987*, p. 105.
24. Author's interview with Georgi Shakhnazarov, 30 March 1998.
25. According to Anatoli Chernyaev, the total cost of economic aid to the socialist countries of Eastern Europe amounted to 41 billion gold roubles each year. Cuba received 27 billion annually. Syria 'cost' the Soviet Union 6 billion every year (*V Politburo Ts K KPSS* . . . , p. 94).
26. Author's interview with Georgi Kornienko, 8 December 1997.
27. Author's interview with Vladimir Kryuchkov, 11 August 1999.
28. Author's interview with General Mahmud Gareev, 29 April 1999.
29. Preface to the *Dictionnaire de la Perestroika*, ed. by Marc Ferro and Yuri Afanasiev (Paris: Payot, 1989).

30. Mikhail Gorbachev, *Razmyshlenia o proshlom i buduschem* (Moscow: Terra, 1998), pp. 179–80.
31. Aleksandr Yakovlev, *The Fate of Marxism in Russia* (New Haven: Yale University Press, 1993), p. 111.
32. Author's interview with Georgi Arbatov, 2 December 1997.
33. Author's interview with Valeri Musatov, 12 December 1997.
34. Valentin Falin, a leading Soviet diplomat, Ambassador in West Germany (1971–8), later Deputy Head of the Information Department and Secretary of the Central Committee after the 28th Party Congress (1990–1).
35. Author's interviews with Arbatov, December 2 1997 and Falin, 7 September 1998.
36. Author's interview with Georgi Shakhnazarov, 30 March 1988.
37. This most probably accounts for the fact that in February 1985, several weeks before Konstantin Chernenko's death, Anatoli Gromyko, at that time Director of the Institute for African Studies, had a meeting with Aleksandr Yakovlev, recently appointed to the post of Director of IMEMO, during which they discussed the possibility of election of Gorbachev to the post of General Secretary. Anatoli Gromyko claims that, having reported this conversation to his father, he persuaded him to make a choice in favour of supporting Gorbachev's candidacy during the crucial Politburo session (Gromyko, *Andrei Gromyko v Labirintakh Kremlia*, pp. 94–6). Gorbachev's own version provides further details to the story. According to Gorbachev, he was unaware of various behind-the-scene consultations regarding his candidature that were engaged between various members of the Party leadership and different go-betweens. He mentions among those who claim to be his promoters apart from Yakovlev also Evgeny Primakov, Yegor Ligachev and even Vladimir Kryuchkov – one of the future putschists. As he told the author, it was he personally who took the initiative to call Gromyko on the night of Chernenko's death:

> I found him in the airport and suggested that we meet briefly before the Politburo session. He immediately agreed. When we met the conversation was very short. I told him: Andrei Andreevich, we are on the eve of important decisions. I have the feeling that we have to work together. He answered that he was of the same opinion. We certainly understood each other. (Author's conversation with Gorbachev, 27 October 2006)

38. According to Evgeny Primakov, when Andropov was Secretary of the Central Committee directing the Socialist Countries Department (before he became Head of the KGB), 'his team', which included experts such as Fedor Burlatsky, Oleg Bogomolov, Georgi Arbatov, Georgi Shakhnazarov, Gennadi Gerasimov and Nikolai Shishlin, was stronger than that of Ponomarev. In later years 'Ponomarev's men', Vadim Zagladin, Anatoli Chernyaev, Karen

Brutents, Vadim Sobakin, Yuri Zhilin, Aleksandr Veber and others, took the unofficial lead (author's interview with Evgeny Primakov, 17 February 2000).

39. Author's interview with Anatoli Chernyaev, 7 September 1999.
40. Even during the *perestroika* years the 'internal antagonism' between the traditional party apparatus and the *mezhdunarodniki* led Yegor Ligachev, who occupied the second position in the Party hierarchy next to Gorbachev, to suggest that new functionaries in the International Departments should be recruited in the same way as the rest of the Central Committee – exclusively on the basis of their previous 'party career' – a suggestion that almost stopped the inflow of professionals into the central Party structures and risked paralysing the competent functioning of the International Departments (author's personal recollection).
41. Author's interview with Chernyaev, 7 September 1999.
42. Author's interview with Primakov, 17 February 2000.
43. Robert D. English *Russia and the Idea of the West: Gorbachev, Intellectuals, and the End of the Cold War* (New York: Columbia University Press, 2000), p. 107.
44. *Understanding the End of the Cold War, 1980–1987*, p. 192.
45. Author's interview with Sergei Tarasenko, 1 December 1997.
46. Author's interview with Anatoli Kovalev, 27 March 1998.
47. Author's interview with General Nikolai Detinov, 8 February 2000.
48. *Understanding the End of the Cold War, 1980–1987*, p. 54
49. We will never know in what direction Soviet military doctrine would have evolved had Ogarkov gained the support of the Politburo (which, in view of the close personal relations between Ustinov and Brezhnev, seems highly improbable) or replaced Ustinov as the Defence Minister (a possibility that apparently was worrying Ustinov). His at times overt dispute with the Minister ended with Ogarkov's removal from the position of the Chief of General Staff in November 1984 and subsequent appointment to a decorative post as Commander of the Western group of the Soviet army in Berlin, after which came his early death.
50. Author's interview with Vitali Kataev, 25 May 1997.
51. Author's interview with Anatoli Kovalev, 27 March 1998.
52. Anatoli Chernyaev, *Moya zhizn' i moe vremya* (Moscow: Mezhdunaronye otnosheniya, 1995), p. 443.
53. Author's interview with Arkady Volsky, 15 February 2000.
54. For reasons that remain unknown a civil South Korean aeroplane on a KAL flight strayed into the Soviet airspace over Kamchatka and flew for several hours over the sensitive strategic area along the Soviet Pacific coast. The Soviet military authority, assuming it was a spy plane, ordered it to be shot down, killing 269 passengers, 63 of them American, including a US Congressman. For the analysis of the 1983 Soviet 'war scare', see Ben B. Fischer, 'A Cold War Conundrum: The 1983 Soviet War Scare', *Intelligence Monograph* CSI

97-10002, Central Intelligence Agency (Center for the Study of Intelligence, September 1997).

55. Anatoli Gromyko and Vladimir Lomeiko, *Novoie politicheskoe myshlenie v iadernyi vek* (Moscow: Mezhdunarodnye otnosheniya, 1984).
56. Jack F. Matlock, Jr, *Reagan and Gorbachev: How the Cold War Ended* (New York: Random House, 2004), p. 85.
57. Confirmed by Anatoli Chernyaev during the Merson Conference in Bavaria, October 1999 (author's notes).
58. Yuli Kvitsinski, *Vremia i sluchai: Zametki professionala* (Moscow: Olma Press, 1999), p. 416.
59. Anatoli Gromyko, *Nezavisimaya gazeta*, 1 March 1997.

## Chapter 2  Ambitions and Illusions of the 'New Political Thinking'

1. Mikhail Gorbachev and Daisaku Ikeda, *Moraljnye uroki XX veka* (Moscow: Blue Apple, 2000), p. 23.
2. Author's interview with Arkady Volsky, 15 February 2000.
3. Author's interview with Yegor Ligachev, 18 February 2000.
4. Author's interview with Arkady Volsky, 15 February 2000. Volsky's story has been corroborated by Peter Boenisch, former spokesman of German Chancellor Helmut Kohl, who accompanied Kohl during his meeting with Andropov in 1983 and heard the Soviet leader name Gorbachev as his desired successor (interview with Peter Boenisch, 19 November 2002).
5. Author's interview with Aleksandr Yakovlev, 16 August 1999.
6. Boris Pankin, *Preslovutaya epokha* (Moscow: Eksmo Publishers, 2005), p. 19. Pankin was the former editor-in-chief of *Komsomolskaya Pravda* – a liberal youth newspaper of the Khrushchev years. He later turned to diplomacy and served briefly as the Soviet Foreign Minister after the failed coup of August 1991.
7. Author's interview with Anatoli Chernyaev, 10 September 1998.
8. Author's interview with Aleksandr Yakovlev, 16 August 1999.
9. Author's interview with Anatoli Chernyaev, 10 September 1998.
10. *Newsweek*, 25 March 1985, p. 15.
11. Author's interview with Mikhail Gorbachev, 22 June 2000.
12. Author's interview with Victor Rykin, 14 November 1998.
13. Lilly Marcou, *Le defi de Gorbatchev* (Paris: Plon, 1988), pp. 200–2.
14. Author's interview with Vadim Zagladin, 1 December 1997.
15. Anatoli Chernyaev, *My Six Years with Gorbachev* (University Park: Pennsylvania State University Press, 2000), p. 9.
16. Archie Brown notes that when foreign politicians gathered in Moscow for Chernenko's funeral in March 1985, 'Gorbachev, who had meetings with the major Western leaders, found time to meet only one European Communist leader – the Secretary-General of the Italian Communist Party, Alessandro Natta' (Archie Brown, *The Gorbachev Factor*, Oxford: Oxford University Press, 1996, p. 75).

17. Chernyaev, *My Six Years with Gorbachev*. p. 16.
18. Author's interview with Georgi Arbatov, 2 December 1997.
19. See the information on this in Brown's *The Gorbachev Factor*, pp. 77–8.
20. Author's interview with Anatoli Kovalev, 27 March 1998.
21. Author's interview with Mikhail Gorbachev, 28 April 1999.
22. Author's interview with Roland Dumas, 25 January 2000.
23. Archie Brown, 'Gorbachev and the End of the Cold War', in Richard K. Herrmann and Richard Ned Lebow (eds), *Ending the Cold War: Interpretations, Causation, and the Study of International Relations* (New York: Palgrave Macmillan, 2004), pp. 32, 37.
24. *Pravda*, 15 March 1985.
25. *V Politburo Ts K KPSS* [Records of Politburo sessions according to notes of Anatoli Chernyaev, Vadim Medvedev, Georgi Shakhnazarov (1985–1991)] (Moscow: Alpina Business Book, 2006), p. 17.
26. Chernyaev, *My Six Years with Gorbachev*, pp. 29–30.
27. Author's interview with Mikhail Gorbachev, 22 June 2000.
28. Author's interview with Anatoli Chernyaev, 10 September 1998.
29. Author's interview with Mikhail Gorbachev, 28 April 1999.
30. *Newsweek*, 15 July 1985, p. 15.
31. *Newsweek*, 25 March 1985, p. 27.
32. Aleksandr Yakovlev, *'Gor'kaia chasha': Bol'shevizm i Reformatsia v Rossii* (Yaroslavl: Verhne-Volzhskoe izdatel'stvo, 1994), p. 386.
33. Author's interview with Yuli Vorontsov, 18 February 2000.
34. Mikhail Gorbachev, *Zhizn' i reformy* (Moscow: Novosti, 1995), vol. 1, pp. 180–1.
35. Eduard Shevardnadze, *Moi vybor: V zaschitu demokratii i svobody* (Moscow: Novosti, 1991), p. 81.
36. *Newsweek*, 15 July 1985.
37. Author's interview with Yuli Vorontsov, 18 February 2000.
38. Author's interview with Anatoli Kovalev, 27 March 1998.
39. Chernyaev, *My Six Years with Gorbachev*, pp. 24–5.
40. Gorbachev, *Zhizn' i reformy*, Vol. 1, p. 266.
41. Claude Estier, *Dix ans qui ont changé le monde* (Paris: Bruno Leprince editeur, 2001), p. 35.
42. Author's interview with Roland Dumas, 25 January 2000.
43. Author's interview with Vadim Zagladin, 1 December 1997.
44. Shevardnadze, *Moi vybor*, p. 146.
45. For the first time Gorbachev used the formula 'a common European home' in December 1984 during his visit to Great Britain, when speaking to the British parliamentarians.
46. See Jack F. Matlock, Jr, *Reagan and Gorbachev: How the Cold War Ended* (New York: Random House, 2004).
47. Author's interview with Aleksandr Yakovlev, 16 August 1999.
48. Chernyaev, *My Six Years with Gorbachev*, p. 43.
49. Author's interview with Georgi Arbatov, 2 December 1997.
50. See Matlock, *Reagan and Gorbachev*, p. 165.

51. *Pravda*, 11 December 1985.
52. Mikhail Gorbachev, *Razmyshlenia o proshlom i buduschem* (Moscow: Terra, 1998), p. 73.
53. Gorbachev, *Zhizn' i reformy*, Vol. 2, p. 7.
54. Author's interview with Anatoli Chernyaev, 10 September 1998.
55. Gorbachev, *Zhizn' i reformy*, Vol. 2, p. 22.
56. Author's interview with Pavel Palazchenko, 19 April 1999.
57. Author's interview with Nikolai Chervov, 7 November 1998.
58. Author's interview with Viktor Starodubov, 26 April 1999.
59. *Understanding the End of the Cold War, 1980–1987*, transcript of an oral history conference, Brown University, 7–10 May 1998, ed. by Nina Tannenwald, Watson Institute for International Studies, p. 136.
60. *V Politburo Ts K KPSS . . .*, p. 32.
61. Author's interview with Mikhail Gorbachev, 6 July 2000.
62. Gorbachev, *Zhizn' i reformy*, Vol. 2, p. 8.
63. Chernyaev, *My Six Years with Gorbachev*, p. 51.
64. In the autumn of 1985, Falin, who had fallen into disgrace during Andropov's reign, had been expelled from the Central Committee and became an editorialist on the government newspaper, *Izvestia*.
65. Author's interview with Valentin Falin, 11 August 1999.
66. Author's interview with Nikolai Kosolapov, August 15, 1999
67. Robert D. English, *Russia and the Idea of the West: Gorbachev, Intellectuals, and the End of the Cold War* (New York: Columbia University Press, 2000), p. 5.
68. Georgi Arbatov was an active member of the International Palme Commission. Evgeny Velikhov and Roald Sagdeev regularly participated in Pugwash and Dartmouth meetings with outstanding Western scientists. Evgeny Chasov (head of the 4th department of Ministry of Public Health responsible for the health of the Soviet *nomenklatura*) co-chaired with Professor Bernard Lawn the organization Physicians Against the Nuclear War.
69. Author's interview with Mikhail Gorbachev, 28 April 1999.
70. 'Political Report of the Central Committee of the CPSU to the XXVIIth Congress of the Communist Party of the Soviet Union', Moscow, Politizdat, 1986, p. 21.
71. Author's interview with Anatoli Chernyaev, 7 September 1999.
72. Jacques Lévesque, 'The Emancipation of Eastern Europe', in Richard K. Herrmann and Richard Ned Lebow (eds), *Ending the Cold War: Interpretations, Causation, and the Study of International Relations* (New York: Palgrave Macmillan, 2004), p. 109.
73. Chernyaev, *My Six Years with Gorbachev*, p. 54.
74. Ibid., p. 57.
75. Shevardnadze, *Moi vybor*, p. 103.
76. Gorbachev, *Zhizn' i reformy*, Vol. 2, p. 8.
77. *V Politburo Ts K KPSS . . .*, p. 50.
78. Ibid., p. 43.

79. Ibid., p. 50.
80. Ibid., p. 66.
81. Author's interview with Mikhail Gorbachev, 28 April 1999.
82. Chernyaev, *My Six Years with Gorbachev*, p. 76.
83. Ibid., p. 81. Original emphasis.
84. *V Politburo Ts K KPSS* . . . , pp. 79, 83–5.
85. Author's interview with Mikhail Gorbachev, 28 April 1999.
86. *V Politburo Ts K KPSS* . . . , p. 87.
87. George P. Shultz, *Turmoil and Triumph: My Years as Secretary of State* (New York: Macmillan, 1993), p. 690.
88. Still, as Jack Matlock claims, 'if we had stayed one more day in Reykjavik, we might have been able to work out a formula that would have been acceptable to both sides' (*Understanding the End of the Cold War, 1980–1987*, p. 186).
89. Gorbachev, *Zhizn' i Reformy*, Vol. 2, p. 26.
90. Chernyaev, *My Six Years with Gorbachev*, pp. 86–7.
91. Shevardnadze, *Moi vybor*, p. 158.
92. Chernyaev, *My Six Years with Gorbachev*, p. 85.
93. Chernyaev, *Nezavisimaya gazeta*, 3 September 1994.
94. Author's interview with Alexei Obukhov, 26 March 1998.
95. Author's interview with Mikhail Gorbachev, 12 July 2000.
96. Author's interview with Sergei Tarasenko, 1 December 1997.
97. Author's interview with General Nikolai Chervov, 7 November 1998.
98. Interview with Vitali Kataev, 5 May 1997.
99. Author's interview with General Viktor Starodubov, 26 April 1999.
100. Author's interview with Vitali Kataev, 5 May 1997.
101. Author's interview with Nikolai Detinov, 15 February 2000.
102. Author's interview with Mikhail Gorbachev, 28 April 1999.

## Chapter 3  Breaking the Ice

1. Mikhail Gorbachev and Daisaku Ikeda, *Moraljnye uroki XX veka* (Moscow: Blue Apple, 2000), p. 34.
2. Author's interview with Mikhail Gorbachev, 28 April 1999.
3. Author's interview with Evgeny Velikhov, 9 September 1998.
4. Author's interview with Vitali Kataev, 20 May 1997,
5. Author's interview with Anatoli Chernyaev, 7 September 1999.
6. Mikhail Gorbachev, *Zhizn' i reformy* (Moscow: Novosti, 1995), Vol. 1, p. 475.
7. Author's interview with Vitali Kataev, 20 May 1997.
8. *V Politburo Ts K KPSS* . . . [Records of Politburo sessions according to notes of Anatoli Chernyaev, Vadim Medvedev, Georgi Shakhnazarov (1985–1991)] (Moscow: Alpina Business Books, 2006), p. 79.
9. Author's interview with Mikhail Gorbachev, 28 April 1999.
10. Eduard Shevardnadze, *Moy vybor: V zaschitu demokratii i svobody* (Moscow: Novosti, 1991), p. 87.

11. Author's interview with Vitali Kataev, 20 May 1997. (In August 1991 Baklanov joined the *putsch* against Gorbachev and was one of its most active participants.)
12. Author's interview with Nikolai Detinov, 8 February 2000.
13. Gorbachev's speech at the press conference in Washington, *Pravda*, 12 December 1987.
14. In three years, by 31 May 1991, the Soviet Union and the United States eliminated 2,692 intermediate- and shorter-range missiles with 4,000 warheads. Out of them the Soviet Union liquidated 1,846 missiles: 889 intermediate-range missiles, including 654 SS-20 missiles, as well as 957 shorter-range missiles, including 239 SS-23 'Oka' missiles. The United States during that time liquidated 234 Pershing-II and 443 cruise missiles and 169 Pershing-I missiles. With hindsight many of the Soviet generals admitted that it was 'historically correct' to sacrifice the 'Oka'. Despite the fact that this missile was never tested at a distance of 500 km, hypothetically it could indeed be used at this range. Also, its conservation could have served as an excuse for the deployment of equivalent American missiles, thus undermining the basic philosophy of the INF Treaty. (Author's interview with Nikolai Detinov, 8 February 2000.)
15. Ponomarev's collaborators, Chernyaev, Brutens and Rykin, have testified that their boss expressed serious reservations concerning the decision to invade Afghanistan within his close circle of colleagues and even shared his doubts with Brezhnev's foreign affairs adviser, Aleksandrov-Agentov. But since as a 'deputy' member of the Politburo he was junior in status, he could not openly challenge the heavyweights, Andropov, Ustinov and Gromyko. As for Brezhnev himself, by 1979 he showed evident signs of dramatic physical and intellectual deterioration; apparently by that time he had abandoned his previous practice of seeking the largest possible consensus inside the Politburo and, above all, no longer sought the view of the International Department on crucial foreign policy issues. (Author's interview with Viktor Rykin, 14 November 1998.)
16. See Diego Cordovez and Selig S. Harrison, *Out of Afghanistan: The Inside Story of the Soviet Withdrawal* (New York: Oxford University Press, 1995).
17. Author's interview with Yuli Vorontsov, 15 February 2000.
18. The total figure for Soviet military casualties – army, interior, border and KGB troops – amounted to 14,453 persons, reaching a peak between 1982 and 1985, the period of the most intensive combat action (Mahmud Gareev, *Afganskaia strada: S Sovetskimi voiskami i bez nih*, Moscow: Insan, 1999, pp. 327–8). The USSR was supplying more than 60 per cent of the country's oil products and offering the Afghan government annual long-term credits on favourable terms covering up to 80 per cent of its needs. During the period of the first five years since the beginning of the conflict the total sum of the economic aid amounted to 1.5 billion roubles (Pierre Allan and Dieter

Klay, *Afgansky kapkan: Pravda o sovetskom vtrozhenii*, Moscow: Mezhdunarodnye otnosheniya, 1999, p. 72) while the total cost of the war for the Soviet Union represented, according to the figure given by Gorbachev, 6 billion roubles annually (*V Politburo Ts K KPSS* . . . , p. 313).

19. In December 1979 the Kremlin had installed Karmal in the President's palace in Kabul to replace Hafizullah Amin, assassinated in a bloody coup orchestrated by the Soviet *'spetznaz'* ('special missions forces', which in the case of the coup in Kabul were jointly commanded by the Soviet Ministry of Defence and the KGB). See Gareev, *Afganskaia strada*, p. 71.
20. Allan and Klay, *Afgansky kapkan*, p. 285.
21. Anatoli Chernyaev, *My Six Years with Gorbachev* (University Park: Pennsylvania State University Press, 2000), p. 42.
22. Author's interview with Mikhail Gorbachev, 6 July 2000.
23. Report to the 27th Congress of the CPSU, Moscow, Politizdat, 1986, p. 92.
24. Jiří Valenta and Frank Cibulka (eds), *Gorbachev's New Thinking and Third World Conflicts* (New Brunswick, NJ, and London: Transaction Publishers, 1990), p. 40.
25. *V Politburo Ts K KPSS* . . . , p. 110.
26. See Jack F. Matlock, Jr, *Reagan and Gorbachev: How the Cold War Ended* (New York: Random House, 2004), p. 114.
27. Valenta and Cibulka (eds), *Gorbachev's New Thinking and Third World Conflicts*, p. 40.
28. *V Politburo Ts K KPSS* . . . , p. 108.
29. Author's interview with Nikolai Detinov, 8 February 2000.
30. Jacques Lévesque, *L'URSS en Afghanistan: De l'invasion au retrait* (Paris: Éditions complexe, 1990), p. 231.
31. *V Politburo Ts K KPSS* . . . , p. 136.
32. Ibid., p. 191.
33. James A. Baker, III, with Thomas M. DeFrank, *The Politics of Diplomacy: Revolution, War and Peace, 1989–1992* (New York: G.P. Putnam's Sons, 1995), pp. 71–4.
34. *Understanding the End of the Cold War, 1980–1987*, transcript of an oral history conference, Brown University, 7–10 May 1998, ed. by Nina Tannenwald, Watson Institute for International Studies.
35. Author's transcription of Gorbachev's statement.
36. In 1980 the CIA spent $30 million providing weapons to the Afghan resistance. The aid reached $250 million in 1985 and rose to $630 million in 1987. In February 1986, the US decided to provide to the opposition Stinger anti-aircraft missiles that started to be used in September. (Cordovez and Harrison, *Out of Afghanistan*, pp. 53–4, 157.)
37. Najibullah's regime eventually collapsed in April 1992 under the pressure of Islamic radical opposition after the new Russian government cancelled its economic and military support to Kabul.

38. *V Politburo Ts K KPSS* . . . , pp. 337–8.
39. Baker with DeFrank, *The Politics of Diplomacy*, pp. 71–4.
40. Richard K. Herrmann, 'Regional Conflicts as Turning Points', in Richard K. Herrmann and Richard Ned Lebow (eds), *Ending the Cold War: Interpretations, Causation, and the Study of International Relations* (New York: Palgrave Macmillan, 2004), p. 67.
41. Author's interview with Anatoli Adamishin, 12 December 1997.
42. A Special Report on the proceedings and conclusions of the conference 'Madrid Fifteen Years Later: Towards Peace in the Middle East' (10–12 January 2007), p. 23.
43. Author's interview with Georgi Shakhnazarov, 30 March 1998.
44. Author's interview with Valeri Musatov, 20 December 1997.
45. *V Politburo Ts K KPSS* . . . , p. 61.
46. COMECON (the CMEA) – Council for Mutual Economic Assistance – founded by the USSR and five East European States (Bulgaria, Czechoslovakia, Hungary, Poland, Romania) in January 1949. The CMEA gradually expanded to encompass ten full members from June 1978 as well as one associate member (Yugoslavia). It was liquidated in June 1991.
47. Author's interview with Vadim Medvedev, 9 December 1996.
48. *Pravda*, 21 July 1985.
49. Georgi Shakhnazarov, *S Vozhdiami i bez nikh* (Moscow: Vagrius, 2001), p. 277.
50. Author's interview with Valeri Musatov, 20 December 1997.
51. Author's interview with Georgi Shakhnazarov, 30 March 1998.
52. Author's interview with Valentin Falin, 11 August 1999.
53. Author's interview with Valeri Musatov, 20 December 1997.
54. 'The prevailing view in Washington as well as in European capitals on both sides of the Cold War divide was that the the USSR would never voluntarily relinquish its sphere of influence there' (John Lewis Gaddis, *The Cold War: A New History*, New York: Penguin Press, 2005, p. 235).
55. Mikhail Gorbachev, *Perestroika and New Political Thinking for Our Country and the World* (New York: Harper and Row, 1987), pp. 43, 148.
56. 19th Party Conference, Documents and Materials, Moscow, Politizdat, 1988, p. 37.
57. Mikhail Gorbachev, *Razmyshlenia o proshlom i buduschem* (Moscow: Terra, 1998), p. 48.
58. Notes of Anatoli Chernyaev, session of Politburo, 20 June 1988.
59. ' "Non-interference" was also a way for Gorbachev to avoid taking direct, personal responsibility if anything went wrong as a consequence of an imposed change,' rightly observes Jacques Lévesque ('The Emancipation of Eastern Europe', in Herrmann and Lebow (eds), *Ending the Cold War*, p. 113).
60. Author's interview with Valeri Musatov, 20 December 1997.
61. Ibid.

62. Chernyaev, *My Six Years with Gorbachev*, p. 61.
63. Author's interview with Valeri Musatov, 20 December 1997.
64. J.F. Brown, *Surge to Freedom: The End of Communist Rule in Eastern Europe* (Durham, NC, and London: Duke University Press, 1991), p. 59.
65. *Le Monde*, 20 August 1988.
66. Vojtech Mastny, 'Did Gorbachev Liberate Eastern Europe', in Olav Njølstad (ed.), *The Last Decade of the Cold War: From Conflict Escalation to Conflict Transformation* (London and New York: Frank Cass, 2004), p. 403.
67. *V Politburo Ts K KPSS* . . . , p. 419.
68. Chernyaev, *My Six Years with Gorbachev*, p. 63.
69. Author's interview with Valeri Musatov, 20 December 1997.
70. Author's interview with Georgi Shakhnazarov, 30 March 1998.
71. Author's interview with Valeri Musatov, 20 December 1997.
72. Vadim Medvedev, *Raspad* (Moscow: Mezdunarodnyie otnosheniya, 1994), p. 288.
73. Warsaw Pact military structures were dissolved in April 1991 and the official dismantling of the Pact was announced on 1 July 1991.
74. George Bush and Brent Scowcroft, *A World Transformed* (New York: Alfred A. Knopf, 1998), p. 165.
75. Author's interview with Valeri Musatov, 20 December 1997.
76. See the text of the original note in: Jussi M. Hanhimaki and Odd Arne Westad (eds), *The Cold War: A History in Documents and Eyewitness Accounts* (Oxford: Oxford University Press, 2003), pp. 39–40.
77. Baker with DeFrank, *The Politics of Diplomacy*, p. 40.
78. Robert D. English *Russia and the Idea of the West: Gorbachev, Intellectuals, and the End of the Cold War* (New York: Columbia University Press, 2000), p. 228.
79. The Romanian dictator and his wife Elena were executed by a firing squad after an expeditious trial on Christmas Day, 1989.
80. Author's interview with Viktor Rykin, 14 November 1998.
81. Author's interview with Valentin Falin, 7 September 1998.
82. Author's interview with Valentin Kopteltsev, 9 September 1998. See also Yuli Kvitsinski, *Vremia i sluchai: Zametki professionala* (Moscow: Olma Press, 1999).
83. *V Politburo Ts K KPSS* . . . , pp. 206–7.
84. Chernyaev, *My Six Years with Gorbachev*, p. 115.
85. Author's interview with Valentin Falin, 17 March 2000.
86. Author's personal notes.
87. Author's interview with Vadim Zagladin, 1 December 1997.
88. Author's interview with Viktor Rykin, 14 November 1998.
89. Author's interview with Valentin Falin, 11 August 1999.
90. Author's interview with Vladimir Kryuchkov, 11 August 1999.
91. Author's interview with Valentin Falin, 17 March 2000.
92. Author's interview with Georgi Shakhnazarov, 16 September 1999.
93. Author's interview with Valentin Falin, 17 March 2000.

94. Author's interview with Georgi Shakhnazarov, 16 September 1999.
95. Author's interview with Anatoli Kovalev, 27 March 1998.
96. Author's interview with Valentin Falin, 17 March 2000.
97. Already in early 1989, Gorbachev declined to interfere when Hungarian Prime Minister Miklos Nemeth informed him that Hungary intended to remove its border controls for Hungarian citizens leaving for Austria. On 2 May this decision was realized.
98. *Pravda*, 7 July 1989.
99. On that night, following the confusing information given to the press by a member of the East German Politburo, Günter Schabowski, about the new rules relaxing the travel of GDR citizens to the West, crowds of Berliners began to gather at the crossing points. Having no instructions and, at a certain moment, realizing that the crush of people was too large to control, the border guards at Bornholmer Strasse took it upon themselves to open the gates. (Gaddis, *The Cold War*, pp. 245–6.).
100. See on this Frank Elbe and Richard Kiessler, *A Round Table with Sharp Corners: The Diplomatic Path to German Unity* (Baden-Baden: NOMOS, 1996).
101. Jacques Attali, *Verbatim III. 1988–1989* (Paris: Fayard, 1995), p. 425.
102. Author's interview with Vadim Zagladin, 1 December 1997.
103. Author's interview with Anatoli Chernyaev, 10 February 2000.
104. Author's interview with Anatoli Chernyaev, 7 September 1999.
105. The signing of the Soviet–German Treaty on the re-establishment of diplomatic relations and development of economic cooperation in 1922 (in the small Italian village of Rapallo) produced a political earthquake during the Genoa Peace Conference convened by the victor powers of the First World War to impose their conditions of the economic reconstruction on the defeated Germany.
106. Attali, *Verbatim III. 1988–1989*, p. 432.
107. Author's interview with Anatoli Chernyaev, 10 February 2000.
108. Author's interview with Nikolai Portugalov, 9 February 2000.
109. Elbe and Kiessler, *A Round Table with Sharp Corners*, p. 48.
110. Ibid.
111. Ibid.
112. Philip Zelchow and Condoleezza Rice, 'German Unification', in Kiron K. Skinner (ed.), *Turning Points in Ending the Cold War*, forewords by Pavel Palazhchenko and George P. Shultz (Stanford: Hoover Institution Press, 2007), p. 232.
113. Elbe and Kiessler, *A Round Table with Sharp Corners*, p. 51.
114. Bush and Scowcroft, *A World Transformed*, p. 195.
115. Author's interview with Aleksandr Bessmertnykh, 3 April 1999.
116. Author's interview with Sergei Tarasenko, 1 December 1997.
117. Author's interview with Anatoli Chernyaev, 10 February 2000.
118. Author's conversation with Roland Dumas, 25 January 2000.
119. Author's interview with Vadim Zagladin, 1 December 1997.
120. Ibid.

121. Author's interview with Anatoli Chernyaev, 10 February 2000.
122. Author's interview with Sergei Tarasenko, 1 December 1997.
123. Mikhail Gorbachev, *Zhizn' i reformy* (Moscow: Novosti, 1995), Vol. 2, p. 148.
124. Bush and Scowcroft, *A World Transformed*, p. 199.
125. Ibid., p. 200.
126. Ibid., p. 201.
127. Margaret Thatcher, *The Downing Street Years* (New York: HarperCollins, 1993), pp. 795–6.
128. See Attali, *Verbatim III. 1988–1989*, p. 466.
129. In a meeting with Gorbachev on 9 February 1990 US Secretary of State James Baker on behalf of George Bush promised that 'there would be no extension of NATO's jurisdiction one inch to the east'. Helmut Kohl, received by Gorbachev in the Kremlin the next day, declared: 'We consider that NATO should not expand the sphere of its action' (Chernyaev's notes of the two conversations transmitted to the author).
130. Author's interview with Vadim Zagladin, 1 December 1997.
131. Author's interview with Valentin Kopteltsev, 9 September 1998.
132. Author's conversation with Roland Dumas, 25 January 2000.
133. Author's interview with Vadim Zagladin, 1 December 1997.
134. Author's interview with Anatoli Chernyaev, 10 February 2000
135. Rodric Braithwaite, *Across the Moscow River: The World Turned Upside Down* (New Haven and London: Yale University Press, 2002), p. 136.
136. Author's interview with Anatoli Chernyaev, 10 February 2000.
137. Chernyaev's transcript of Gorbachev's conversation with Mitterrand, Moscow, 25 May 1990, transmitted to the author.
138. Braithwaite, *Across the Moscow River*, p. 137.
139. Author's interview with Anatoli Chernyaev, 10 September 1998.
140. See for it Mikhail Narinsky. 'M.S. Gorbachev i Obiedinenie Germanii', *Novaia i noveishaia istoria*, 1 (2004), pp. 48–54.
141. Author's interview with Valentin Falin, 17 March 2000.
142. Ibid.
143. Author's interview with Anatoli Chernyaev, 10 September 1998.

## Chapter 4  Up to the Peak and Down the Slope

1. *A Millennium Salute to Mikhail Gorbachev on his 70th Birthday* (Moscow: R. Valent, 2001), p. 127.
2. In Gorbachev's speech a public commitment was made to reduce unilaterally the Soviet armed forces by 500,000 men. Of these, 10,000 were to be withdrawn from armoured divisions in three East European countries bordering with the West (GDR, Czechoslovakia and Hungary) by 1991, as well as from airborne assault units from those countries. In addition, 5,000 Soviet tanks, half the Soviet total in those countries, were to be withdrawn.

3. *Pravda*, 8 December 1988.
4. Eduard Shevardnadze, *Moi vybor: V zaschitu demokratii i svobody* (Moscow: Novosti, 1991), p. 12.
5. Thesis for the 19th Party Conference, *Pravda*, 27 May 1988.
6. Author's interview with Jack Matlock, *Obschaia Gazeta*, 17–23 April 1997.
7. In Mikhail Gorbachev, *Zhizn' i reformy* (Moscow: Novosti, 1995), Vol. 1, pp. 402–3.
8. *Sovetskaya Rossia*, 6 August 1988.
9. Anatoli Chernyaev, *My Six Years with Gorbachev* (University Park: Pennsylvania State University Press, 2000), p. 172.
10. Yegor Ligachev, *Inside Gorbachev's Kremlin* (New York: Pantheon, 1993), p. 321.
11. *V Politburo Ts K KPSS. . .* [Records of Politburo sessions according to notes of Anatoli Chernyaev, Vadim Medvedev, Georgi Shakhnazarov (1985–1991)] (Moscow: Alpina Business Books, 2006), pp. 418–23.
12. Mikhail Gorbachev. *Zhizn' i reformy*, Vol. 2, p. 132.
13. Anatoli Gromyko, *Andrei Gromyko v Labirintakh Kremlia* (Moscow: IPO 'Avtor', 1997), p. 123
14. Chernyaev, *My Six Years with Gorbachev*, pp. 201–2.
15. *A Millennium Salute to Mikhail Gorbachev on his 70th Birthday*, p. 127.
16. Karabakh – a mountainous region of Azerbaijan with a predominantly Armenian population.
17. While keeping a majority of seats for the communists and satellite parties, the agreements allowed Solidarity to enter Parliament and eventually to enter a coalition government.
18. Author's interview with Wojciech Jaruzelski, 23 October 2004.
19. Jacques Lévesque, 'The Emancipation of Eastern Europe', in Richard K. Herrmann and Richard Ned Lebow (eds), *Ending the Cold War: Interpretations, Causation, and the Study of International Relations* (New York: Palgrave Macmillan, 2004), p. 116.
20. Interviews with Anatoli Chernyaev, 10 February 2000, and Georgi Shakhnazarov, 16 September 1999.
21. Author's interview with Gyula Horn, the former Hungarian Minister of Foreign Affairs and Prime Minister, 23 October 2004.
22. Vojtech Mastny, 'Did Gorbachev Liberate Eastern Europe?', in Olav Njølstad (ed.), *The Last Decade of the Cold War: From Conflict Escalation to Conflict Transformation* (London and New York: Frank Cass, 2004), p. 413.
23. Author's personal notes
24. *Moskovskie Novosti*, no. 46, 1999.
25. Gromyko, *Andrei Gromyko v Labirintakh Kremlia*, p. 182.
26. Author's interview with Georgi Kornienko, 8 December 1997.
27. Dobrynin's speech in the Moscow Institute of International Relations, 29 June 1999, author's notes.
28. Author's interview with Anatoli Adamishin, 12 December 1997.

29. Author's interview with Anatoli Chernyaev, 7 September 1999.
30. Chernyaev's notes of the meeting shared with the author.
31. Author's interview with Chernyaev, 22 October 1999.
32. Jack F. Matlock, Jr, *Reagan and Gorbachev: How the Cold War Ended* (New York: Random House, 2004), p. 302.
33. CIA Cold War Intelligence documents declassified in March 2001. *Washington Post*, 11 March 2001.
34. Michael R. Beschloss and Strobe Talbott, *At the Highest Levels: The Inside Story of the End of the Cold War* (Boston: Little, Brown, 1993), pp. 72–3.
35. Ibid., p. 74.
36. Author's interview with Yuli Vorontsov, 15 February 2000.
37. *A Millennium Salute to Mikhail Gorbachev on his 70th birthday*, p. 127.
38. Daniel Vernet, 'Mitterrand, L'URSS et la Russie', in Samy Cohen (ed.), *Mitterrand et la sortie de la guerre froide* (Paris: Presses Universitaires de France, 1998), p. 44.
39. Chernyaev, *My Six Years with Gorbachev*, p. 215.
40. Ibid., p. 221.
41. Ibid., p. 223.
42. Author's interview with Roland Dumas, 25 January 2000.
43. Author's interviews with General Jaruzelski and Guyla Horn, 23 October 2004.
44. James A. Baker, III, with Thomas M. DeFrank, *The Politics of Diplomacy: Revolution, War and Peace, 1989–1992* (New York: G.P. Putnam's Sons, 1995), p. 168.
45. Author's interview with Anatoli Chernyaev, 7 September 1999.
46. Author's interview with Vadim Zagladin, 1 December 1997.
47. Author's interview with Anatoli Chernyaev, 7 September 1999.
48. The decision was taken during the Politburo meeting on 13 April 1989 on the basis of Gorbachev's report of his visit to Cuba and his meeting with Fidel Castro, who also agreed to recall Cuban military advisers from Nicaragua (*V Politburo Ts K KPSS . . . .* p. 469).
49. George Bush and Brent Scowcroft, *A World Transformed* (New York: Alfred A. Knopf, 1998), pp. 172, 165.
50. Chernyaev, *My Six Years with Gorbachev*, p. 235.
51. Author's interview with Anatoli Chernyaev, 7 September 1999.
52. Baker with DeFrank, *The Politics of Diplomacy*, p. 171.
53. Chernyaev, *My Six Years with Gorbachev*, p. 234.
54. Jacques Attali, *Verbatim III. 1988–1989* (Paris: Fayard, 1995), pp. 447–8.
55. Shevardnadze, *Moi vybor*, p. 12.
56. Author's interview with Anatoli Adamishin, 12 December 1997
57. Ligachev, *Inside Gorbachev's Kremlin*, p. 153.
58. *Sovetskaya Rossia*, 21 June 1990.
59. *Pravda*, 26 June 1990.
60. Nikita S. Khrushchev, the first Secretary of the CPSU, was sent into retirement following the unanimous vote of the members of the

Presidium of the Central Committee (the equivalent of the Politburo) in October 1964.

61. Author's interview with Anatoli Chernyaev, 10 September 1998.
62. Author's interview with Victor Starodubov, 26 April 1999.
63. Author's interview with Vadim Medvedev, 17 July 1999.
64. Author's interview with Sergei Tarasenko, 23 April 1998.
65. Valentin Falin, *Konflikty v Kremle* (Moscow: Tsentrpoligraf, 1999), p. 150.
66. Author's interview with Anatoli Chernyaev, 10 September 1998.
67. Author's interview with Sergei Tarasenko, 23 April 1998.
68. Ibid.
69. Author's interview with Anatoli Adamishin, 12 December 1997.
70. Author's interview with Ambassador Oleg Grinevsky, Soviet chief negotiator at the Vienna talks, 10 October 1999.
71. Valeri Boldin, Director of Gorbachev's Secretariat, who joined the team of putschists conspiring against Gorbachev in August 1991.
72. Chernyaev, *My Six Years with Gorbachev*, p. 283.
73. Ibid.
74. Author's interview with Sergei Tarasenko, 23 April 1998.
75. Author's interview with Georgi Arbatov, 2 December 1997.
76. Shevardnadze, *Moi vybor*, p. 179.
77. Chernyaev, *My Six Years with Gorbachev*, p. 334.
78. Author's interview with Anatoli Chernyaev, 10 September 1998.
79. Author's interview with Sergei Tarasenko, 23 April 1998.
80. Shevardnadze, *Moi vybor*, p. 181.
81. Out of five permanent members of the Security Council, four voted in favour of the resolution. The Chinese representative abstained.
82. Author's interview with Valentin Falin, 17 March 2000.
83. Author's interview with Anatoli Chernyaev, 10 September 1998.
84. Author's interview with Evgeny Primakov, 17 Febuary 2000.
85. Author's interview with Aleksandr Bessmertnykh, 3 April 1999.
86. Author's interview with Evgeny Primakov, 17 February 2000.
87. Author's interview with Mikhail Gorbachev, 15 July 1999.
88. Chernyaev, *My Six Years with Gorbachev*, p. 313.
89. On the night of 12–13 January 1991, Soviet troops in Vilnius, the capital of the Lithuanian Republic, moved to take over the local television station and clashed with the massive demonstration of supporters of Lithuanian nationalists. In this confrontation fourteen people were killed and many more wounded. Several days later, on 20–1 January in Riga, the capital of another Baltic republic, Latvia, the troops of OMON (the Special Ministry of the Interior) in a similar incident killed four people. Both violent provocations, which apparently were organized by the conservative forces against Gorbachev's will, were intended to give a signal for a forceful rebuff to the offensive of 'separatists' in national republics and the imposition of 'order' within the Soviet Union.

90. Chernyaev, *My Six Years with Gorbachev*, p. 329.
91. On 28 March a huge demonstration of supporters of Yeltsin marched through the streets of Moscow heading toward the Kremlin and brought the Soviet capital to the brink of civil conflict.
92. Author's interview with Vadim Zagladin, 1 December 1997.
93. Author's interview with Vagif Guseinov, former Chairman of the KGB of Azerbaijan, 10 August 1999.
94. See Beschloss and Talbott, *At the Highest Levels*, p. 176.
95. Author's interview with Aleksandr Bessmertnykh, 3 April 1999.
96. Beschloss and Talbott, *At the Highest Levels*, p. 188.
97. Author's interview with Aleksandr Bessmertnykh, 3 April 1999.
98. Ibid.
99. Author's conversation with Jack Matlock, 22 October 1999.
100. Gorbachev. *Zhizn' i reformy*, Vol. 2, p. 285.
101. Beschloss and Talbott, *At the Highest Levels*, p. 93.
102. Author's interview with Evgeny Primakov, 17 February 2000.
103. Author's conversation with Jack Matlock, 22 October 1999.
104. Beschloss and Talbott, *At the Highest Levels*, p. 237.
105. On 17 March 1991 an overwhelming majority of Soviet citizens (76.4 per cent) voted in favour of maintaining the Union State in a form of a 'renewed federation'. The referendum took place in nine out of fifteen soviet republics.
106. Interviews with Grigori Yavlinsky, 27 April 2004 and Nikolai Petrakov, 15 September 1999.
107. Beschloss and Talbott, *At the Highest Levels*, p. 378.
108. Author's interview with Anatoli Chernyaev, 10 September 1998.
109. Author's conversation with Jack Matlock, 22 October 1999.
110. Author's conversation with Roland Dumas, 25 January 2000.
111. Ibid.
112. Author's interview with Anatoli Chernyaev, 10 September 1998.
113. John Lewis Gaddis, *The Cold War: A New History* (New York: Penguin Press, 2005), p. 255.
114. Author's conversation with Roland Dumas, 25 January 2000.
115. Mikhail Gorbachev resigned from the post of the President of Soviet Union on 25 December 1991 after four months of desperate attempts to save the Union state by negotiating a new Union Treaty with the republican leaders.

## Chapter 5  The Winds of Change

1. Archie Brown, *Seven Years That Changed the World: Perestroika in Perspective* (Oxford: Oxford University Press, 2007), p. 240.
2. Ibid., p. 241.
3. Matthew Evangelista, 'Turning Points in Arms Control', in Richard K. Herrmann and Richard Ned Lebow (eds), *Ending the Cold War: Interpretations, Causation, and the Study of International Relations* (New York: Palgrave Macmillan, 2004), p. 95.

4. Author's interview with Anatoli Chernyaev, 10 September 1998.
5. James A. Baker, III, with Thomas M. DeFrank, *The Politics of Diplomacy: Revolution, War and Peace, 1989–1992* (New York: G.P. Putnam's Sons, 1995), p. 16.
6. *Time*, 28 January 1991.
7. The original Treaty on Conventional Armed Forces in Europe (CFE) established comprehensive limits on key categories of conventional military equipment in Europe (from the Atlantic to the Urals). The Treaty proposed equal limits for the two 'groups of states-parties', NATO and the Warsaw Pact.
8. Jacques Lévesque, 'The Emancipation of Eastern Europe', in Herrmann and Lebow (eds), *Ending the Cold War*, p. 111.
9. Baker with DeFrank, *The Politics of Diplomacy*, p. 221.
10. Author's interview with Aleksandr Bessmertnykh, 3 April 1999.
11. Baker with DeFrank, *The Politics of Diplomacy*, p. 603.
12. Ibid, p. 326.
13. Lévesque, 'The Emancipation of Eastern Europe', p. 110.
14. Baker with DeFrank, *The Politics of Diplomacy*, p. 254.
15. Anatoli Chernyaev, *My Six Years with Gorbachev* (University Park: Pennsylvania State University Press, 2000), pp. 361–2.
16. Author's conversation with Mikhail Gorbachev, 25 October 2006.
17. See on this Archie Brown, 'Gorbachev and the End of the Cold War', in Herrmann and Lebow (eds), *Ending the Cold War*, p. 53.
18. Author's interview with Mikhail Gorbachev, 6 July 2000.
19. John Lewis Gaddis, *The Cold War: A New History* (New York: Penguin Press, 2005), p. 257.
20. See James W. Davis and William C. Wohlforth, 'German Unification', in Herrmann and Lebow (eds), *Ending the Cold War*, p. 144.
21. Baker with DeFrank, *The Politics of Diplomacy*, p. 157.
22. See, for example, Aleksandr Sheviakin, *Zagadka gibeli SSSR: Istoria zagovorov il predateljstv* (Moscow: VECHE, 2005).
23. Archie Brown's book with this title (*The Gorbachev Factor*, Oxford: Oxford University Press, 1996) remains probably one of most complete and convincing reflections on this subject, despite the piles of volumes, including the Russian ones, that have been produced on the exceptional phenomenon of *perestroika* and the singular reformist endeavour of its leader.
24. Jack F. Matlock, Jr, *Reagan and Gorbachev: How the Cold War Ended* (New York: Random House, 2004), p. 318.
25. See Mikhail Gorbachev, *On my Country and the World* (New York: Columbia University Press, 2000), p. 206.
26. Baker with DeFrank, *The Politics of Diplomacy*, p. 652.
27. Brown, *Seven Years That Changed the World*, p. 245.
28. See Evangelista, 'Turning Points in Arms Control', p. 98.
29. Lévesque, 'The Emancipation of Eastern Europe', p. 124.
30. Gaddis, *The Cold War*, p. 230.

31. Vladislav Zubok, 'German Unification from the Soviet (Russian) Perspective', in Kiron K. Skinner (ed.), *Turning Points in Ending the Cold War*, forewords by Pavel Palazhchenko and George P. Shultz (Stanford: Hoover Institution Press, 2007), p. 272.
32. Author's interview with Anatoli Chernyaev, 7 September 1999.
33. Mikhail Gorbachev in a conversation with the author, 26 October 2006.
34. Chernyaev, *My Six Years with Gorbachev*, p. 76.
35. See Brown, 'Gorbachev and the End of the Cold War', p. 52.
36. Ronald Reagan, *An American Life: The Autobiography* (New York: Simon and Schuster, 1990), p. 635.
37. See Matlock, *Reagan and Gorbachev*, pp. 237–50.
38. Jacques Attali, *Verbatim III. 1988–1989* (Paris: Fayard, 1995), p. 485.
39. See Baker with DeFrank, *The Politics of Diplomacy*, pp. 172–3.
40. George Bush and Brent Scowcroft, *A World Transformed* (New York: Alfred A. Knopf, 1998), p. 370.
41. Lévesque, 'The Emancipation of Eastern Europe', p. 126.
42. Baker with DeFrank, *The Politics of Diplomacy*, p. 475.
43. Ibid., p. 210.
44. Gaddis, *The Cold War*, p. 251.
45. Baker with DeFrank, *The Politics of Diplomacy*, p. 251.
46. *V Politburo Ts K KPSS* . . . [Records of Politburo sessions according to notes of Anatoli Chernyaev, Vadim Medvedev, Georgi Shakhnazarov (1985–1991)] (Moscow: Alpina Business Books, 2006), p. 632.

# BIBLIOGRAPHY

Sergei Akhromeev and Georgi Kornienko, *Glazami marshala i diplomata*, Moscow: Mezhdunaronye otnosheniya, 1992.

Pierre Allan and Dieter Klay, *Afgansky kapkan: Pravda o sovetskom vtrozhenii*, Moscow: Mezhdunarodnye otnosheniya, 1999.

Sorin Antohi and Vladimir Tismaneanu (eds), *Between Past and Future: The Revolutions of 1989 and Their Aftermath*, Budapest: Central European University Press, 2000.

Georgi Arbatov, *Zatyanuvsheesya vyazdorovlenie (1953–1985): Svidetel'stvo sovremennika*, Moscow: Mezhdunarodnye otnosheniya, 1991.

Jacques Attali, *Verbatim III. 1988–1989*, Paris: Fayard, 1995.

James A. Baker, III, with Thomas M. DeFrank, *The Politics of Diplomacy: Revolution, War and Peace, 1989–1992*, New York: G.P. Putnam's Sons, 1995.

Michael R. Beschloss and Strobe Talbott, *At the Highest Levels: The Inside Story of the End of the Cold War*, Boston: Little, Brown, 1993.

Archie Brown, *The Gorbachev Factor*, Oxford: Oxford University Press, 1996.

Archie Brown, *Seven Years that Changed the World: Perestroika in Perspective*, Oxford: Oxford University Press, 2007.

George Bush and Brent Scowcroft, *A World Transformed*, New York: Alfred A. Knopf, 1998.

Anatoli Chernyaev, *Moya zhizn' i moe vremia*, Moscow: Mezhdunaronye otnosheniya, 1995.

Anatoli Chernyaev, *My Six Years with Gorbachev*, University Park: Pennsylvania State University, 2000.

Anatoli Chernyaev, *Shest' let s Gotbachevym: Po dnevnikovym zapisyam*, Moscow: Kultura, 1993.

Samy Cohen (ed.), *Mitterrand et la sortie de la guerre froide*, Paris: Presses Universitaires de France, 1998.

Diego Cordovez and Selig S. Harrison, *Out of Afghanistan: The Inside Story of the Soviet Withdrawal*, New York: Oxford University Press, 1995.

Anatoli Dobrynin, *In Confidence: Moscow's Ambassador to America's Six Cold War Presidents (1962–1986)*, New York: Random House, 1995.

Frank Elbe and Richard Kiessler, *A Round Table with Sharp Corners: The Diplomatic Path to German Unity*, Baden-Baden: NOMOS, 1996.

Robert D. English, *Russia and the Idea of the West: Gorbachev, Intellectuals, and the End of the Cold War*, New York: Columbia University Press, New York, 2000.

Claude Estier, *Dix ans qui ont changé le monde*, Paris: Bruno Leprince editeur, 2001.

Valentin Falin, *Bez skidok na obstoyatel'stva: Politicheskiye vospominaniya*, Moscow: Respublika, Sovremennik, 1999.

Valentin Falin, *Konflikty v Kremle*, Moscow: Tsentrpoligraf, 1999.

André Fontaine, *La tache rouge: Le roman de la guerre froide*, Paris: Éditions de La Martinière, 2004.

John Lewis Gaddis, *The Cold War: A New History*, New York: Penguin Press, 2005.

Mahmud Gareev, *Afganskaia strada: S Sovetskimi voiskami i bez nih*, Moscow: Insan, 1999.

R.L. Garthoff, *The Great Transition: American–Soviet Relations and the End of the Cold War*, Washington, DC: Brookings, 1994.

Robert M. Gates, *From the Shadows*, New York: Simon and Schuster, 1996.

Mikhail Gorbachev, *Gody trudnykh resheniy*, Moscow: Al'fa-Print, 1993.

Mikhail Gorbachev, *Izbrannye rechi i stat'i*, Moscow: Politizdat. 1987.

Mikhail Gorbachev, *Kak eto bylo*, Moscow: Vagrius, Petro-News, 1999.

Mikhail Gorbachev, *On My Country and the World*, New York: Columbia University Press, 2000.

Mikhail Gorbachev, *Perestroika and New Political Thinking for Our Country and the World*, New York: Harper and Row, 1987.

Mikhail Gorbachev, *Zhizn' i reformy*, Moscow: Novosti, 1995.

Mikhail Gorbachev and Zdeněk Mlynář, *Conversations with Gorbachev: On Perestroika, the Prague Spring, and the Crossroads of Socialism*, New York: Columbia University Press, 2002.

Andrei Grachev, *Final Days: The Inside Story of the Collapse of the Soviet Union*, Boulder, CO: Westview Press, 1995.

Andrei Grachev, Chiara Blengino and Rossella Stievano (eds), *1985–2005: Twenty Years that Changed the World*, Rome: World Political Forum and Editoria Laterza, 2005.

Anatoli Gromyko, *Andrei Gromyko v Labirintakh Kremlia*, Moscow: IPO 'Avtor', 1997.

Jussi M. Hanhimaki and Odd Arne Westad (eds), *The Cold War: A History in Documents and Eyewitness Accounts*, Oxford: Oxford University Press, 2003.

Richard K. Herrmann and Richard Ned Lebow (eds), *Ending the Cold War: Interpretations, Causation, and the Study of International Relations*, New York: Palgrave Macmillan, 2004.

Georgi Kornienko, *Kholodania voina: Svidetel'stvo ee uchastnika*, Moscow: Mezhdunaronye otnosheniya, 1995.

Vladimir Kryuchkov, *Lichnost i vlast'*, Moscow: Prosveshchenie, 2004.

Yuli Kvitsinski, *Vremia i sluchai: Zametki professionala*. Moscow: Olma Press, 1999.

Jacques Lévesque, *The Enigma of 1989: The USSR and the Liberation of Eastern Europe*, Berkeley: University of California Press, 1997.

Jack F. Matlock, Jr, *Autopsy on an Empire: The American Ambassador's Account of the Collapse of the Soviet Union*, New York: Random House, 1995.

Jack F. Matlock, Jr, *Reagan and Gorbachev: How the Cold War Ended*, New York: Random House, 2004.

V.A. Medvedev, *V komande Gorbacheva: Vzgliad iznutri*, Moscow: Bylina, 1994.

Sarah E. Mendelson, *Changing Course: Ideas, Politics and the Soviet Withdrawal from Afghanistan*, Princeton: Princeton University Press, 1998.

Valeri Musatov, *Predvestniki buri: Politichskie krizisy v Vostochnoi Evrope (1956–1981)*, Moscow: Nauchnaia Kniga, 1996.

Dan Oberdorfer, *The Turn: From the Cold War to a New Era. The United States and the Soviet Union, 1983–1990*, New York: Simon and Schuster, 1991.

Pavel Palazchenko, *My Years with Gorbachev and Shevardnadze: The Memoir of a Soviet Interpreter*, University Park: Pennsylvania State University Press, 1997.

Richard Pipes, 'Misinterpreting the Cold War: The Hard-liners Had It Right', *Foreign Affairs*, 74/1 (Jan.–Feb. 1995).

Ronald Reagan, *An American Life: The Autobiography*, New York: Simon and Schuster, 1990.

Georgi Shakhnazarov, *Tsena svobody: Reformatsiya Gorbacheva glazami ego pomoshchnika*, New York: Rossika Zevs, 1993.

Eduard Shevardnadze, *The Future Belongs to Freedom*, London: Sinclair-Stevenson, 1991.

Eduard Shevardnadze, *Moi vybor: V zaschitu demokratii i svobody*, Moscow: Novosti, 1991.

George P. Shultz, *Turmoil and Triumph: My Years as Secretary of State*, New York: Macmillan, 1993.

Georges-Henri Soutou, *La guerre de cinquante ans: Les relations Est–Ouest 1943–1990*, Paris: Fayard, 2001.

Margaret Thatcher, *The Downing Street Years*, New York: HarperCollins, 1993.

*Understanding the End of the Cold War, 1980–1987*, transcript of an oral history conference, Brown University, 7–10 May 1998, ed. by Nina Tannenwald, Watson Institute for International Studies.

*V Politburo Ts K KPSS* . . . [Records of Politburo sessions according to notes of Anatoli Chernyaev, Vadim Medvedev, Georgi Shakhnazarov (1985–1991)], Moscow: Alpina Business Books, 2006.

Jiří Valenta and Frank Cibulka (eds), *Gorbachev's New Thinking and Third World Conflicts*, New Brunswick, NJ, and London: Transaction Publishers, 1990.

Hubert Vedrine, *Les Mondes de François Mitterrand*, Paris: Fayard, 1996.

Markus Wolf, *Igra na chuzhom Pole: Tridtsatj let vo glave razvedki*, Moscow: Mezhdunarodnye otnosheniya, 1998.

Aleksandr Yakovlev, *'Gor'kaia chasha': Bol'shevizm i reformatsia v Rossii*, Yaroslavl: Verhne-Volzhskoe izdatel'stvo, 1994.

Philip Zelikow and Condoleezza Rice, *Germany Unified and Europe Transformed: A Study in Statecraft*, Cambridge, MA: Harvard University Press, 1995.

# INDEX